THE TWO SHALL BECOME ONE

THE TWO SHALL BECOME ONE

God and His People from Genesis to Revelation

"Let us rejoice and exult and give him the glory,
for the marriage of the Lamb has come, and his
Bride has made herself ready;
it was granted her to be clothed with fine linen, bright and pure"
– for the fine linen is the righteous deeds of the saints.
Rev 19:7--8

By Lenora Grimaud

XULON PRESS

Xulon Press
2301 Lucien Way #415
Maitland, FL 32751
407.339.4217
www.xulonpress.com

Printed in the United States of America.

ISBN-13: 9781545636381

CONTENTS

Part One — Marriage between One Man and One Woman;
Brought Together By God

Part Two—Marriage between Jesus and His Church;
Beginning with a Promise

ENDORSEMENTS

The Three characteristics of Christ's love for His bride, the Church, are also at the heart of Christian marriage: faithfulness, perseverance, and fruitfulness. Christ himself is the model and measure of these three loves of Jesus: for the Father, for His Mother, and for the Church. "Pope Francis' Little Book of Wisdom" by Andrea Kirk Assaf

How well Lenora has expressed the above sentiments in her book, "The Two Shall Become One." Her journey of faith; the struggles in her own marriage; her annulment; and her temporary experience in living religious life as a Nun, have enabled her to be a writer who presents us with a profound wisdom and insight into family and married life.

This book opens up the treasures of the Sacrament of Matrimony. It is a must book for anyone contemplating marriage. Each page a gold nugget each chapter a gold bar.

—Father Pat Crowley, ss.cc.

DEDICATION

$\mathcal{I}$ humbly dedicate this book to the Most Sacred Heart of Jesus; to his most holy will, his Divine Providence, his Divine Mercy, and to the Immaculate Heart of Mary, my mother. I also dedicate it to all my Magnificat sisters throughout the world; to all the Women of Grace throughout the world; to all the priests I have known, especially those who have been my spiritual directors; and last but not least, my beloved children: Dan, Carrie, Nicole, and Jeanine.

ACKNOWLEDGEMENTS

$\mathcal{I}$ want to acknowledge and thank all those who have prayed for me and this book, as well as those who have encouraged me through their support, assistance, comments, suggestions, and editing. I especially want to thank: Dan Grimaud, Nicole Lesher, Carrie Reid, Jeanine Allen, Avon Stevens, Angela Sarvis, Vanessa Browne, Colleen Swiatek, Donna Ross, Madelene Balloy, Msgr. Robert Ecker, Fr. Rafael Partida, Fr. Howard Lincoln, Fr. Lou Cerulli, and Fr. Pat Crowley, ss.cc.

DISCLOSURE

$\mathcal{J}$n December, 2017, Pope Francis's prayer for the Church was that the elderly would be given opportunities to share their wisdom. His prayer, along with the urging of my spiritual director, gave me the courage to publish this book. I have been writing for years but was always afraid to write a book for the public. I was afraid of writing something that might be heretical, misunderstood, or that might offend someone. Yet, I have a passion within me to witness, and to give away all that the Lord has given to me. I am a firm believer in Jesus Christ as the Son of God, of all that he has said and done; and in Scripture and the teachings and guidance of the Catholic Church. I have included in this book, many personal insights, experiences, and even some speculation, so I ask the reader to do as I do: "test everything you hear and read" (1 Thes 5:21). If it is helpful or beneficial to you, bringing you closer to the Lord and his love, then hold onto it; if it contradicts Scripture or the teachings of the Church, or leads you away from Jesus and his love, then dismiss it; and forgive me.

Writing is a part of my prayer life. I write when I am inspired to write, and my writing is mostly confined to the spiritual life. I am not, however, a theologian, doctor, scientist, or psychologist;

and certainly, not infallible. My intention is only to share all that my faith tells me is good and true; to respond to the call to evangelize. You will find that this book is saturated with Scripture; my primary resource. It is my witness to Jesus Christ and to the Gospel. My hope is that this book will reach readers within the Catholic Church, those who have left the Church, and those who are non-Catholic Christians; as well as all those that the Lord wants to hear this message.

—Lenora Grimaud

ABOUT THIS BOOK

$\mathcal{T}$his book is not your typical book on "marriage." Beginning with Genesis and ending with Revelation, it is about God's plan for *two becoming one* in a marriage between one man and one woman, and *two becoming one* in the marriage between Jesus and his Church. The main focus is on our relationship with God, in marriage and in the Church. This book takes the reader on a roller-coaster journey through the many *rise and falls* of marriage and the Church. It ends with the call to be awake and to be prepared for what is coming. The hope is that this book will be an instrument of reconciliation and unity, as well as an instrument of evangelization; and that it will challenge readers to "Seek the Lord while he may be found, call him while he is near." (Is 55:6)

INTRODUCTION

$\mathscr{I}$was born and raised in the Catholic Church; baptized as an infant. My parents both came from strong Catholic families, but once they moved to California, their faith became very weak. They did, however, make sure that their children went to church and to catechism. My grandparents had a great spiritual influence on me, so while I was not outwardly religious, growing up, I did have a strong faith. My relationship with God was personal and private most of the time. I had a strong loyalty to the Catholic Church, a strong faith in the goodness of God and his love for me, and a strong desire to love everyone. I believed wholeheartedly in Divine Providence and the need for conformity to the will of God. I also had a great love for the Eucharist, but did not really know why. I did not know Jesus, or have a personal relationship with him. I saw God as the Spirit of *Love* and *Truth*, but he was very distant; beyond reach and beyond knowing. I was in love with *Love* and *Truth*.

In the late 60's, I experienced a spiritual awakening and a desire to learn everything I could about God and about my Church. One of the first things I learned was that the worst thing I could ever do would be to become a heretic. That became my greatest fear.

At this same time, I came in contact with the charismatic renewal through some non-Catholic women. They also introduced me to Scripture, which I devoured with a passion. Because of my fear of heresy, I had a lot of resistance to what they called, the "baptism of the Holy Spirit" and being "born again." I was not familiar with this terminology. This presented for me, at that time, the greatest risk and challenge I had ever experienced, and I struggled with it for months. I believed that any teaching from God would be revealed to the Church before it would be revealed to anyone else. I thought that if what they were saying was really from God, my Church would have told me about it. I believed that the Church taught everything that was handed down by the Apostles and their successors. What these women were telling me seemed to be totally new and foreign to me. They told me about miracles, miraculous healing, prophecy, visions, and dreams—happening to ordinary people in our day and time.

After reading scripture, however, I discovered that I had an even greater fear of resisting the Holy Spirit, so I finally surrendered to this experience of God. Jesus became the center of my life. I fell in love with him, and this radically changed me—and my life. As I read more about the lives of the saints, I discovered that this experience of the Holy Spirit was not new, and was always a part of Church teaching; even if I had not heard about it in my religious training. I also became aware that the way I interpreted scripture, and what the Holy Spirit was saying to me, was very different than that of my friends. In fact, they seemed to differ amongst themselves, as well. I visited various protestant churches and discovered the same inconsistencies in interpreting scripture. I had the belief that the Holy Spirit would bring all Christians to be of one mind, one heart, one belief, and one common purpose. I asked my friend how she could be sure what the scriptures were really saying. She replied, "The Holy Spirit will reveal the real meaning of Scripture, and he reveals the same thing to all of us." I did not find this to be true, however. It became evident to me that "Scripture Alone," was not enough, even with a personal experience of the Holy Spirit, to make us all of one mind. I came to the realization that tradition and church authority were also necessary. It seemed rational to me that Jesus had to give the Church, as well as the Apostles, authority to interpret Scripture and tradition, or we would never be one Church, all believing the same thing. So, after this experience of the Holy Spirit, I became more involved and committed to Jesus and my Church. In the years that followed I seemed to grow, considerably, in wisdom and grace, as well as ministry in the Church and the charismatic renewal; but, seventeen years later, everything fell apart, including my marriage.

At this time, I went through a desert experience, a very dark night of the soul; a time of transition, loss, blindness, sin, and purification. I felt lost—like Abraham who blindly followed the Lord through the desert, not knowing where he was going. I had no maps for the journey. I felt like I could not discern good from evil. The "Law" and Church teachings did not seem to make sense to me anymore. All I could be sure of was that God loved me and his will was my perfect good, but I did not know what his will was or how to find it. It was as though I had *spiritual amnesia*. When the darkness lifted, almost four years later, I returned home to the Church. I saw that *desert experience* as a fall from grace, at the time. Later, I realized that in some ways, I was probably closer to God in that desert than any other time of my life. More spiritual and psychological growth took place within me during that exile than before and after my return to the Church. It forced me to become like a little child again, and put me in touch with my need for God and dependency on him for everything. I grew in self-knowledge. That exile also led me to prepare for a vocation to religious life.

I spent the next ten years as a nun, determined to live for God and to do his will in obedience and fidelity to the Church. When it came time for me to profess final vows, my superiors made known to me that they did not think I was called to their congregation, and did not accept my request to take final vows. They agreed to allow me to renew my vows for one year to give me time for discernment, in seclusion, in Ireland. I could not believe what I was hearing! After all those years, with so many confirmations of my calling, I was being sent home. But, by the time the year was up, I also came to the realization that God was not calling me to final vows with that congregation; and that he had a different plan for me, even though I had no idea of what it could be. So, I returned home to family, to wait for the Lord to lead me. God never closes one door without opening another, if we are willing to wait.

Nevertheless, I found myself going through another transition — back into the secular world. I was *literally* back in the desert again, experiencing another dark night of the soul, and more purification and change. I felt as though I had gone full circle, facing many of the same doubts and needs I had during my previous exile. I found myself having to, once again, come face to face with loneliness; and all the contradictions, ambiguity, and paradoxes within me and within the Church. During my previous experience, I was not able to fully integrate these contradictions. Instead, I chose one over the other. One day I was a liberal, and the next day, a conservative. I went back and forth between the Law and the Spirit, causing me to be somewhat double-minded.

Once again, I felt like I was on a journey through the desert with no map; none of the old maps worked anymore. This was also a time of awakening for me; of learning to trust the God within me to teach and guide me. I needed to learn how to integrate religious life and secular life. I was still in a process of coming to understand the role of the Church in the world, today; of seeing the Church through the eyes of Jesus. I discovered that my knowledge was not as important as my response to the Lord's invitation; my obedience, trust, and acceptance of the cross.

The invitation to fullness of life, to enter into the kingdom of God, comes in many forms and languages. God meets every person where they are at, and is never at a loss for ways to get our attention. The Lord began to prepare me for a new vocation—as a religious woman living in the world—to become a *handmaid of the Lord* and his witness to people in the Church and in the world. I was also led to become involved in *Magnificat, A Ministry to Catholic Women*. This has been my vocation for the past fourteen years.

Now I am faced with a call to share my spiritual journey, knowledge, and experience in this book. As far back as I can remember I wanted to write. It was not for achievement or to create something, but to discover who I am, and to share that person with others. I was always wondering: Who am I? Where did I come from? Why am I here? Where am I going? I remember when I was in High School, thinking, there is so much more to me than what people can see, more than what I can see. I wished I could turn myself inside out so that others could know me, and so that I could know me. I thought about writing an autobiography, but then, realized that I had barely begun to live. What would I write about? So, the motivation of this book is to share my story, and to witness to the one who made me. I am a "handmaid of the Lord," and this is how I became a *handmaid of the Lord*.

After my conversion in 1969, I begin writing—by keeping a spiritual journal. At the time, (almost fifty years ago) I did not have a spiritual director to go to. So, I began to pour out my heart and mind to Jesus, through my journal. I poured out my feelings, insights, experiences, questions, fears, doubts—everything that filled my mind and heart. As I did, I received answers to some of my questions, as well as new insights and wisdom. My gift of writing grew out of this. Over the years, I shared many of my writings with friends, those who I ministered to, and whoever was interested in reading them. But, for some reason, I always resisted writing a book. It seemed to me that there are millions of books on the market, regarding spirituality, and I figured that whatever I had to say has already been said by others. Nevertheless, for years people have been asking me, "When are you going to write a book?" This question has hounded me for most of my life, like the *hound of heaven*. Recently, however, my spiritual director put the question more in the form of a command: "Write a book! What do you want to say to the world?"

My greatest desire in life is to become a saint; by loving God with all my heart, soul, mind, and strength; and loving my neighbor as myself. To me, this means I need to use all that God has given me; my talents, skills, experiences, joys, sufferings, and spiritual gifts as instruments of spreading the love of God to others. I can do this through writing, teaching, and sharing what I have received and experienced with others. I can do this by surrendering to the will of God and trusting him in all events and circumstances of my life. I can do this by accepting all that God allows to happen to me with joy, praise, and thanksgiving.

⊿ see my mission as a *handmaid of the Lord;* whether it is as a mother, sister, or grandmother; as a wife, friend, or nun; in the kitchen or in the classroom; in the Church or in the street; with the word at the tip of my tongue or at the tip of my pen; in sickness and in health; richer or poorer; in joy and in sorrow; all the days of my life. I see myself as a messenger of hope to others through faith and love. This book reflects much of what I have learned and understood from my life experiences, from my studies, from what I have received from the Church, and from what I have received through prayer at the feet of Jesus. I am not a theologian, nor do I claim to be a biblical scholar, and I make no claim that all I have written is due to the authentic promptings and inspiration of the Holy Spirit. I leave that to the good judgment and discernment of the reader.

This book begins with the marriage between one man and one woman, as revealed in the book of Genesis; and ends with the marriage between Christ and his bride, the Church, in the book of Revelation. The book of Genesis is an introduction to the Bible, and to salvation history, as we understand it through the revelation of Jesus Christ. The Bible begins and ends with allegorical stories (Genesis and Revelation) that are historical in essence, as well as prophetic; using figurative and symbolic language. The first three chapters of Genesis focus on the story of creation. When it comes to interpreting prophetic or symbolic language, *hindsight is better than foresight.* Life has a way of confirming, denying, or fulfilling what was said and done in the past. Personally, I hold to the

Catholic interpretation of the *creation story* in the Catechism of the Catholic Church (CCC 337—421). The creation story reveals to us: the creation of the world by God; the creation of man and woman in a state of original goodness and innocence; the unity of the human race; the institution of marriage—two becoming one flesh; the personal and intimate relationship between God and humans; the testing and fall of Adam and Eve (original sin); the future promise of salvation; the spiritual warfare between Satan and the people of God; the victory over Satan and sin by Jesus Christ and Mary; the kingdom of God and the kingdom of the world; and the mission of humans to multiply and care for the earth and all the inhabitants of the earth.

The book of Genesis is our story, the story of humankind; our beginning. It started with one man and one woman, who were made one flesh; joined together by God in marriage. Throughout the Bible, the reference to *man* is not just referring to Adam, the male, but to Adam and Eve, male and female. Whatever is said to the man is also said to the woman, unless it is directed specifically to the man or woman by name. The term, *man,* is used to include both sexes, rather than the term, *woman*, because man was created first and woman came forth out of man. At least, this is what we are told in Genesis, and no one has yet proved otherwise.

Genesis gives us a hint of the kind of relationship God intended for a man and a woman to have in marriage, as well as their relationship with God, and other humans. It also shows the consequences of sin upon the relationship between the man and the woman, as well as their relationship with God. These two relationships, with God and with each other, are interdependent. Adam and Eve needed to be in a covenant relationship with God, in order for their relationship with each other to be in the image and likeness of God. The break in the relationship between God and humans caused a break in the relationship between Adam and Eve, as well. The book of Genesis tells us about the creation and fall of Adam and Eve, and the consequences that followed. (Read Genesis, chapters two and three).

In spite of the shame, darkness, and blindness that Adam and Eve experienced, due to sin, God broke into their consciousness and gave them a promise; a promise of deliverance and reconciliation; a promise of transformation and reunion with God and creation. Though they were unfaithful, God would always be faithful to them. However, they were not yet ready for a relationship with God. They were not free for a marriage with God, or for the gift of eternal life: a permanent, interdependent relationship with God. Thus, they were expelled from the Garden of Eden. God would have to lead them into the desert and speak to their heart. They would have to be purified before they could be a faithful wife to Yahweh. (See Hos 2:14—21)

From the beginning, God wanted to form a people to be his *bride;* a people that would spread and expand, and eventually include all of humankind. God wanted to establish the kingdom of God over all the earth; and to also, establish his kingdom within the souls of all humans. The earth and everything in it belongs to God. It is his creation and he is the one creator and Lord, over all of heaven and earth (Mt 11:25). The marriage between one man and one woman prefigures the marriage between Christ and his bride.

Humanity inherited original sin and its consequences from Adam and Eve. The *Good News* is that humanity also inherited the experience of God that Adam and Eve had before they fell, as well as the promise of salvation and reconciliation. Deep within the heart of every human is the knowledge of God, who spoke face to face with Adam and Eve. Because of Jesus and the Holy Spirit, our longing for God need no longer be that of unrequited love, but the joyful longing of a bride for her husband. We look forward with longing and hope for the Lord's return and the full manifestation of the kingdom of God. We look forward with longing and hope to the *Marriage feast of Jesus and his bride*. (Rev 19:7)

—Lenora Grimaud

Part 1

Marriage between One Man and One Woman
Brought Together By God

1

Marriage In The Beginning

Therefore a man leaves his father and mother and clings
to his wife, and they become one flesh.
(Gen 2:24)

The story of creation, especially of Adam and Eve, in the book of Genesis, is viewed by many as simply a fable or a myth. Although we cannot interpret it literally, because it is an allegory, yet, if we look closely, we can see that it embodies a timeless truth about life that has been enacted in every society throughout time. It is kind of a blue-print of human nature. Let me share with you my personal interpretation of the creation of humanity.

In the beginning, there was God; Father, Son, and Holy Spirit. This Holy Trinity was a relationship of love, power, energy, unity, harmony, beauty, truth, and order. The Father loved the Son so much that he wanted to give him a gift. He wanted to create for him, a beautiful bride who would have the potential of becoming divine, like his Son. In the beginning, driven by love, God spoke love, and all creation came into existence, out of nothing. First, he created the heavens and the earth, plants and trees, and animals; a place for this bride to live and grow in order to be prepared for a marriage to his Son. Then, God formed a body from the earth, and breathed spirit into him from the spirit of his Son, giving him life. He called this body, Adam, and made him king over all the earth. Then, while Adam was asleep, God drew forth from him, a helpmate; making two bodies from the one; and called her Eve. God created them male and female, in his own image and likeness. Adam and Eve, the man and the woman, were interdependent and delighted in each other. They were inseparable.

In the beginning, God provided everything for man and woman. He placed them in a garden that they did not create, and gave them all they needed to sustain life. He protected them from predators by giving them knowledge of what would nurture them and what would harm them; what would increase life and what would destroy life in them. As long as man and woman lived together in unity and harmony, with God, their image and likeness would live forever.

God gave Adam and Eve everything that they would need that was life-giving, including the *tree of life* which would enable them to live forever; to be immortal. In addition, he warned them of what was not life-giving; of what would bring death. He provided for them and protected them. He also gave them a free will, and the freedom to choose among all the good things of the earth. Humans were his *final hour* of creation. The rest of creation would be done through Adam and Eve, cooperating with God.

Together, man and woman would be *one flesh,* radiating love to each other. Man would love woman by being her provider and protector. Woman would love man by bringing forth new life from his love, and nurturing it. Through their unity and love for one another, man and woman would glorify God. They would worship God by being with God and never forgetting their beginning; never losing sight of the one whose image and likeness they bore; loving each other and living always in an attitude of gratitude. Gratitude is to love one's own life, and to love the one who gave us that life. Love is being true to our own nature and to the life our nature calls us to, as man and woman. Love is being the person we were created to be; being our true self.

God made them one again through marriage. Together, they represented humanity. Together, they would become the bride for the Son of God. Although they were two, they were still one; in perfect harmony and unity, completing and complementing each other. Together, they would be the leaders and protectors of the earth and all the inhabitants of the earth, as King and Queen, Mother and Father. He gave them authority over all and made them responsible for the care of everyone. God made them his representatives to the people, and the people's representatives to God.

God's plan for Adam and Eve was that they would learn how to be parents and leaders by being parented by him. They would become like little children; loving, trusting, obeying, and following their parent's example. They would learn to be the kind of parents he was; serving, nurturing, guiding, directing, teaching, and loving; ready to lay down his life for the sake of his children. This was the kind of parents and leaders God wanted for all of humanity.

God never left their side. Adam and Eve enjoyed continual communion with God and with each other. They walked and talked with God. What happened? When did they leave God's side? What distracted them? Why were they not aware of God being with them; aware of God's presence? Perhaps this was not a deliberate act of

their free will, in the beginning. Perhaps it was due to their immaturity, their need to grow and develop. But, gradually they stopped
communicating with God and with each other.

Adam and Eve were not yet complete. They were still immature and had to learn to make wise choices. It never even occurred
to them to eat of the *tree of life,* which would have made them
immortal. Adam and Eve were always free to reject God. If they
disobeyed God and ate of the forbidden tree, the consequence
would be death; loss of communion with God and the gift of eternal
life. God had warned them of that.

For some reason Adam and Eve forgot about God, that he was
with them. They forgot about their own humble beginnings. They
were no longer grateful for what they had or what they had been
given. They were no longer present to each other or to God. They
yearned for their own independence from each other and from
God. They forgot about their need for God and each other. They
stopped loving and started living for themselves, because they were
distracted by their own self-awareness. They each started going
their own way.

It was Adam's duty to protect Eve from all predators. Where
did he go? Perhaps he was out chasing after illusions of grandeur;
seeking fame and fortune; seeking his own glory. Perhaps he forgot
that his glory was in glorifying God by loving and protecting his
spouse. His ambitions took priority over his relationship with Eve.
Perhaps Eve was distracted by curiosity; seeking knowledge of
things beyond her understanding; excitement, something new and
extraordinary, something more.

Adam and Eve became estranged from each other because they
were not communicating with God. Eve was no longer satisfied by

6

Adam's love and Adam was no longer satisfied with Eve's love. Then, *evil* entered into the garden in the form of a serpent, to tempt them to choose to replace God with their own self. The serpent was the personification of Satan, of Lucifer, and of evil. The *original sin* of Adam and Eve was *unbelief;* choosing to believe Satan instead of God. Their sin was not simply disobedience and a lack of trust in God, it was also replacing God with a false god; it was idolatry. The sin of Adam and Eve was not just breaking their covenant with God, but adultery. They thought they were choosing independence, but they chose slavery to evil, instead. Evil is the consequence of a free-will choice to divorce God and replace him with something else. The *serpent* represents Satan, the destroyer and father of lies; the Anti-Christ or false god; the false prophet; the false teacher; and false leader. He infiltrates the whole culture of a nation: Church, religion, government, academics, ideologies, and human sexuality (morality); he leads the way for *the principalities, the powers, the world rulers of darkness, and the spiritual hosts of wickedness* to come into the world. (Eph 6:12)

Adam and Eve listened to the serpent and ate of the one forbidden tree; breaking their covenant with the one true God. The consequence of breaking their covenant with God led to the fall of their kingdom and to exile. It led to an adulteration of the marriage between man and woman and brought about the great divorce. It takes three to sin, just as it takes three to get married. Sin involved a man, a woman, and Satan, who divided them and set them against each other. Marriage required a man, a woman, and God, who brought them together and made them one with each other and with him.

7

Satan, or Lucifer, is evil. He is not a void, or something that is random. He is a calculating power; a fallen angel, who once was good. He did not lose his power. He used his power for evil. Through the power given to Lucifer, evil was not just an absence of good, but was a power and force beyond the imagination of man; something that keeps expanding and multiplying, bringing death to the living. Evil is not just the absence of love, but the replacement of love with hatred; not just the absence of truth, but the replacement of truth with lies and deception; not just the absence of life, but the replacement of life with death; not just the absence of beauty, but the replacement of beauty with disorder and corruption; not just the absence of God, but the replacement of God with the devil, the demonic. Evil is not an empty void. Satan does not come merely to tempt us to make selfish choices. He comes to possess and destroy us with evil; to replace God in our lives. Evil is like a deadly drug that makes us insane.

Adam and Eve sinned first, through ignorance and immaturity. They drifted apart. This was not through their free will, so they were not fully culpable. They had two choices. If they returned to God, they would increase in love, wisdom, and strength. If they did not return, they would be vulnerable to be tempted by Satan; tempted to rebel against God and put their own desires in place of him.

Adam and Eve both ate of the forbidden fruit, choosing not to serve God. Their disobedience could be forgiven, but they ate of the tree that would change their whole composition. They would become like "dry bones" (Ezek 37), unfit for the kingdom of God. God banished Adam and Eve from the Garden of Eden, his kingdom, for their own sake; lest they eat of the *tree of life* and make their present condition permanent; a condition of impurity because they lost their original innocence through sin, through disobedience and eating of the forbidden tree. Even so, God promised to deliver them over time, and to bring them home.

This is not the end of the story, however. From the descendants of Adam and Eve, God would raise up a new Adam and a new Eve, and redeem all the inhabitants of the earth. They would destroy Satan and overcome his power in the world with the power of the Holy Spirit. They would prepare the world to become the *bride of Christ*. But, first God would need to prepare the way for the *New Adam* to emerge. He would form a new people and make a covenant with them. He would give them the Law and teach them what is good and what is evil. He would raise up good leaders, prophets, teachers, and holy sages to form and guide them. He would prepare a kingdom for them, a new Garden of Eden, a new earth. This, he promised them. From out of this people, he would raise up the new Eve, Mary. Through her, God would send his own Son, the *Bridegroom*, to become the New Adam. Together, they would crush the head of the serpent and save the people.

From the beginning of time, God has revealed to those who have ears to hear and eyes to see, that creation was destined to go from mortality to immortality. After sin entered the world, creation would have to go from life to death and from death to eternal life, through the death and resurrection of the Son of God. God sent prophets into the world, not to create the future, but to prepare the world for the future; to prepare humanity for the future. We do not know what the future holds, but we do have a divine blue-print of God's plan for creation. We know that God desires that all humans have the fullness of life, in the present as well as in the future. We know that God wants only good for creation, and that with his help, we can conquer evil in the world. We know that God desires to establish his kingdom on earth as it is in heaven, and that it is already in process. We know that every person is a part of God's divine plan and has a role and purpose to bring God's plan to fulfillment. We know that the *cross* is a part of this fulfillment, enabling humans to develop and fulfill their mission in life. We also know that for every door that closes, another one opens. There are no limits or lack of options to how we fulfill our mission. God works all things for good when we trust in him; even our sins, imperfections, bad choices, and failures. If we have faith, hope, and love in the present, we will be prepared for whatever the future brings us.

In conclusion, marriage in the beginning meant that a man and woman, brought together by God, would become one flesh. They would love each other as God loved them—unconditionally. They would be willing to make any sacrifice for each other, out of love; even to laying down their life. Scripture tells us what love is: "Love is patient and kind; love is not jealous or boastful; it is not arrogant or rude. Love does not insist on its own way; it is not irritable or resentful; it does not rejoice at wrong, but rejoices in the right. Love bears all things, believes all things, hopes all things, endures all things." (ICSB 1 Cor 13:4—7)

2

Marriage After The "Fall"

After the Fall of Adam and Eve, marriage went through many transitions; each one worse than the last. Polygamy, rape, incest, concubines, slavery, cohabitation, and disordered unions of all types made their way into the marriage bed and family life. So, God called Abraham and Sara, and began to form a family. He made a covenant with Abraham, based on his faith in God. After Abraham and Sara, God called Isaac and Rebekah, and Jacob and Rachel. Gradually, after many trials and errors, they began to see a glimpse of what marriage and family life was meant to be. From this family, God formed a nation.

When the children of Abraham were captured and made slaves of Egypt, God called Moses to deliver them. But, God had to cleanse and purge his people from the effects of sin before they could enter the *Promised Land*. They had lost sight of the difference between good and evil. They called evil, good, and good, evil. So God gave Moses the Law, the Ten Commandments, to reform them.

The Ten Commandments can be summed up in the *Two Great Commandments*. The first is: "You shall love the Lord your God with all your heart, and with all your soul, and with all your mind" (ICSB Mt 22:37). This was the commandment that Adam and Eve disobeyed which resulted in sin and death and brought all of humanity under condemnation; severing the relationship between God and all of humanity. Adam and Eve rejected the one Lord through their disobedience and lack of reverence and trust in God—a manifestation of *unbelief*. They turned to idolatry by listening to the serpent and deciding to form their own conscience, apart from God. This commandment includes the first three of the Ten Commandments.

The second great commandment is like the first, and contingent on it. If you cannot keep the first, you will not be able to keep the second: "You shall love your neighbor as yourself" (Mt 22:39). This commandment includes the last seven of the Ten Commandments. Adam and Eve were *one flesh*, interdependent. Whatever they did to each other, they did to their own self. Together, they represented the marriage between Christ and his Church. When they sinned against God, they also sinned against each other. Their original sin against God radically affected their relationship with each other, as well as the rest of humanity; and even all creation. All the people of God are intended to become the *bride of Christ*.

Through Moses, God gave the Law to his people. Through Jesus, God gave the Spirit; as well as the forgiveness of sin and the grace needed to keep the Law. The Law, alone, cannot save people; we need grace, the Holy Spirit. It is only through forgiveness and grace from the Holy Spirit that we can fulfill and live in accordance to the fullness of the Law; live the Spirit of the Law. To break one commandment, one time, is to break all of them, and leads to death. In fact, at the time of Moses, the punishment for breaking most of the commandments was death. The Law signified God's covenant with his people.

We are told that there are two judgments that every person faces at death; the judgment of our sin against God, and the judgment of our sin against humanity. It is not only important for us to receive forgiveness from God, but we also need to forgive others, and to be forgiven by others. Jesus revealed to us that God is a relationship, and he created humans for relationship—with him and with each other. Jesus forgave us our sins against him and against God as an example for us to forgive one-another. If we do not forgive others, we will not be forgiven. God's love cannot remain in those who refuse to forgive—even their enemies. When we refuse to forgive anyone who has intentionally hurt us, we condemn them to prison, as well as ourselves. It is like placing a curse on them, unless they repent and are set free by the mercy of God. In that case, they will be set free but we will remain in prison. When we hate anyone or seek revenge, we hate God. When we cling to hatred, we choose hell. Perhaps the main reason why some people choose hell is that they are so unwilling to forgive others, or even to receive forgiveness.

St. Paul explains the difference between living under the Law and living under the Spirit in his letter to the Romans, "For sin will have no dominion over you, since you are not under law but under grace" (Rom 6:14). Those under the Spirit have the *forgiveness of sin*. Paul tells us that the Law was given to form our conscience. If there was no Law, there would be no sin. Sin entered the world through the Law. Sin is the breaking of the covenant. If God had not told Adam and Eve not to *eat of the tree* they would not have been guilty of sin if they ate of the tree, and would not be accountable for sin. Sin is *unbelief*, the rejection of God and lack of trust in him. Nevertheless, if they ate of that tree, in their ignorance, they still would have suffered death in their body; as with some kind a virus that gets into their cells and changes their whole genetic structure. The Law warns us of what will destroy us and what will bring us life. (See Romans Chapters 4—8)

One of the consequences of *original sin* is that when we are told not to do something, sin takes advantage of that, and causes us to do the very thing we do not want to do, that which we are forbidden to do. Sin produces temptation, guilt and shame. As St. Paul tells us, "I can will what is right, but I cannot do it. For I do not do the good I want, but the evil I do not want is what I do. Now if I do what I do not want, it is no longer I that do it, but sin which dwells within me" (ICSB Rom 7:18—20). We need forgiveness and the gift of the Holy Spirit in order to strengthen and exercise free will; in order to will what is good and do it; in order to restore our covenant with God.

Does this mean that the Law is bad, because it produces sin, temptation, guilt, and shame? Of course not! We cannot know what love is or freely choose to love without being formed by the Law. We would have no warning against evil and that which can destroy us. Without the Law, we would not be able to form our conscience. We would not know the difference between good and evil. We need God to form our conscience through the Law. Otherwise, we could not have the freedom to choose, and to develop our will. We would have no free will or choice. Love is a free choice of the good. We were created for love, to love, and through love. But, we need the

Spirit to understand the Law and to follow it, to love as God loves; to freely choose to obey out of love.

Therefore, the Law alone, cannot save us; just as faith or works, alone, cannot save us. We are still under condemnation, and subjected to futility: "for the creation was subjected to futility; not of its own will but by the will of him who subjected it in hope" (ICSB Rom 8:20). Without the Law, we are without a conscience, and though we may not be held accountable for sin, we are barbarians and not fit for community life or relationship with others. We are not fit for heaven. St. Paul continues, saying, "Wretched man that I am! Who will deliver me from this body of death? Thanks be to God through Jesus Christ our Lord!" (ICSB Rom 7:24—25). Only Jesus, through the forgiveness of sin, and grace through the gift of the Holy Spirit can save us. If we live in the Spirit, we will live all that the Law commands, naturally, and without living under the law of sin and death, "For the law of the Spirit of life in Christ Jesus has set me free from the law of sin and death" (ICSB Rom 8:2). The Law will have served its purpose, and we will not even need it. The Law is necessary to form our conscience according to the mind of Christ, and grace and the Holy Spirit are necessary in order to live according to our conscience. The *law of sin and death* brings condemnation instead of mercy.

God, however, cannot be contained in a book. That would be idolatry. God is greater and beyond anything we can know about him. He is unknowable as God. Scripture says, "For who has known the mind of the Lord or who has been his counselor?" (ICSB Rom 11:34). Yet, we can know what God has revealed to us. Revelation, Scripture and Tradition, reveals all that we need to know about God in regards to our salvation. Nothing new will ever contradict or cancel what God has already revealed, because he is *Truth*. God never changes, but reveals himself through his relationship with humanity. God meets every person where they are at.

The purpose of correction and judgment is love; that all may have life and have it to the fullest. This includes correction and judgment of the individual as well as of the community; for the sake of the individual as well as for the community.

A mother meets each of her children where they are at. She teaches the same laws and rules to all of them, but corrects them according to their nature. She knows their potential, capacity, and needs. One child may require firm discipline and punishment, which will make them strong and healthy. For another child, firm discipline would crush their spirit. They require that she embrace them, hold them, and allow them to release their bad energy through tears and comfort. The mother's intention for both children is the same; that they may have life. She does not change her values or love one more than the other. She merely changes her method of correction according to the needs of the child. God gives the same laws for the rich and the poor, alike, but he is much more lenient and merciful with the poor; whereas, the world is much more lenient with the rich.

Scripture tells us that Jesus is Lord of the Sabbath and of the Law. The Law was given for the good of humans, not God. The commandments are meant to restore order and peace, to enable the people of God to live in harmony with one another and to keep their covenant relationship with God. The Law is meant to lead us to love, to Jesus, not slavery or bondage. God brought his people, gradually, to the fullness of the understanding of the Law. He also brought them, gradually, to a full understanding of his plan and purpose for marriage.

In summary of Paul's teaching in Romans 7, it seems to me that Paul is saying that three things are necessary for our salvation: First, in order to will what is good, we need the Law, fulfilled in Jesus Christ, to show us what is good and what is evil; we need Jesus, the Word of God. Jesus is the model of perfect love in human form. He models the perfect goodness and will of God for us, and reveals it for all time in the Gospels. He perfects for us, the commandments that prepared the way for him to come. He is the perfect image of the Father.

Second, we need conversion. We need to reject the lies of Satan that tell us what is good is evil and what is evil is good; that tell us we cannot trust God because he does not love us. We have to truly want what is good and choose it with our will; and hate what is evil. We have to believe in Jesus and choose to follow him. Our relationship with Jesus is personal and communal. He meets each one of us where we are at and leads us forward. He knows each of us by *name*. We are not just a number or part of a group. When we stray from the community, he comes after us. His love for us is personal. He does not love us just because we belong to a group or community; nevertheless, he wants to save us as a whole family. Together, with the whole Church, we become his bride.

Third, when we fail to do the good that we want, and instead, do the evil we do not want, we need the forgiveness of sin, purchased for us by Jesus. We need to receive this forgiveness, as well as the gift of the Holy Spirit that empowers us to do the good that we want instead of the evil that we hate; empowers us to even love our enemies. We need to be baptized in the Holy Spirit. Without grace, we can do nothing. Without the Holy Spirit, we cannot become the *bride of Christ*.

In conclusion, divorce was initiated after the *Fall,* because of the separation from God. We can never justify divorce, but we can help people to be better prepared for marriage; and to choose the right mates. Nevertheless, unless God brings a couple together, there is little hope for the marriage to be blessed. In addition to Adam and Eve and the patriarchs and their wives, Scripture gives us many examples of how God has brought men and women together and joined them in marriage; making them one flesh, and bringing many blessings from their union. Some of these examples are: Tobias and Sarah, Ruth and Boaz, Elizabeth and Zacharias, and Mary and Joseph. Their lives and relationships give us a further glimpse into the mystery of marriage, which is meant to be a sacrament, reflecting the relationship between Christ and his bride.

3

Marriage over Time

arriage and family life are under severe attack today. Separation, divorce and remarriage, and annulment of marriages have directly affected almost every Christian family. Many Christians today do not have, or have never had a fully formed conscience, and have not been able to live a life in full accordance with the teachings of Jesus. They are not accountable for what they do not know or have not learned. When they learn the truth, they are not accountable for sins committed in ignorance in the past, or for bad choices. But, once they know and understand the truth, they are accountable for what they do thereafter; as in baptism, it is a new beginning. Nevertheless, even if they are not accountable for sin, they still suffer the consequences of all their choices; past, present, and future; unless the Lord in his mercy intervenes. We still have to carry our cross, unless the Lord sends someone to help us.

Many Christians today have well-formed consciences but lack the fullness of the Holy Spirit in order to live the truth. They need to be *baptized in the Holy Spirit*. Many Christians today suffer from psychological, physical, or mental impediments, which render them not culpable or only partially culpable for sins committed. They are dependent on God's mercy and the mercy of others. There are some Christians whose only option for marriage is cohabitation; and some Christians who are forced into unsuitable marriages by their culture, family, or circumstances in life. Many Christians still have deep faith in God but have lost their faith in the Church due to bad example and teaching.

This is a great challenge for the Church. She must always teach the whole truth, in accordance with the stages of growth, and never water down or teach falsehoods. She cannot change Divine Law or make exceptions to the Law. She cannot fall into the trap of *situation ethics* when it comes to the Law. Yet, she must be able to meet everyone where they are and show mercy where it is most needed. The Law never changes, but expectations for people vary according to the individual. All priests and pastors need to be baptized in the Holy Spirit; to have the gifts of counsel, discernment, wisdom, knowledge, and understanding. They even need these gifts, in some measure, in order to grant absolution of sins in confession and to counsel sinners; to know if someone is truly repentant or dishonest. They need to be able to discern between malice and immaturity or ignorance; between compulsion and intention; between sin and disability.

Jesus taught that when two people get married, they are no longer two but one flesh. What does that mean? It does not mean that they are somehow fused together and lose their personal identity or personhood. If that were true, then when one died the other would also die, or only be half a person. It means they share the same life in this world. They share the same children, extended families, friends, community, and tribes. They share the same family goals and values. They share the same concerns and problems. Everything they have belongs to both of them. They become a couple, and that is how everyone sees them. They are of one mind and heart. Whatever happens to one happens to both of them; including poverty or riches, suffering or joy, success or failure, sickness or health, good times or bad. The whole of their lives is interdependent. To be *one flesh* means to be interdependent, to be an exclusive couple, and capable of complementarity; one man and one woman, with the same purpose. Divorce is not one of the commandments, but adultery is. Jesus said: "What therefore God has joined together, let no man put asunder" (ICSB Mt 19:6). In the case of adultery, the punishment was death by stoning, or one could quietly divorce their spouse. Adultery shatters the relationship. It shatters trust and unity. Marriage was intended by God to be a permanent, life-long commitment of love and fidelity. When one party dies, the other party is free to marry again, but not before. Divorce was especially terrible in Jesus' day because if a man divorced his wife, she was left with nothing, including her name, children, and reputation. She was labeled an adulteress or unfit. She was often forced into prostitution in order to survive. Only men were allowed to divorce their spouse; and we may presume that those who divorced their wives did not do so until they found a replacement for her. This is nothing more than legalized adultery. Divorce, even if one does not remarry another, can be just as damaging to the couple and the family as divorce and remarriage. Divorce is unnatural for marriage.

Today, one problem with remarriage after divorce, and also even after an annulment, is that when people divorce and marry someone else they take their former spouse with them into that marriage, along with the problems, pain, hurt, anger, and expectations. They take the whole life of their spouse with them, the life they shared together. They project their former spouse onto the new spouse. Because they take their former spouse with them, they are not really free when they enter that second marriage. They are still attached to their former spouse.

In the Catholic Church, two people can get a divorce but they are not free to remarry without an annulment. They are still married and the divorce merely represents a separation. If they remarry, it is considered habitual adultery. We may not understand how two people can still be one flesh after a divorce, but according to Jesus, they are still bound to each other. They are held accountable for each other before God. That accountability does not end with divorce, unless they receive an annulment. They are not free to remarry, or free of their responsibility to and for each other. They are still responsible for the well-being of each other; physically, mentally, emotionally, and spiritually. They still affect each other's life.

A valid marriage, in which *two become one flesh*, requires that both parties are free to get married, and also free in their heart and mind to make a life-time commitment; free to give their self to the other and free to receive from the other. This is not possible if they are still married to their former spouse. This is also why Jesus said: "whoever divorces his wife, except for unchastity, and marries another, commits adultery; and he who marries a divorced woman, commits adultery" (Mt 19:9). Even if they are divorced, they are still one flesh, unless there was some impediment preventing them from truly becoming one; which would mean they were never really married, and they cannot be held accountable for what they are incapable of doing. They would be like little children who have not reached the age of reason and who are incapable of marriage. In this case, that judgement would still need to be confirmed by the Church, and the marriage annulled, in order for the couple to be *free* for another relationship. The couple would also need to go through a process of healing before they could be free to move on. But, a divorce from a valid sacramental marriage would make another marriage nothing more than an adulterous relationship. As a sacrament, marriage makes a man and a woman one spirit in Christ. It is like an invisible cord uniting their spirits, until it is removed by God. When God joins two people together, it is a three-way covenant with God. We can be forgiven when we break our covenant with God, but we also have a covenant with our spouse. We may not be forgiven or able to ever restore that covenant. Marriage is not a contract; it is a covenant, sealed by our mutual vows and the consummation of our marriage. Our bodies are no longer our own. The woman's body belongs to her husband and the man's body belongs to his wife. *For the wife does not rule over her own body, but the husband does; likewise the husband does not rule over his own body, but the wife does.* (ICSB 1Cor.7:4—7)

4

The Two Shall Become One Flesh!

When a man and a woman, joined together by God, become *one flesh*, their marriage is indissoluble; it is impossible for them to be separated until death. The marriage is indissoluble, not because the law says so, but because it is an actual fact. Whether they obtain a divorce or annulment, they cannot be separated, if God joined them together. How do we know when a couple has been joined together by God? What evidence should we look for?

It seems to me that marriage has gone through many transitions over the past centuries, but I think that from the very beginning, God intended for marriage to be a sacrament; *two becoming one flesh,* in Jesus Christ, the true image of God. As Bishop Sheen has said, *it takes three to get married: a man, a woman, and Jesus Christ.* (Sheen 1951)

The twentieth century has produced a very dramatic shift in our understanding of the theology of marriage, and marriage as a sacrament. Before this shift took place, our culture, including most Christians, had a very different concept of marriage. Our culture had a very different concept of what it means to be a whole man and what it means to be a whole woman, as well. Naturally, this concept would also distort the meaning of two becoming *one flesh*. Women were not regarded as having equal worth and dignity to men; at least, in practice. At best, the attitude of society regarding newly married women was rather like that of *mail-order brides*—a woman who was contracted to be a wife in exchange for security and the basic necessities of life. Women were regarded as an asset or possession of their husbands; to serve his needs and goals in life. Women were not equal partners with individual or equal rights of their own. The well-being of the man was top priority, and the well-being of the woman was not really even a consideration. The world revolved around the man. These concepts were usually not preached or spoken out loud, but in reality, this was the mind-set of society and our culture. This kind of mind-set could never produce a truly sacramental marriage; it is a contradiction to the Gospel of Jesus Christ. This kind of mind-set is contrary to the kingdom of God, and is a consequence of original sin.

Nevertheless, in spite of the cultural mind-set of the times, many Christian couples, after having a total conversion of hearts and receiving the sacramental grace of marriage, were able to become *one flesh* and one heart. Even though they lacked an intellectual conversion and still had the cultural mind-set of the times, their conversion of heart changed their reality, attitude, and vision of life, and the two became one flesh. When two become one flesh, each spouse loves the other as much, or more than their own self. Their marriage is a covenant, rather than a contract. They see themselves as equal in dignity and worth. Their lives do not revolve around only the husband, but also the wife, and every child that is brought into the family. No longer is the well-being of the man the primary consideration. The physical, mental, emotional, and spiritual well-being of every member of the family is equally important. This mutual well-being is the basis for every choice and decision the couple has to make regarding the sanctity of the marriage and the good of each member of the family; and every decision and choice is made together, not just the choice of one of them. They are *one*, united in everything; not divided or dominated by one or the other of them.

I believe that in a true marriage, everything must be held in common; what belongs to one belongs to both. Their income, property, possessions, awards, honors, accolades, status, position, as well as present and future benefits (earnings, promotions, and savings) belong to both of them. Not only do they have an equal share of all their goods, talents, and gifts, they also share in each other's sufferings, losses, weaknesses, and disabilities. Any duties or responsibilities one spouse has to family, friends, community, Church, or country, belong to both spouses. Whatever sacrifices that one spouse makes to family, friends, community, Church, and country, are made by both spouses. Whatever happens to one of them happens to both of them. Even their own individual body belongs to both of them, because they are no longer two, but *one flesh.*

I see the human family as a *micro-Church.* The marriage between a man and a woman prefigures the marriage between Christ and his Church. Just as a man and woman become one body in Christ, through marriage, the Church becomes one body, the *body of Christ,* through her union with Jesus. There is no separation between Jesus and the Church because they are one body.

If our life in Christ means anything to you, if love can persuade at all, or the Spirit that we have in common, or any tenderness and sympathy, be united in your convictions and united in your love, with a common purpose and a common mind. That is the one thing which would make me completely happy. There must be no competition among you, no conceit; but everybody is to be self-effacing. Always consider the other person to be better than yourself, so that nobody thinks of his own interests first but everybody thinks of other people's interests instead. (JB Phil 2:1—5)

From my observation, when the shift in the cultural mind-set came about—at least in theory—and women were seen to have equal worth and dignity, when women were seen as persons instead of objects, this shift had a radical affect upon marriages of couples, where one or both of them lacked a conversion of hearts. Intellectually, they bought the new mind-set, but their reality, vision of life, and attitudes remained the same. They became confused and divided, and divorce was on the rampage. Battles over custody of children and divorce settlements ensued. Women resisted the equal rights and entitlements of their husbands, regarding their children and custody of them. Men resisted the equal rights and entitlements of their wives, regarding community property, alimony, and retirement. Those who lacked a conversion of heart saw themselves as *victims* and felt violated by their spouse.

In a marriage where the *two become one flesh*, there is no place for revenge, retribution, competition, jealousy, or envy between the spouses; there is nothing that they cannot forgive each other for. Whatever they do to their spouse, they do to themselves. Love cannot exist in a person who refuses to forgive another person; they can neither receive nor give love because their heart is hardened.

Divorce and the consequences of divorce still plague our society, today. We cannot forgive because we do not want to forgive. We want to hold onto our desire for retribution and revenge; and our distorted perception of justice. Unless a person is willing to forgive and let go of their desire for retribution, revenge, and what they perceive to be justice, they will remain in the prison of their own pain. The healing of the wounds and suffering caused by divorce and unjust mind-sets can only come from a conversion of hearts and forgiveness. We cannot forgive those who have hurt us, except through the grace of the Holy Spirit and the will to forgive. But, if we do not forgive we will continue to live in a prison of pain; a prison that we have built ourselves.

It still takes three to make a truly authentic marriage—a man, a woman, and Jesus Christ. A true marriage needs the mind-set that comes from Christ; to "put on the new man" (Eph 4:24). Both, the man and the woman, need to have a conversion of heart; to love each other unconditionally until death, as Jesus loves us. An authentic, true, and sacramental marriage still requires that the *two become one flesh*.

The Church, as the *bride of Christ*, is made up of many members. She is made one through her union and covenant with Jesus, the one *Bridegroom*, who is God. The Church could never be joined with anything less than God; a mere man, or even many men. Only God can make the Church his bride. The covenant relationship between Jesus and the Church is prefigured by the model of a marriage where *two become one flesh*.

5

The Permanence of Marriage

As I reflect upon the need for permanence in marriage in the midst of change, I cannot help but think that sometimes it seems that *arranged marriages* have a better chance of remaining permanent, until death, than marriages that are based on attraction and personal preference. I think that the reason for this is because the spouses, more often, enter into marriage for the right reasons, or at least better reasons. Their desire is for a marriage and a family, and to provide for the well-being of the family together, as parents. They do not seem to have false expectations for one-another. They seem more able to love each other unconditionally. I am not advocating that we go back to arranged marriages, but I see a need to return to the purpose of permanent marriage.

Marriage was designed to be permanent for this life, but the only thing about the spouses that can be permanent is their soul, and their commitment to one another in faith, hope, and love. The physical body is constantly changing, sometimes for better, sometimes for worse, but in the end, it dies. The brain and intellectual capacity is constantly changing, sometimes for better, sometimes for worse, but in the end, it becomes feeble or senile and dies. The same is true of psychological growth, our emotional balance, and our personalities. We are always in a process of change, growth, and dying. The things that people have in common, and the things that attracted them to each other, are constantly changing. Our abilities, capacities, gifts, talents, and strengths are all in a process of change; of growth and decline until finally, death. Most of us go up and down for a long time. Nevertheless, a man and a woman are never really the same person that they were on the day they got married. To expect otherwise is futile.

When a couple get married, they share many of the same values, beliefs, likes and dislikes, goals, ideas, politics, and views on life. But, over time, only the core of those values, beliefs, likes, dislikes, goals, ideas, politics and views on life remain. Marriage is not based on temporary or changing commonalities.

Marital love begins with the will to love. Feelings come and go, and are up and down. Commitment is made with the will. Of course it takes more than commitment and the will to sustain love; and to make a happy, permanent marriage. As long as there is life in our bodies, we love through our bodies. There needs to be a deep affection, touching and hugging, on-going forgiveness, and a deepening of trust from both spouses. These things never die, as long as we are alive and have love. This cannot happen unless a couple is capable of intimacy; able to be fully present to each other, to give their full attention to each other. Many marriages fail because other things and people take precedence over their spouse, and they are seldom able to be present to each other. They are too distracted by career, projects, goals, and other persons. Last, but not least, is the spiritual life of the couple. Praying together is a necessity for a happy and permanent marriage.

The essence and purpose of marriage is *family life*. The mutuality that a couple should share, that is not meant to change, is the fact that they will always be parents together; a mother and a father. They will always have a mutual love and concern for the well-being of their children at every stage of their growth. They will always share a mutual love for each other, which never dies. The foundation of marriage is a mutual commitment; fidelity to each other and the promises made to each other; trust in the good will of each other, in all circumstances; openness to life; and the desire to grow in holiness and virtue. The love that a couple has for each other should become unconditional, and unaffected by change.

A sacramental marriage is an elevated form of marriage, based on our relationship with God in the person of Jesus Christ. It is based on a mutual understanding of the purpose of life; union with God, and growth in holiness and virtue. It is based on our understanding of faith, hope, and love. It is based on our awareness of our need of salvation, and openness to grace; to the free gift of God that comes to us through our spouse, and through us to our spouse. This is why St. Paul and St. Peter urged married couples to submit to one another as to the Lord. How can one be an instrument of Jesus if they are not in communion with him? Married couples are intended to sanctify each other. Sacramental marriage is also based on our openness to life, to participate in the creation of new life. It is based on the motherhood and fatherhood of that life. It is based on our relationship with the Church and the sacraments. The family is a *domestic Church*, with the same mission and purpose of the universal Church.

God is the one who instituted marriage, revealed to us in Genesis; and he has always had a plan and purpose for marriage, which never changes. His purpose was for the creation and sustaining of human life in the midst of a constantly changing world. Marriage is and always has been the only truly viable way of doing this. The parenting of a mother and father is the most ideal means of nurturing and protecting life within the family. It takes families to build a community, and communities to build a world. From the beginning, God's purpose was for one man and one woman to become one flesh; to participate in creation and populate the earth; to nurture and protect their family; to be his stewards over the earth; and for them not to be alone.

In our present times, marriage has gone from being a covenant to being a contract. Marriage has become a commodity, and the spouses and children have become either assets or liabilities. People marry for companionship, security, prestige, shared responsibilities, need for sex, or need for a caretaker. It lasts only as long as both parties fulfill their obligations. Of course, there is usually a physical attraction that brings them together, but that does not last or keep them together. That initial attraction, as well as sex drive, diminishes over time. Only authentic love, trust and commitment, aided by the grace of God and prayer, can keep them together. After all, the body and mind cannot be separated from the spirit, and spiritual life of both spouses. We need to get back to marriage as a covenant, like the covenant between Christ and the Church. This is the model of a true marriage, one that is permanent and life-giving.

6

The Sacrament of Marriage

$\mathcal{P}$art of Jesus' mission was to restore marriage to its original form as God intended it to be in the beginning. This involved much more than ending divorce and irregular marriages; more than baptism and making vows before the witness of a priest and congregation. It also required that man rediscover himself as man, with all his masculine and paternal gifts, and what it means to be a husband and a father. It required that woman rediscover herself as woman, with all her feminine and maternal gifts, and what it means to be a wife and mother. Marriage is a sacrament when it becomes a sign and a witness of the relationship and love of Jesus for his bride, the Church. It requires a total self-donation of both spouses to each other, motivated by the authentic love that comes from God. The spouses see each other as persons and desire the highest good and well-being for each other.

Only authentic love, sacramental love, can sustain a marriage until death. Only a marriage between one man and one woman has the potential of being a sacramental marriage. Only a marriage open to new life, such as procreation, has the potential of being a true and authentic marriage; a covenant of love. Only a marriage that grows in holiness and virtue, especially chastity and fidelity, has the potential of being a sacramental and authentic marriage.

In contrast, our cultural understanding of marriage today seems to be that of a "utilitarian marriage," which sees the partner as an object to fulfill one's physical and emotional needs and desires. It is a contract, rather than a covenant; based on what a person can get from another person, rather than give; based on pleasure and security, rather than on love and family. A utilitarian marriage between two or more persons of the same sex or opposite sex has no hope of ever becoming a true marriage, or growing into a sacramental marriage and authentic love. A couple cannot grow in holiness without virtue; without chastity and fidelity. They will become an "unholy alliance." Instead of becoming a sign for the world, of authentic love, and covenant love, it will become a sign to the world of tyranny, slavery, victimization, and idolatry.

Everyone agrees that it takes much more to make a true mother or father than simply donating an egg or sperm; more than just being the biological mother or father. It also takes much more than providing for a child's basic needs and raising them, in order to be a true mother and father. A true mother and father should be a sign and witness to their children, of covenant love, authentic love. Every child deserves to know and bond with their natural mother and father. They need to know they are loved by their parents and that they were conceived in love. Children have a natural innate longing to know their natural mother and father. This is not always possible, due to divorce and death; nevertheless, it is a deprivation for children not to have their biological parents. Fortunately, however, there are many childless couples who can provide a loving and nurturing family life for them. But, to encourage homosexual couples to adopt children is not for the good of children.

The Church is opposed to the parenting of children by homosexual couples. In this environment, children cannot help but grow up with a lot of confusion; about what it means to be a family; the role and nature of man and woman; and the meaning and purpose of marriage. Children are made vulnerable to growing up with a loss of their own identity as a male or female. This is what the Church believes and teaches; not the present culture.

Surely the Church must oppose any kind of marriage that does not have the potential or possibility of becoming a covenant of authentic love. This would include cohabitation, incest, and polygamy, as well as same-sex marriages. The sanctity of marriage is such a crucial issue today, and cannot be ignored. The institution of marriage and family life are at risk. Wherever the sanctity of a marriage has been compromised or destroyed, the relationship may become abusive. We either grow in holiness and virtue, or we increase in vice and sin.

Many people think that the teachings of the Church are unjust, intolerant, and bigoted; and that the Church is persecuting those with a homosexual orientation or divorced; those who disagree with her teaching on morals. This is not so! The Church has a responsibility to teach the facts of life, and to enforce them for members of the Church. The facts of life come from God. Every human being is born with various impediments that deprive us of some of the goods of life. We cannot grow in holiness by denying that we have impediments, or by not accepting the deprivations in life that come from them. This is what it means to take up our cross and carry it. Not every man is called to be a priest; not every person has a vocation to a religious community; not every woman is able to give birth; not every person has a vocation to marriage and family life; not every couple is capable of having a sacramental marriage, a true marriage; not every person is capable of parenting children.

For Catholics, it takes a lot more than simply getting married in Church, before a deacon or priest, to make a sacramental marriage. It presupposes that the spouses are mature Christians, with a strong commitment to Jesus and the Church. It presupposes that the spouses have a developed character; that they live the virtues, especially fidelity and chastity. It presupposes that there are no spiritual, physical, psychological, mental, emotional, or moral impediments that would be an obstacle to a sacramental marriage. The reason that there are so many divorces and annulments amongst Catholics, today, is because there was a lack of formation, maturity, and spiritual growth. In some cases, there may have been serious impediments that were not seen at the time of marriage. This is also why, even among those who are still married, probably only one in ten marriages are healthy and happy marriages; nevertheless, if a couple is committed to each other, have good will, and believe in God, God can bring good out of their marriage, in spite of their limitations and crosses they have to bear.

There was a time, during my lifetime, when "no-fault divorce" was illegal in America. Once it was made legal, divorce became a promise for happiness, and easily accessible; even for Catholics. The Church adapted to the times by establishing a more accessible annulment process, because so many Catholics were affected by this cultural change, and getting divorced.

It seems to me that when the Church opened the door to annulments and widened the boundaries for impediments, many saw this as the first step towards approving or accepting divorce. The number of annulments and divorces among Catholics, however, has something to tell us about the number of Catholics who were not formed in the *faith*, and not ready for a sacramental marriage. Most Catholics, who get married in Church, as well as those in *irregular* relationships, have good will in accordance with their spiritual formation and conscience. Perhaps this is the reason for the good fruit that we see in many irregular relationships. No Christian intentionally wants to be separated from God or his grace when they enter any kind of relationship with another person.

When a couple gets divorced, it should be a *red flag* to the Church that something is missing in their adult conversion process. Instead, we are too quick to judge it as sin and pass judgment. Catholics should really not be encouraged to enter a sacramental marriage unless they are fully formed adults and fully converted. Sacramental marriage is not for children. In the early Church, St. Paul saw an impediment to a sacramental marriage between two non-Christians, when only one of them converted and became a follower of Jesus. He permitted dissolution of the marriage, releasing the couple from their commitment if the non-believing spouse refused to stay in the marriage due to their different mindsets. (ICSB 1 Cor 7:13—15)

To me, the preparation for a sacramental marriage has to do with faith formation, not cultural formation. A sacramental marriage should require a full conversion:

- A mature faith formation; knowledge of the teachings of the Church and marriage preparation
- A commitment to follow the teachings of the Church
- A commitment to intentional discipleship

- A commitment to live the Gospel of Jesus Christ in faith and morals
- A personal relationship with Jesus as Lord, and a regular prayer life
- A personal experience of the baptism of the Holy Spirit, or release of the Holy Spirit
- Free will and consent of one man and one woman to enter a sacramental marriage
- A commitment to a permanent, sexually exclusive, and intimate relationship of marriage
- Freedom from all moral, physical, psychological, emotional, and mental impediments
- Desire and intention to procreate, and to maintain Catholic family life

Of course, this is the ideal, rather than the reality. It could be argued whether any Christians, today, are fully mature (psychologically or spiritually) when they first get married. The danger is that divorce will become the norm for Catholics, regardless of faith formation; and that Catholics will continue to leave the Church, or be Catholics in name only, without growing in formation and being able to benefit by the sacraments.

Personally, I think that annulments should only be encouraged for those who are evangelized first, and receive counseling and healing; those who have come to a full conversion since their divorce. Otherwise, it really is of no spiritual benefit to them. They are still not free for a sacramental marriage. If there are impediments to the faith, for which they are not seen to be culpable or responsible, they should be encouraged to receive the sacraments, but also offered every pastoral help to grow and mature in their faith; to experience a total conversion.

The present annulment process may be able to determine a person's lack of culpability for divorce, as far as psychological and moral formation, but it does not encourage conversion and growth in the faith as adult Catholics, or determine their spiritual formation. I think that it is fair to presume that most Catholics who are divorced and remarried, or who have had an annulment, are still not psychologically mature; have impediments to marriage; have not been formed in the faith; and have not experienced a total conversion of mind and heart.

Today, we cannot even prevent mentally handicapped adults from getting married; and it may be a reproach against their dignity to even try, because their conscience and understanding cannot accept it. But, we know they will be severely handicapped as far as the expectations for a mature marriage and family life are concerned. They do not have the capacity for it. The Church does not allow them to enter into a sacramental marriage because of this impediment. This is also why *age* can be an impediment. The faith and capacity to trust, of a child, is not the same as an adult. They are not mentally or emotionally mature and cannot make wise choices.

In our present time, for those who are psychologically immature adults, uneducated, poor, or from unstable family backgrounds, a permanent, healthy marriage is impossible without a radical conversion and faith in Jesus Christ. Even those who are psychologically mature adults, educated, financially secure, and from stable family backgrounds, are finding it almost impossible to have permanent, healthy marriages and family life. Natural gifts and talents are not enough. We need grace from God, and the gifts and fruits of the Holy Spirit, in order to save marriage and family life. Formation and conversion are necessary to be open to the grace given through the sacrament of marriage.

At the time of my marriage, I did not know that I needed Jesus to be Lord in my life, to be the center of my life. I did not know that I was only a pilgrim in this world, preparing for eternal life in heaven. I did not know that I was involved in a spiritual warfare, and not fighting only enemies of flesh and blood. I did not know that the Gospel is usually counter-cultural to the prevailing culture in which we live. I did not know about the power and gifts of the Holy Spirit; how to recognize the leading of the Holy Spirit, and how to respond to the gifts or to use them. I did not have an adequate prayer life, or example of Christian living in my family. I did not know the Scriptures, the full Gospel of Jesus. I did not know the example of all the saints. I did not know the difference between a sacramental marriage and a non-sacramental marriage. I did not have discernment; know how to discern between my will and God's will. I did not know how to *test the spirit*. I did not know myself; my defects or my gifts and talents. My husband and I were both more like Old Testament Jews who had not yet really entered into the new covenant. We heard about Jesus but did not know him intimately. Without full conversion and formation, our hearts were not open to the fullness of truth. A sacramental marriage is not just a covenant between two people, but three. Jesus has to be the center of the marriage. We have to be spiritually awake or we will not be able to prevent *the thief who comes in the night to rob and steal* (Mt 24:43) from robbing us of our marriage.

The only thing I knew about marriage was that it was *until death do you part*, that it was an exclusive sexual relationship between one man and one woman, that the purpose was for procreation, that we had a joint checking account and shared everything in common, that we needed to raise our children Catholic, and that we had to be married in a Catholic Church, by the priest. I wanted to be married and to raise a large family. That was my dream! I wanted to be the perfect wife and mother.

Moses allowed for the Israelites to divorce because of their *hardness of heart*. They were incapable of marriage according to the mind and will of God; incapable of even understanding what marriage is. We often assume that Jesus was saying that Moses was wrong to allow divorce for the Israelites. But, this is not what Scripture says. It seems to me that Jesus was simply stating why Moses allowed divorce and what God intended from the beginning (Mt 19:8 — 9). Jesus did not come to change the Law of Moses, but to change the hearts of the people through grace and truth: "For the law was given through Moses; grace and truth came through Jesus Christ." (Jn 1:17)

A legitimate marriage between one man and one woman was a sacrament and a covenant, from the *beginning*. Divorce and remarriage was adultery, from the *beginning*. The people were closed to *grace and truth* because of the *hardness of their hearts,* and because Jesus had not yet come into the world. Being a baptized Catholic is not enough to make one capable of living the sacrament of marriage. It seems to me that unless we are open, and disposed to receive grace and truth, at the time of marriage, there is no marriage covenant. Unless we first know and desire the *truth,* we will not be able to live it. This is part of the formation of a Catholic conscience. In addition to this, some people are emotionally or mentally handicapped, which also affects the formation of their consciences, and is an impediment to a sacramental marriage. This should not however, exclude them from full communion with the Church.

If a couple is not mature or not ready to follow the Church, they are not ready to enter a sacramental marriage. They probably will get married anyway, outside the Church, but at least, when their marriage fails and they repent and return to the Church, they will be admitted to the sacraments. Many people today reject the *teaching of the Church* because they have lost faith in those who have authority; due to abuse, bad example, and false teaching. These representatives will be held accountable for the sins of many people; just as some parents will be held accountable for the sins of their children.

7

The Good Shepherd

Is there ever a time or circumstance when remarriage after divorce, without a formal annulment, is not adultery? Is there ever a time when their second marriage could be holy, and not considered adultery? Is there ever a time when the couple would not be judged as living in a *state of habitual mortal sin?* Can a person or couple manifest the fruit of the Spirit if they are in a state of mortal sin? Is there ever a time when they could receive the sacraments? What do we mean by *mortal sin?* Do we really understand what sin is? Why do we need the Eucharist and on-going sanctifying grace? Do we really understand what it means to be properly disposed to receive the Eucharist? Why do we still need Jesus? What is a sacramental marriage? How do we reach out to all the baptized Christians, lost in the world, and bring them back into the fold?

I believe that these are the kinds of questions and issues that Pope Francis is grappling with in his recent encyclical, *Amoris Laetitia,* and why he appears to be begging the Church to enter into discernment in the Holy Spirit. It seems to me that he is suggesting an *internal forum* for pastors to use in counseling couples in irregular relationships, in order to lead them back into the Church. He may also be suggesting this as an option to the annulment process—in some cases. I believe that Pope Francis is trying to find a way to feed all the sheep from the table of the Lord; all those who sincerely want to follow the Lord; all those who are hungry for God; all those who believe in Jesus and desire what he has to offer; all those who seek healing and new life. He represents the *Good Shepherd* who leaves the ninety-nine and goes in search of the lost sheep. (Pope Francis 2016)

I cannot presume to know what is going on in the mind and heart of Pope Francis, but his writings have raised a lot of questions for me. I asked myself, what was Pope Francis really trying to say in *Amoris Laetitia*? He was not teaching people to break or disrespect the Law. He was not saying that we should change our doctrines. The Church can never condone adultery, or say it is not a sin. She can never call evil, good, or say that God leads us to divorce and adultery. But, can we ever know for sure who is an adulterer in the eyes of God? Can we ever know for sure who God has *joined together*, and made *one flesh*? Can we ever label anyone an *adulterer* with certitude? Francis was not saying that divorce is ever good; that homosexual unions or behavior is ever good; that adultery and immoral behavior are ever good. Pope Francis was very direct in saying that all divorce is evil; all break-ups of the family are evil; all homosexual behavior is evil, and same-sex unions are illicit. He also condemned all attempts to change or distort divine revelation. He was also saying that although we cannot "do evil that good may come," it is also true that God can bring good out of evil, and even sin, for those who trust in him; those who repent and receive the *forgiveness of sins*. He was also saying what marriage should be like, and what family life should be like; what children should be taught and how they should be formed. Divorce is evil, but so is an unholy marriage without peace and joy; marriages that are abusive, slavery, immoral, demeaning, and seedbeds for hatred and violence. Family life that resembles a mob, a gang, or a terrorist group is also evil. Surely, God did not join these couples in marriage? Marriage requires sacrifice and hard work, and is not always easy, but God never intended it to be a prison or hell on earth. Marriage should also include the fruit of the Spirit: "love, joy, peace, patience, kindness, gentleness, faithfulness, and self-control" (Gal 5:22). Those who are yoked unevenly really cannot become one flesh.

It seems to me that Pope Francis was challenging the Church to see the divorced and remarried, everyone in an irregular relationship, as individual persons and children of God, instead of *adulterers;* especially the poor who have no advocate. He challenged us to look at the nature of sin. As I reflect on the nature of sin, it seems to me that sin always causes us to go from bad to worse; not from bad to good; from belief to unbelief. There are many divorced couples who experience, not just one divorce, but several. This is also true among many who have their marriages annulled. They end up repeating the same bad choices and behavior. But, if someone goes from a bad marriage and divorce to a good marriage, even though they did not get an annulment, can we really say that they are living in a state of habitual adultery? Would not sin make the second marriage even worse than the first? What happened? How can this be? Is this even reasonable? Can we be sure that the second marriage really is better than the previous marriage? How can we help people recognize that their illicit relationship is not good for them, that it is a sin? Otherwise, how can they leave it, or even repent? Sin begets sin. Some people want to leave their illicit relationship but do not have the strength or the power; they are in bondage and need deliverance. Some people find it hard to believe that they are in an adulterous relationship because their life is better than their previous marriage and they see good fruit; perhaps they are blind and need to be healed, or perhaps the Church is blind. Is it possible that the Lord has seen their hearts and situation and granted them *forgiveness of sin*? If they are forgiven, can they still be adulterers; especially if their former marriage never was a true marriage? If they are forgiven by God, can we deny them the sacraments? Pope Francis never suggested that they immediately return to the sacraments. These are hard questions, questions that cannot be answered with *yes* or *no*. These are questions that Pope Francis is asking the Church to consider.

Pope Francis acknowledged that homosexual behavior is evil, and produces more sin and more suffering; but, so is isolation, loneliness, hatred, rejection, judgment, condemnation; the lack of discernment, understanding, compassion, and love for the human person. He challenged us to see each person through the eyes of Jesus, and do what he would do. The Church must teach the Law, doctrines, and Scripture; everything that Jesus commanded us to teach. But, it is also necessary to teach the purpose, meaning, values, morality, and virtues of the Law and doctrines. It is necessary for the Church to give grace in order to conquer sin. The Law cannot save us. The Jews had the Law; they knew what was sin and what was not sin, but it was not enough. They needed grace. They needed the very life blood of Jesus to flow into them. How can we punish people for breaking the law by refusing them the grace they need to change their lives? How can people, living a homosexual lifestyle, let go of it unless they are offered something better in its place?

Pope Francis was not advocating that we permit, excuse, defend, or encourage sin. He was saying that we need to search for the lost sheep, carry them home, tend their wounds, and feed them. We do this by helping them to form their conscience; by healing them; by listening to them; by giving them good catechesis; by giving them the good news of the Gospel; by giving them hope of salvation and heaven; and by giving them the sacraments when possible.

Pope Francis condemned division and apostasy. He also condemned the leaders of the Church who drive the people away by sexually abusing children; by their lust for power, praise, and honor; by their greed and lack of poverty; by their pride, arrogance, and self-righteousness; and by their abuse of authority and power. He condemned both, the teaching of immorality and hedonism, and the rigid, pharisaic legalism in interpreting the Law. Like St. Paul, he condemned those who wanted the Church to be *under the law* instead of *under the Spirit*; to return to the old covenant. He did not call out anyone by name. Those who are guilty know who they are.

Do we really trust that Pope Francis is *Peter*, and that he was chosen by God and given authority for this mission in time; that he was duly elected by the bishops; that he is a man of morals, holiness, faith, and love for the poor and the Church; that there are more prayers and grace allotted to him than anyone else in the world? Then, why are we so quick to disagree and judge his words as wrong? Why are we not able to give him the benefit of the doubt, and seek to hear what he is really trying to say? Why do we seem to

trust more in our own knowledge and understanding, our own perception, than we do the one that God chose to be Peter? Why do we
trust more in the written word than in Jesus, the true Word of God?
Why do we trust more in rules and laws than we do the Holy Spirit?
Surely, there must be a solution to this dilemma; one that does not
violate the revelation of truth, and is one that people can live with,
within reason? Perhaps what needs to change, or rather develop, is
our understanding of sin, and the proper disposition for receiving
the sacraments. If the annulment process is a valid gift of the Holy
Spirit, and not just legalized divorce, then surely, the *internal forum*
by ordained authority is just as valid and trustworthy.

Jesus said, of the Holy Spirit, "And when he comes he will convince the world of sin and of righteousness and of judgment: of sin,
because they do not believe in me; of righteousness, because I go
to the Father, and you will see me no more; of judgment, because
the ruler of this world is judged" (Jn 16:8—11). Sin is basically,
unbelief; they crucified Jesus as a criminal, although he was innocent, because they did not believe in him.

Pope Francis has challenged me to reflect more on the Eucharist,
as well as the kind of disposition we should have when we receive
the Eucharist. I cannot help wondering how the Church has gone
from St. Paul's exhortation to the Corinthians about the *unworthy
manner* of receiving the Eucharist and the factions and divisions
in the community—to our present understanding of an unworthy
state, such as the *state of mortal sin*. It seems to me that anyone
who is truly in a *state of mortal sin*, cut off from sanctifying grace,
would be in a spiritual state of death, and would not want to go
anywhere near a Church, unless it was to deliberately mock God
or the Church.

When St. Paul reproaches the Corinthians, regarding the Lord's Supper, he points out two problems. First, he points out the divisions and factions among them. At that time, the Eucharist was combined with the sharing of a common meal, in homes. Those who arrived first were well-fed and some were even drunk; while, others received nothing to eat or drink. It is suggested that perhaps the divisions were between the poor and the more prosperous; or between those who had more prestige and were well known and those who were unknown; or between those who claimed they followed Paul, or Peter, or Apollos, or Christ; or between conservatives and liberals. These divisions and discriminations were a contradiction to the very meaning of the Eucharist: "Because there is one bread, we who are many are one body, for we all partake of the one bread" (ICSB 1 Cor 10:17). Secondly, Paul reprimanded them for their "unworthy manner" of receiving Eucharist. They ate and drank as though they were only partaking of ordinary bread and wine; without acknowledging the body of the Lord. This is unbelief, and "profaning the Body and Blood of the Lord" (ICSB 1 Cor 11:27). This is why many of them were getting sick, and even dying; bringing judgment upon themselves. We seem to have the same divisions, factions, and discriminations, today; as well as unbelief, not acknowledging Jesus; and lack of humility and desire for grace when we receive him. (1Cor 11:17—34)

The Eucharist is "the source and summit of the Christian life" (CCC 1324). It is not only the body, blood, soul, and divinity of Jesus, but it is his whole life; what he was about and what he did for us; why he came to us and where he came from. Eucharist is an act of thanksgiving to God, in union with Jesus, as well as communion with our neighbor. It is the fulfillment of the Two Great

Commandments of God—love of God and love of neighbor; and unites us with the whole body of Christ, all baptized Christians throughout the world. Jesus is the bread of heaven, sent by God, to feed and nourish us with the very life-blood of Jesus; given for all his sheep and lambs; the broken and the lost. He is wheat that has been broken, crushed, and ground into dust; then resurrected into bread. The passion, death, and resurrection of Jesus are timeless events, spread out over the history of the world, over all people, until the end of time when he comes again. The Eucharist reopens the window to Calvary, showing us his love by pouring out his body and blood on the cross, laying down his life for us, while we are yet sinners. We continue to reap the benefits and experience the effects of his great sacrifice, for all time.

The Eucharist is no ordinary bread and wine that we receive; it is the very life, Body and Blood, soul and divinity of Jesus. It is Jesus; gathering us together, touching us, being with us, healing us, and filling us with grace and power that will transform us into his likeness.

The Eucharist is not a reward for holiness or goodness. It is not bread and wine to fill the bellies of a few. It is not reserved for the elites of the world. It is not ordinary bread, shared as a sign of fellowship. It is a gift, given freely; the gift of Jesus. It is *God with us*. The proper or worthy disposition to receive Eucharist is receptivity and humility; to recognize and acknowledge Jesus' presence in the Eucharist; to hunger and thirst for God; to yearn for healing and new life. The proper disposition does not have to do with worthiness or sinfulness. No one is worthy. The proper disposition is faith and humility. We need to say from our heart, "Lord, I am not worthy that you should enter under my roof; say but the word and I shall be healed" (Canon of the Mass). We need to know that we need Jesus. We need to desire to be made whole, and desire the grace that will change our life. Those who do not believe the Eucharist is the body and blood of Jesus should not receive. Those who have hardened their heart against God should not receive. I believe that if we really understood how powerful the Eucharist is, and what a great miracle it is, we could not deny it to anyone of good will who really wanted to receive. I must add that this is only my opinion. Good will, to me, has to do with conscience and motivation of the heart. It has been the teaching of the Church, however, that anyone in an objective state of adultery or serious sin cannot receive the sacraments; the reason being that they would not be in communion with the mind of the Church, and because it would give scandal to the faithful. If the Church is right, then the sacraments would not be of benefit, and may even be detrimental to these recipients. Nevertheless, Jesus gave the Church authority *to loose and to bind*, not me. (Mt 16:19)

Jesus is literally present with us at every Mass we attend. The Eucharist makes Jesus present among us. Jesus never turned anyone away who came to him, including Gentiles, Romans, Pharisees, and even his enemies. The Eucharist, under the appearance of bread and wine, is the greatest visible miracle that Jesus gave us. Miracles happen every day, but we fail to recognize them. Sometimes, even very ordinary and natural experiences that happen to people turn out to be miracles. They are miracles because, through them, God produces extraordinary or supernatural changes in them through their experience. For instance, someone with a hardened heart who has blocked their relationship with God because they are unable to forgive someone who hurt them, may hear the Word of God preached in the power and authority of the Holy Spirit, and suddenly that Word penetrates their hardened heart and they are able to forgive and to receive God's love in a way that radically transforms their life. This is a miracle. I believe that there are also visible, supernatural miracles that happen every day, but we fail to recognize them because we do not expect to see miracles in our times. For example, we could walk down the street and pass a close relative that we have not seen for years, and not recognize them because we do not expect to see them in that place and time. Perhaps, this was the disciples' experience of Jesus on the road to Emmaus.

I recall a miracle that I witnessed many years ago. I was part of a non-denominational charismatic prayer group, and I was the only Catholic in the group. I felt very close to these women and shared wonderful fellowship with them. One of the women, the leader of the group, was a special inspiration to me. Her relationship with the Lord was very deep, and she seemed to have all the fruits of the Holy Spirit. After a while, she challenged me on some of my Catholic beliefs; especially in regards to the Eucharist, the pope, and the saints. I was very defensive at first, and found myself reacting by trying to convince her of the validity of my beliefs. She would gently say, "Just take it to the Lord in prayer," convinced that the Lord would show me the error of my ways. I followed her advice and took it to prayer. At first, I experienced a lot of turmoil and struggle. As a Catholic, I always believed that the Eucharist was a very important means of grace in order for us to grow in holiness. But, my friend did not partake in the Eucharist, and she seemed to be much holier than I was. I found myself faced with doubts about my faith. I began to think that maybe the Eucharist wasn't as important as I thought it was, or that she was not as holy as I thought she was. One minute I was judging her and looking for faults in her, and the next minute I doubted my own beliefs. It was a very painful and difficult struggle. I felt so confused. Finally, with many tears, I cried out to the Lord and told him that all this was beyond my understanding. I prayed that he would not let me doubt or reject any gifts he gave me, especially my faith in the Eucharist, and that I would continue to love my friend and not judge her. I turned it over to God, and believed that he would straighten everything out for me because he knew my will was good. I felt at peace.

The next day I went to Mass. Our chaplain had a particular problem with controlling his anger. Before Mass started, he would always set out a plate for unconsecrated hosts, for those who wanted to receive Communion. He wanted to be sure he had enough for everyone who wanted to receive, and did not want to have extra consecrated hosts. Invariably, people would forget to put a host on the plate and then when they came to Communion, he would have to break the hosts in halves or quarters. This made him furious. This particular day was the same. He was so angry throughout the Mass. I put my hand on his shoulder and he pulled away in anger. After the Mass, he came to me and said, "You are going to have to pray for me. I get so angry when this happens and I cannot control myself. I feel like such a hypocrite saying the Mass while being so angry." I told him I would pray for him. In the meantime, we were preparing to go on a pilgrimage to Rome. There were about fifteen people from our parish going, including our chaplain. When we got to Rome, our priest prepared to say the Mass for us in the little chapel over the tomb of St. Peter. Our priest started by asking us how many wanted to receive Communion. Then, he counted out the hosts. After he began the Mass, other people who were not part of our group, saw that there was a Mass going on and began to pack into that little chapel. After Communion, I said to my husband, "the Lord multiplied the hosts!" My husband said, "No, I did not go because I did not think there would be enough, and others probably did not go either." I said, "No, I know that the Lord multiplied the hosts!" After Mass, our priest came up to my husband and myself and said, "You do not have to believe this, but I counted out fifteen hosts to consecrate, and at Communion time, I broke five in half; then, I got angry and thought to myself, if there is not enough, they can just go without. There were at least sixty people that came up to receive, and I had exactly enough for everyone. I think the Lord is trying to tell me, "All those who come to me hungry, will not go away empty." The priest was healed of this problem of anger; it no longer bothered him if there were not enough hosts.

Two days later, my husband and I went to Sunday Mass at St. Peters on our own. Every altar in the Basilica was packed with people. Finally, I saw two young priests carrying a ciborium. I told my husband, "Lets follow them; they must be going to say Mass." They found an empty altar and began to prepare for Mass. They were American. People began to gather around the altar, and the young priest asked, "How many would like to receive Communion?" Then he counted out the hosts. After he began the Mass, more people arrived and packed around the altar. When the young priest got to his homily, he seemed to trip over his words; nothing came out right. I thought to myself, "I bet this is his first Mass." It just seemed to me as though the priest looked up to God to say, "Why did you ever choose me?" This priest also ended up with exactly enough hosts for everyone who came up to receive.

This time, my husband recognized the miracle and acknowledged that the Lord had multiplied the hosts. The next day, our group went on a tour of the North American Seminary. Suddenly, our priest came running up to my husband and me. He had been talking to one of the priests who were at the Mass that my husband and I had gone to the day before. Our priest said, "You will never believe what happened! I was talking to that young priest, and he said that his friend was saying his first Mass at St. Peters' the day before, and the Lord multiplied the hosts. I told him that the same thing happened to me."

As far as I know, no one other than my husband, me, and the priests that celebrated the Masses, noticed these miracles. In both of these miracles of multiplication of the hosts, the priests experienced spiritual healing; which was the greater miracle. It amazed me that these miracles could take place right under our noses, with so many people present, yet, only a few of us were able to see it. Not only were the priests healed, but I also experienced a healing. It was as though scales fell from my eyes. I realized that the Eucharist is a gift, and my faith in it is a gift. I realized how powerful a gift this is to those who have faith. At the same time, I realized that the Lord meets everyone where they are at and that he will use any means he can to give grace to those who believe in him. I realized that my friend could become holy, become a great saint, as long as she is faithful to what the Lord gives to her, even without the Eucharist. When I returned home, I was able to love and accept my friends without giving up my own faith or beliefs. In fact, my devotion to the Lord's presence in the Eucharist was increased a hundred fold.

I dare to say, there are some people who are in bondage to sin, such as those who suffer from addictions and uncontrollable situations and behaviors, that may be truly disposed to receive Eucharist, while others who are in an objective *state of grace* and receive every day, may not be disposed to receive at all. There are many Christians of good will who cannot become free of their bondage to serious sin on their own. But, Jesus can set them free if they ask him. However, it may not happen immediately. Sometimes, something else has to be healed first. As long as they remain within the fold, and are given every means of grace and nourishment, they will eventually be set free. A parable comes to mind, that seems to illustrate this:

> "The kingdom of heaven may be compared to a man who sowed good seed in his field; but while men were sleeping, his enemy came and sowed weeds among the wheat, and went away. So when the plants came up and bore grain, then the weeds appeared also. And the servants of the householder came and said to him, 'Sir, did you not sow good seed in your field? How then has it weeds?' He said to them, 'An enemy has done this.' The servants said to him, 'Then do you want us to go and gather them?' But he said, 'No; lest in gathering the weeds you root up the wheat along with them. Let both grow together until the harvest; and at harvest time I will tell the reapers, 'Gather the weeds first and bind them in bundles to be burned, but gather the wheat into my barn.'" (ICSB Mt 13:24—30)

We know that marriage and family life, today, are undergoing severe spiritual warfare. There are many victims. Pope Francis has recognized this, and does not want to lose any of the wheat, or sheep. Many people who are in situations such as irregular marriages, same-sex unions, divorced and remarried, drug and alcohol addictions, homosexual relationships, confused gender identity, abortions, etc. are victims of spiritual warfare; they are prisoners of war. The real enemies are those who are strong advocates of these things and do all they can to publicly promote them as something good and natural, and to make them available to all; those who want to make laws that will punish anyone who is opposed to these things.

Night and day are very different. It is not easy to walk or journey at night, without stumbling and falling. We are living in a time of great darkness upon the earth. I recall a vision that the Lord gave me almost forty years ago. It is as clear, now, as it was then. My children were all very young. I had just returned from a pilgrimage to the Holy Land. On the plane coming home, I was especially drawn to reflect on this scripture:

> Hear, O Israel! The Lord is our God; the Lord alone! Therefore, you shall love the Lord, your God, with all your heart, and with all your soul, and with all your strength. Take to heart these words which I enjoin on you today. Drill them into your children. Speak of them at home and abroad, whether you are busy or at rest. Bind them at your wrist as a sign and let them be as a pendant on your forehead. Write them on the doorposts of your houses and on your gates. (NAB Dt 6:4—9)

That evening, as I was praying, my eyes became very heavy and I could not keep them open. As soon as I closed them, I had an *intellectual vision*. By this, I mean that I did not see any images with my imagination, or as in a dream. I saw the vision with my understanding. It was like a *knowing;* something infused. I was standing before a tunnel, and told that everyone would have to go through that tunnel. I was told that I would have to take my children through the tunnel, but I was allowed to go into the tunnel first to see what it was like. I went into the tunnel and it was total darkness. It went for thousands of miles in every direction. I knew that there was a light at the end of the tunnel, but it was too far off to be seen. This light at the end of the tunnel represented the kingdom of God, the New Jerusalem, and heaven.

One could get lost in this tunnel, going around in circles. There was a light in my heart, however, and I was told that all I needed to do was start walking and trust that the light within me would lead me through the tunnel. I also perceived that there were many thieves within the tunnel, waiting to steal my children and take them off into slavery. I would have to keep my children close to me because the light within them was not fully formed, and they did not know how to trust the light to lead them.

When I came out of the tunnel, I asked, "Lord, how can I keep my children close to me? I have four children and only two hands?" Then, I reflected that I would get a rope and tie them to me, forming a circle, like beads on a rosary. Then, I heard a voice say, "A rope will not be strong enough. The thieves can cut through the rope. You will need a chain that cannot be cut." At that moment, my husband came over to shake me because he thought I had died. I went back to pray and asked the Lord, "What does the rope symbolize, and what does the chain symbolize?" I was given to understand that the rope symbolized my natural gifts and talents, which would not be strong enough. I would need the gifts of the Holy Spirit, to connect and hold us together. I was then reminded of the scripture from Deuteronomy. I needed to make this my life, and give it to my children.

I also understood that this vision was personal for me and my children, but also universal. The *woman* represented the Church and the sacraments, and the children are the people of God, the body of Christ. The Church on earth would also have to go through this tunnel of darkness, but the Holy Spirit would guide her through. As long as her children stayed together, in the Church, trusting in her and not going their own way, we would all get through this darkness together. The *woman* also represented Mary, the mother of the Church and the mother of Jesus. The circlet was the rosary. Mary would bind us together through the rosary, and take us through the tunnel, if we turn to her. She always leads us to Jesus.

Dreams and visions, as well as allegories and parables, can be multidimensional and have multiple meanings. They are teaching tools. I was not Mary, nor was I the Church. I was only a symbol, called to become like Mary, and like the Church. The reality is that I am very imperfect and have failed many times to trust in the light and allow it to lead me out of the darkness, and to protect my children from evil.

Hindsight is often much clearer than foresight. My vision was a reminder that my first vocation is to be a handmaid of the Lord; to maintain and nurture my personal relationship with Jesus, the light within me, so that he could lead me. My second priority was to protect my family, as mother and spiritual mother. Nevertheless, I neglected my relationship with Jesus as much as I did with my natural husband, even though Jesus was much more faithful than my husband was. I also frequently neglected the care of my children in order to serve the Church and minister to others. I allowed my priorities to get out of order, which resulted in the loss of my marriage, and my children all leaving the Church. This was not intentional, and I tried to put my family first; but as the Lord warned me, it would take a total commitment and abandonment to the will of God, and the gifts of the Holy Spirit, to overcome the darkness and enter the kingdom of God.

In spite of my failures, the Lord did not abandon me, or my children. He is truly, the *Good Shepherd* (Lk 15:4). Nevertheless, everyone needs to cultivate a personal relationship with Jesus; to be *handmaids of the Lord*. Those who are called to marriage and family life need to become aware that their vocation is to the sanctity of marriage and family. We need to give our children all that the Lord has given to us; then, we will have more to give to others.

Pope Francis reminds us that the family is a *domestic Church*. This is really where the Church started, before and after the Incarnation of Jesus. God could have incarnated as a grown man, a rabbi, an ordained minister of the Church, or a king. But, he did not! He came as an infant; born of a virgin; in a stable. It all started with Mary, not Peter. It started in a *holy family*, a *domestic Church*. It started with family life. The Church needs to retrace her steps, to go back to her roots, to take a good hard look at family life. Without family life, there can be no Church. Family life is under attack and in danger of being destroyed. It is the Church's mission to save and to rescue families; not to leave them for dead.

8

Divorce and Annulment: My Story

I realize how vulnerable I am making myself in sharing my experience of marriage, divorce, and annulment. So, I beg your indulgence and prayers in advance. I speak from experience, as one who was divorced after a long marriage and raising a family; and who then received an annulment several years later.

Before this marriage, I was a victim of *date rape* by a man I was dating, and became pregnant. I was eighteen, at the time, and entered into a civil marriage for the sake of my baby, but never lived with him, or told my parents that I was raped. The marriage was annulled when I married my second husband. I was twenty-one, at the time, and we were engaged for a year before our marriage.

Divorce was such a contradiction to our life. My husband and I were raised Catholic and had always been practicing Catholics. After three years of marriage, I experienced the *baptism of the Holy Spirit,* and from that time on, Jesus was the center of my life. We had been married for twenty-four years, and both, my husband and I were totally committed to serving the Church. My husband was a career officer in the military, as well as a deacon in the Catholic

Church, and I was a spiritual director and involved in many different ministries. Our children went to Catholic school, prayer meetings, youth retreats and conferences. Our family life revolved around the Church. It was not long, however, before we began to experience a lot of spiritual warfare; neither of us was really fully prepared for that. The enemy always knows our weakest spots. Our children came under heavy attack, and we lacked the necessary knowledge and psychological tools to protect them. My husband and I could not even take care of ourselves, or each other.

When my marriage was on the brink of divorce, the military transferred my husband three thousand miles away, for three years. I was left to sell our house, move to a new community—where we planned to retire—and to pick up the pieces of a fractured and wounded family. I went into rehab because I was consuming too much wine. Later, I discovered that this was not my problem, but a symptom of the problem. I was using wine to numb the pain that I was in. This is common with people who are going through a divorce. They look for any means to distract them from the pain and loneliness—alcohol, drugs, gambling, pornography, affairs, food, shopping—even idolatry.

Our marriage ended in divorce before either of us could get the healing we needed to make the necessary changes for a healthy marriage. I discovered that I was suffering from burn-out, change of life, stress, and an accumulation of grief and trauma; not to mention, my own personal weaknesses. One friend of ours referred to me as the feminine counterpart of Job. Together, all these things were slowly killing me; I broke down, physically, mentally, emotionally, and even spiritually. That was when I went for help. Sometimes we have to literally hit bottom—come to the end of our human strength — before we are forced to get the help we need. I literally cried out to God for help, crying buckets of tears. Then, I went for medical help. I discovered that I needed to learn how to say *no* without feeling guilty. I discovered that I needed to learn how to discern between what was my responsibility and what was not my responsibility; I tended to take responsibility for people and things that were not my responsibility. I needed to become aware of my limitations and surrender them to God in humility, instead of punishing myself for them, or blaming others for them. I needed to become aware of my own personal wants, needs, and desires, and to learn how to care for and nurture myself.

I was always very independent and never wanted or expected others to take care of me, but I also did not know how to take care of myself. I thought I did, but actually I seldom even knew what I needed or wanted. I saw my purpose in life as being to serve and love others; to make others happy, not myself. So, I neglected taking care of myself. I did not know how to ask for help, or who to ask. I did not know how to cope with my emotions and feelings. My emotions were out of control and my feelings were suppressed until they became numb. My priorities became confused and out of order. I needed therapy, but even more than that, I needed the Church and pastoral counseling. I did get therapy, but ended up in a worse state — with spiritual amnesia and a divorce. My therapist was also on the brink of a divorce, and was a fallen away Catholic with a lot of anger towards the Church.

Our purpose in life is to love God with all our heart, soul, mind, and strength; and to love our neighbor as ourselves. This is why we were created. Our first priority is our relationship with God, which includes our relationship with our own self, and the salvation of our soul. Self-knowledge and knowledge of God go hand in hand. Humility enables us to know the difference—who God is and who we are. If we are not in right relationship with God, we will not be able to be in right relationship with anyone else. Our second priority is our spouse and children. If we are not in right relationship with God, our relationship with our spouse and children will suffer. We will not have good judgment or be able to make good decisions. We will not be able to provide our family with the right kind of guidance and nurturing. Our love will be disordered. This will affect our relationships with everyone outside our home as well. If our immediate family unit is healthy and ordered, our love will flow out from it to others outside our home—family and relatives, friends, and community. Our priorities will be in order. If our family unit is not healthy, all our other relationships will suffer, as well. It takes two to make a marriage healthy, and two to get a divorce.

It took quite a while for me to get the healing I needed and to make the changes in myself that I needed. When I finally felt that I was healthy enough to resume my marriage, to be committed to my marriage and husband, even if my husband did not or could not change, it was too late. My husband did not want me back and was not ready to make a commitment to me or our marriage. Both partners have to be willing to make a commitment to each other and to the marriage; a commitment to work towards a healthy and fruitful marriage or it will be a marriage in name only.

If one partner is involved with someone else they have to be willing to give that person up or there can be no healing, no marriage. If one partner is violent or controlled by rage they have to be willing to get help—to get therapy. If one partner has a serious addiction that threatens the safety and security of the family, they have to seek healing, or there can be no marriage. In some cases, there is an impediment that makes it difficult or impossible for one or both partners to have a relationship of intimacy and mutuality. Unconditional love does not mean that it is always good or possible to live under the same roof as another person. We need to know our limitations. We need to discover them ourselves. No one else can make our decisions for us. But, we need pastoral and family counseling to hold up a mirror for us so that we can make a free and morally sound choice. Sacrifice is a necessary part of marriage; but, suicide and martyrdom is not. As long as both partners are willing to heal their marriage and to forgive, most other kinds of wounds, defects, or problems, can be healed and over-come.

Most of all we need the power and strength that comes from the sacraments. When we are going through distress, we cannot always pray as we would like; or pray at all. Our prayer is more like some of the psalms of misery and distress. We wonder where God is in all this and why we cannot hear him, or why he does not answer us. We feel lost and abandoned by God, and when we pray we feel numb; like we are just going through the motions. This is when we especially need the Eucharist, regular confession, and family and community support. We come face to face with Jesus in the sacraments, even though we may not experience his presence. When we are in distress, we are bombarded with negative thoughts and emotions—anger, resentment, guilt, fear, judgment, self-pity, and condemnation; and if we do not blame ourselves, we blame others. We need the sacrament of confession to set us free and keep us open to love and grace. Through confession and Eucharist, Jesus gives us what we need; he turns our problems into opportunities for growth, and pours his love into us: "We know that all things work for good for those who love God, who are called according to his purpose." (NAB Rom 8:28)

We may be on the brink of divorce, but we are not without hope. With the help of the Holy Spirit, we can turn things around; and our marriage may even become truly a sacrament, in which we sanctify and make each other holy. We can seek out pastoral counseling as soon as we begin to have problems; we can receive the anointing of the sick and confession; we can turn to other Christians for support. Sometimes we may be too weak even to pray, or to receive Eucharist as often as we need, but we have to reach out to others for help. We cannot just lie down and die, expecting God to come to us. As soon as we call out to the Lord, he hears us; but he sends us help through other people.

There were probably grounds for an annulment on both, the part of my former husband and myself, but the divorce really was due to many outside forces; trials, losses, illness, military separations, relocations, the war in Vietnam, and various crises and problems of our children. All these things led to a rupture in the stability of our family life. We were wounded psychologically, emotionally, and spiritually.

In my annulment process, I never had the opportunity to speak to any of the judges or to hear the response from my former spouse; his experience of our marriage and the divorce. We were separated by three thousand miles due to the military, prior to our divorce and subsequent annulment. We never really had the opportunity for marriage counseling, together. The only persons I spoke to were my pastor and spiritual director; in regards to the annulment process.

I am an articulate and prolific writer, and when going through the process of annulment, was able to answer the questions in a very objective and concise manner. However, because my feelings were numb in regards to my former spouse and our marriage, I was not able to be subjective or to express my true feelings; only my thoughts. I still had confusion and memory loss to cope with, as well, so that my testimony was misinterpreted. On the other hand, my former spouse was filled with rage and pain, at the time, which impaired his perception and ability to be rational. My perception was impaired by the lack of feelings. I felt neither, love or hate. If it had not been for the compassionate pastoral counseling and accompaniment of a priest that I met after I stopped therapy, I may not have returned to the Church for years. If I had to go through the annulment process, today, I think I would answer those questions very differently.

I have discovered that perception is very distorted by loss and grief. A couple can be on the verge of a divorce and have all kinds of problems in their relationship. If one of them suddenly dies, the other spouse only remembers the good in their marriage and in their spouse. To hear them speak, you would think they were married to a saint. The opposite is true when it comes to divorce. The spouses only remember the problems and negative experiences. They do not see how grace was operative throughout their marriage. They make rash or false assumptions in their summations.

My response to the questions in the annulment process was very analytical. Our annulment came through in less than five months. How can this be, when one spouse is a deacon and the other is a certified spiritual director, and they were married for twenty-four years? I went through the diaconate preparation with my husband; we were both interviewed and evaluated; we both had to have letters of reference; and I was always very supportive of his ordination and ministry.

When I was growing up, divorce among Catholics was very rare. When divorce became very prevalent among Catholics, the Church revised and activated the annulment process. It became apparent that for such an increase in divorce among Catholics, there must have been something missing in their marriage that prevented them from having a truly sacramental marriage. When I got married, I believed that my marriage was a sacramental marriage. We were both baptized Catholics. We both believed in the permanency of marriage and wanted a family. None of our friends or family suggested that we should not get married. There were no apparent impediments to our marriage, at the time. I believed that we made this choice freely. We were engaged for a year and I prayed for God's will, that if it was not God's will, he would show me. It was always my belief that if I sincerely wanted only God's will, especially in major life decisions, and asked God for it in prayer, God would show me in some way if it was not his will. He would stand in the way of our marriage. I believe that if my will is surrendered to God's will, he will not let me down. Therefore, when I got married I felt confident that God was blessing our marriage; that we were not alone in this and that he brought us together. I also believe that God permits sin and evil when to intervene would violate our free will, and when he can bring greater good out of it. Evil never has the last word. Nevertheless, my will was for God's will to be done.

After our divorce, and failed attempts to be reconciled, I applied for an annulment at the urging of my pastor. Actually, I did not really believe that the Church would grant me an annulment; but they did, on the grounds of "lack of due discretion." Even after the annulment, I still was not convinced that my marriage was not a sacramental marriage.

At the time of our divorce, our marriage had gone through numerous family challenges, crises and trials. We had to contend with external as well as internal negative forces. My desire at that time was to have my marriage healed or find my true *soul-mate*. I was lonely and felt like I was married in name only. I welcomed the annulment process because it gave me an opportunity to come to know myself better by examining my life before, during, and after my marriage ended. The annulment also gave me the option, or legal freedom, to enter religious life if I did not remarry.

I entered religious life a few years after my annulment, after much discernment and prayer. God revealed his will, one stage at a time. When it came down to taking final vows, he did not allow me to go forward. I left the community after ten years, before final vows, because the Abbess General did not believe that I was called to their particular community. I have no regrets and see my time in religious life, as well as my leaving as a gift. I gave a lot to them and received a lot from them. That is also how I feel about my marriage.

Neither, my husband or I ever remarried. It has been thirty years since our divorce. Although I believed that we were free when we got married, and made the choice with full freedom, I have only just recently discovered that there probably were psychological impediments that would challenge our marriage, at least unconscious ones, but I do not believe they could prevent a sacramental marriage. The biggest challenges in our marriage were ignorance, lack of good parenting skills, unrealistic expectations and communications. My husband was too strict and I was too permissive; he was too conservative and I was too liberal. We were able to meet these challenges until our family was hit with many severe trials from outside. This took its toll on our whole family; emotionally, mentally, and physically. I was also highly influenced by false teaching from popular theologians and priests who taught their own perception of love, marriage and family life, as well as divorce. I do not think I would have ever pursued a divorce, otherwise. We were unable to get the counseling that we both desperately needed because of his military assignment. I could not understand how, even with two courts, the judges could possibly make the determination, after so many years of marriage, to grant us an annulment. I do not think that even my husband and I could make that determination because our testimonies, regardless of our sincerity, were dubious. The duress I experienced prior to our divorce and the numbness I felt, made me even doubt if I was ever in love with my husband; which was without substance. Actually, I no longer believed that he loved me. This, I am sure, clouded my perception and testimony. The duress my husband experienced, along with his anger and rage, clouded his perception. When it comes down to it, the judges cannot make the right determination without the gift of the Holy Spirit.

Only the Holy Spirit can give priests and bishops the power and gifts needed to make such pastoral decisions; as well as to grant absolution in confession with certainty that there is true repentance and honesty. The Holy Spirit often gives them the ability to read souls and to give counsel from the Holy Spirit even when they are not aware of it. All pastors do not have the same degree of these charisms, however. Scripture says, "Having gifts that differ according to the grace given to us, let us use them: if prophecy, in proportion to our faith; if service, in our serving; he who teaches, in his teaching; he who exhorts, in his exhortation; he who contributes, in liberality; he who gives aid, with zeal; he who does acts of mercy, with cheerfulness." (ICSB Rom12:6—8)

I believe that the Church can make mistakes in their prudential judgments, and even with two separate courts, there is always room for error. But, God would not allow it unless he could bring greater good from it. God often writes straight with crooked lines. I have great faith in *divine providence*. God does not need humans to be perfect, only to be faithful. He can work with our limitations and mistakes. He gave Peter authority over the Church, not because he was all-knowing or perfect, but because of his faith. Jesus has great trust in us. Without the Holy Spirit, the Church would be merely a secular institution. Without faith and the Holy Spirit, how could we trust in the validity of apostolic succession, the sacraments, and the power of ordination, which enables priests to forgive sins in *persona Christi;* the infallibility of Scripture and the teachings of the magisterium, the granting of annulments, the *internal forum*, and so forth? Neither could we trust the testimony of the apostles and believe in Jesus and his teachings and deeds.

It took me thirty years to trust that the Holy Spirit was working through the Church in granting me an annulment. As long as my husband or I believed that our marriage was a sacramental marriage, we really were not free to remarry. For me, the annulment was invalid because it went against my conscience. I only filed in order to know whether I should try harder to be reconciled or to move on with my life. An annulment seems to suggest that God was not present in the marriage, and I knew this was not true. It is hard for me to even imagine that we could have lived together for so many years, and brought out the best in each other for most of that time, unless our marriage was a valid sacramental marriage. I often had doubts about the annulment over the years. Even today, I still feel very connected to my husband through our children and the common life we shared. It seems to me that total freedom is both objective and subjective. Just as I was not free to remarry, I was not truly free to enter a religious community for life. I could never have accepted a permanent separation from all my family. My first vocation was to my family. The purpose of marriage is an intimate interdependent relationship between a man and a woman; for procreation, and to raise a family together.

I believed that my marriage was a true and valid marriage because I believed that I was in love with my husband and that he loved me, as well; because I sincerely sought God's will before I married him; and because I took vows, of my own free will. My only desire was to be a good wife and mother, to make my husband happy, and to raise my children to love God and to be good citizens. The first two years were happy, followed by two years of doubt and struggle. We both had a lot of maturing to do. We were both lacking in knowledge when it came to married life and parenting. Then, I experienced a deeper conversion and the *baptism of the Holy Spirit*. After that, for the next twenty years we continued to grow in our faith and service to God and the Church. There was much evidence of the working of grace in our marriage and family; but, eventually our family was torn asunder by many trials and crises, leading to a breakdown in our marriage, and divorce—especially the last three years before our military separation.

I love my former spouse as much today, as I did when I married him, but not in the same way. We still have a relationship, but not the same kind of relationship. We have different duties, goals, and life purpose. We still share the same love and hopes for our children, however, and are truly a *family*. I love him as a brother, and have always prayed for him daily; desiring only good for him, and God's will. I think he feels the same. Our lives, however, are no longer interdependent or intimate; on many levels they never were. I believe that we were *one flesh,* physically, emotionally, and spiritually; but we were not one flesh, mentally.

Do I regret marrying my husband, or believe that it was a mistake and should not have happened? No! I have many happy memories of our life together, and most of those years were the most fruitful years of my life. We created a beautiful family, together. I would not be the person I am today if it was not for my husband and marriage. Do I regret our divorce and my life since then? Something died in our relationship and marriage, due to our neglect, and I sometimes mourn the loss of that. To be honest, something was missing in our relationship from the beginning, but I cannot really articulate it. I regret that we did not get the counseling we needed at the time, but I have come to accept this loss. I believe that I have received a lot of healing, and have continued to grow and to be fruitful. I will always honor him and be grateful for him.

I did not regret getting an annulment, at the time, but would choose to reverse it today if I could. It caused a lot of confusion and pain for my children, even though they were adults. I think it was even harder for them to accept the annulment than it was to accept the divorce. Nevertheless, I can only speak for myself, and from my own experience. I cannot speak for my former husband, and do not really know what was in his mind and heart when we got married, or what his impediments were. If we were meant to be together, we probably would have been reconciled soon after our divorce. And, of course, I would not have been able to enter religious life without an annulment. I believe that ten years in religious life was an important part of my formation and life, so I see the providence of God at work through my annulment. It may also have been my *purgatory*; reparation for my sins against my husband during my marriage. My greatest healing came after I left religious life and was led into the desert. It was here that I discovered the purpose the Lord has for my life: to be a *handmaid of the Lord*, and a *bride of Christ*. It was here in the desert, that I made private vows to the Lord, consecrating my life to him forever:

> Therefore I will hedge up her way with thorns; and I will build a wall against her, so that she cannot find her paths. She shall pursue her lovers, but not overtake them; and she shall seek them, but shall not find them. Then she shall say, 'I will go and return to my first husband, for it was better with me then than now'....

> Therefore, behold, I will allure her, and bring her into the wilderness, and speak tenderly to her. And there I will give her her vineyards, and make the Valley of A'chor a door of hope. And there she shall answer as in the days of her youth, as at the time when she came out of the land of Egypt.

> And in that day, says the Lord, you will call me, 'My husband,' and no longer will you call me, 'My Baal'... And I will make for you a covenant... And I will betroth you to me in righteousness and in

justice, in steadfast love, and in mercy. I will betroth
you to me in faithfulness; and you shall know the
Lord. (RSV Hos 2:6—7, 14—20)

Personally, I think that older couples and those who have older
children should think twice before getting married again. They
need to adjust to being a single person and living alone, first. I think
that they would benefit by the *internal forum* more than by a formal
annulment. The children also need time to heal from the loss of
family life with both parents; even if they are adults. One day, one
of my daughters told me that she was so grateful that my husband
and I never remarried someone else, because we have been able to
stay together as a family. Mixed families bring a host of new problems and adjustments. All of my daughters have been married for
over twenty-five years, and have never been divorced. Family life
is very important to them, as well as the permanence of marriage.

I am very grateful to God for all of my life, and for the family
he has given us. Recently, all our children, grandchildren, spouses,
and great-grandchildren traveled to Albuquerque to celebrate my
husband's 80th birthday. There were thirty-three of us in all. I was
so proud of our family and the honor and respect they have for their
father. Everyone payed tribute to him and shared their most memorable memories of him; including me. They were all so happy to
be all together. The spouse of one of my granddaughters' shared,
with tears in his eyes, that he never really had a family, and he was
so grateful and happy to be a part of this one. Our family is certainly not perfect. We are very diverse in so many ways; but the
fact that everyone wanted to be together, in spite of the sacrifices
they had to make to be there, and the respect they showed to my

former husband and me, and to each other, is a tribute to *family life*. I do regret, however, that all of them have left the Catholic Church and joined other churches. I think our divorce had a lot to do with that. I also regret that the Church did not reach out more, to my husband. He was an ordained deacon who gave a lot to the Church, and was in great need of pastoral counseling and love from the Church. Maybe they did, and I did not know it! That also added to the pain and disillusionment that my children felt towards the Church. They grew up in the Church, and were exposed to some of the hypocrisy and abuse that seeped into the Church.

Jesus said to Peter (the pope): "I will give you the keys of the kingdom of heaven, and whatever you bind on earth shall be bound in heaven, and whatever you loose on earth shall be loosed in heaven" (ICSB Mt 16:19). This was the same authority that God gave to Moses in his time. Jesus was not critical of Moses; he merely explained the reasoning behind Moses' decision. Perhaps the times we live in today, call for annulments and internal forums, but when Jesus comes again, he may say: "For your hardness of heart Moses [Peter] allowed you to divorce your wives [and annul your marriages], but from the beginning it was not so. And I say to you: whoever divorces his wife [or annuls his marriage], except for unchastity, and marries another, commits adultery; and he who marries a divorced woman, commits adultery" (ICSB Mt19:8—9). Jesus was speaking of all marriages made in good faith, sealed by the exchange of vows; not just those of baptized followers. The sacrament gives them additional grace to enable them to keep their vows, but marriage was instituted by God with Adam and Eve, when he made them *one flesh*. Marriage was a sacrament from the beginning. In the garden, Adam and Eve had *truth and grace* available to them.

Except for those who are saints, I doubt if there are many divorced persons who have not fallen into adultery; whether their marriage is annulled and they remain single or remarry; or whether they divorce and remain single or remarry. After a divorce, people are very vulnerable to illicit relationships and adultery. They have not learned how to cope with loneliness and the need for intimacy. They want to be loved, and to love someone else. They are looking for a replacement to what they have lost. They really believe that their marriage just died and had no hope of recovery. Their perception and ability to reason is impaired. Their values and sense of right and wrong is confused. After a divorce, many Catholics automatically excommunicate themselves from the Church. They do not feel worthy to stay. This is usually unconscious. Some just get lost in the world and do not know how to get back home; back to where they were before they fell. This is the way with all serious sin. These are the ones that Pope Francis is searching for.

From the beginning, God intended marriage to be between one man and one woman, for the whole of their life. He intended for them to leave the authority of their parents and begin a new family; to be joined together, and to become one. From the beginning, outside of Paradise, marriage included many so-called impediments, psychological problems, human failings, sin, tragedy, and trials to contend with. Whether a marriage ends in divorce or annulment, there are devastating consequences to face; the same kind of consequences that all sin has. Nevertheless, God can always bring good out of evil, out of sin, and out of all our bad choices, when we turn back to him.

It is not enough to be forgiven by God; we also need to forgive and to be forgiven by our spouses and children. It seems to me that we consign each other to purgatory in this life, and maybe even the next, until satisfaction is made. Satisfaction is forgiveness by those we have wronged or hurt. God is quick to forgive, but humans are not; even if it cost them time in purgatory. It took thirty years of letters, prayers, and reaching out to my former husband, for him to let go of his hurt and anger and actually say, "I forgive you," and mean it. I think that it was only by forgiving me that he was able to see his part in our divorce. Pastoral counseling of divorced and remarried, as well as those seeking annulments, must also include the former spouses and children. Everyone needs healing.

Closing Observations and Comments:

I really do not think that relaxing the rules regarding remarriage and annulments is the answer to the problem, whether the former marriage was sacramental or not. The Jews that Jesus spoke to regarding divorce and remarriage were not in sacramental marriages. They had all kinds of natural, but not illegal, impediments to their marriages. Catholics today, have the same problem that the Jews had. The solution Jesus gave the Jews was conversion and grace. Grace without faith and conversion is not possible. Today, the statistics on second and third marriages ending in divorce are even higher than on first marriages. The families are fragmented and broken. There seems to be just as many annulments among Christians, today, per capita, as there were divorces among the Jews in the time of Jesus. No one is really free of all impediments. Annulments are not the solution. The only thing that can deliver and save us is Jesus Christ. The Church needs to believe it and proclaim it. If everything is an impediment to marriage, then there will be no men and women normal enough to get married.

I think that the Church needs to focus on a deeper understanding of what a sacramental marriage is, in our times; considering the culture change as well as the relevance of faith development to the marriage. Sacramental marriage, in my opinion, is for spiritual adult Christians (1 Cor 2:14—16). The spouses are the only ones who can really testify to their relationship with Jesus and the Church, at the time of their marriage. How did they practice their faith at the time of their marriage? What did they believe about Jesus? In what way, was he their Lord? What does that mean to them? Did they have any kind of personal or interior relationship with Jesus? Were they spiritual Catholics? Did they ever become spiritual Catholics throughout their marriage? Were they unspiritual Catholics? What does it mean to them to be a Christian? Was their perception of marriage a covenant or a contract?

It seems to me that a sacramental marriage must include both, an objective and subjective faith experience. Faith is interior as well as exterior. The subjective faith experience, personal faith encounter with Jesus, is just as necessary for the validity of a sacramental marriage, as what we outwardly profess and believe with our intellect. Unlike the other sacraments, marriage is a sacrament bestowed by the married couple, not the Church. If one or both persons do not have a mature faith, a full conversion, a personal heart-felt relationship with Jesus through prayer and the sacraments, how can they be open to receive from Jesus and bestow grace upon one-another?

Perhaps the Church needs to distinguish between a sacramental marriage and one that has the potential of becoming a sacrament. They should strive to save both, if possible. What kind of outside influences brought about the breakdown of the marriage? What losses, trials, family problems, and illnesses have they experienced? Were there separations involved, due to military service or work? These things can trigger border-line personality problems or psychological impediments that may have been present before the marriage; they also may be new and recent impediments, like PTSD. Were there prior marriages or relationships that might have impeded the sacrament of the marriage? Whenever there is any kind of break-up in a relationship, a person takes that baggage into the next relationship. Were there children from prior relationships? It may be possible for these impediments to be healed with good spiritual and psychological counseling. Many marriages that ended in divorce could have been saved or repaired, even after the divorce if there was adequate counseling.

People need to be healed of prior losses before they are really free to enter a sacramental marriage. They need to know, objectively and subjectively, that they are not bound to someone else before entering into a new relationship; especially a sacramental marriage. This is my own opinion, but I personally believe that there is a psychological or emotional bonding with every sexual relationship that a person has, even in the case of *date rape* or invalid marriages. Scripture says: *Do you not know that he who joins himself to a prostitute becomes one body with her? For, as it is written, "The two shall become one"* (ICSB1 Cor.6:16—20). Previous sexual encounters can be an impediment to a sacramental marriage, especially for women. The separation of the *flesh* has to be cauterized and healed. Otherwise, it is like a person who loses a limb, but still feels the presence or pain of the wounded limb that was removed. It takes much more to constitute a marriage than *two becoming one flesh,* but nevertheless, we become one flesh with every sexual encounter we have. They are adulterous relationships, and only the *forgiveness of sin* can set us free and heal us from the effects.

It is probable that most divorced Catholics gave full consent to their marriage, on a conscious level, at the time of their marriage. Most of them probably also believed that marriage was exclusive and permanent, on a conscious level. Most of their witnesses were probably Christians, practicing Catholics, or nominal Catholics at the time of their marriage, and did not give any reasons why they should not marry. The Church needs to review the annulment process. It does not seem to me that the Tribunals can make a truly reliable judgment based only upon written records. I think the spouses also need to be present so that the judges can examine or question them about their written testimony; as well as their faith development at the time of their marriage, and at the present time. Letters from witnesses may not be very credible if the witnesses are no longer practicing Catholics, and if they affirmed the marriage at the time of the marriage. The most reliable witnesses are the spouses, themselves. If there is dialogue between the judges and the couple, the couple will likely reveal a more authentic witness.

Those who have received annulments, as well as divorced and remarried Catholics, need to be encouraged to put their children and their faith, first; to choose God's will over their own will; before their own personal comfort and happiness, or their own emotional and physical satisfaction. It seems to me that when a couple receives an annulment, it means that one or both of them did not have sufficient faith. They were not free to enter fully into the sacrament. It seems to me that the primary purpose of annulments is not to free people to remarry, but to discover why the marriage failed; if the marriage was ever a sacramental marriage, and why not. A sacramental marriage should never end in divorce, if we are living our faith. An annulment is a sign that one or both spouses need to receive the gift of salvation. They need to be evangelized. Many Catholics today, continue to get divorced and remarried several times, even after annulments, because they are still pagan Catholics. No one reformed their consciences. They continued to have a broken and fragmented family life, as well. They continue to be wounded and are not healed. They cannot forgive because they have not received forgiveness. They cannot receive forgiveness because they do not know they have sinned, or that they need it.

The goal of the Church, today, should be evangelization *and* pastoral care, not one without the other. Evangelization of the divorced should include pastoral care to heal them and help them to understand why their marriage failed, as well as their part in the divorce. It should lead them to repentance and conversion. They need to know that they are not excommunicated; and can and should receive the sacraments. They need to know that they must remain celibate and cannot remarry unless they receive an annulment, or are reconciled with their spouse; that before God and the Church, they are still married. They need to forgive their spouse and be forgiven; be healed and reconciled as fully as possible. They need to know that they are still one flesh with their spouse and accountable for their spousal responsibilities and parental responsibilities; especially to pray for their spouse, "For the unbelieving husband is consecrated through his wife, and the unbelieving wife is consecrated through her husband." (ICSB 1 Cor 7:14)

Evangelization of the divorced and remarried should include suggesting an annulment; and abstaining from sex, if possible, until they receive an annulment and have their marriage ratified; or to live a celibate brother-sister relationship with their spouse, if possible. If both of them are really ready for the sacraments, they will seek an annulment and a chaste life. They also need to be spiritually reconciled with their former spouse; free of all resentment, bitterness, and lack of forgiveness.

Evangelization of those who cannot leave an irregular or sinful state of life, or receive an annulment, should include encouraging them to attend Mass and receive "spiritual communion." It should also include pastoral care: compassion, healing, and counseling; in addition to evangelization. However, in some countries, divorce and annulments are prohibited. There are also some remarried who were refused annulments, yet believe that their prior marriage was not a sacramental marriage. They want to be in full communion with the Church and to receive the sacraments. These people need pastoral counseling, and perhaps, the *internal forum*. It is not reasonable that anyone living in a state of mortal sin would hunger for the sacraments. This has to be discerned. Perhaps they received a conversion after their divorce and remarriage!

The primary need in all of these situations is pastoral care. Pastoral care needs to include encouraging forgiveness and making amends when possible. It needs to include making them aware of God's love for them and the power of prayer and actual grace. We are called to love everyone, and to welcome and treat everyone with dignity and respect. We cannot do that by condoning or excusing sin. That does not mean that we should be pointing out their sins or judging them. It means that we teach what we believe; that others know what our beliefs and values are. We need to give them the freedom to disagree; and to acknowledge their own sins, without judgment and condemnation from others. We need to encourage them to seek for the truth, through prayer and study, and trust that God will reveal the truth to them—gradually. We need to give them hope

9

Prepare the Way of the Lord!

I have often heard it asked: Why did the Son of God choose to be incarnated as a Jew instead of a Gentile or a pagan? Scripture seems to show us that God always prepares the foundation — the way — before he does something. God prepares us to be able to hear him and see him, by announcing his coming. We cannot hear or see God unless we have faith. Faith is initiated in us through the *announcements* of God, brought to us by the messengers that are sent to *prepare the way of the Lord*. Faith comes by hearing and believing, and it is never in vain, because God is always true to his word.

God created the earth and the universe in six days (outside of time), according to his word. He created man and woman on the sixth day, and on the seventh day, he rested. The eighth day was for humans to do what God created them to do. God created the world in stages, each stage preparing the way for the next. Each stage prepared a place for humans to live in relationship with God. Jesus said: "The Sabbath was made for man, not man for the Sabbath; so the Son of man is lord even of the Sabbath" (ICSB Mk 2:27—28).

The Sabbath is for humans to come into union with God and be nourished by him; to remind humans that they are not alone, and that they were created by God.

The pagans believed in many gods, not one; gods who had power over man. They could hold these gods captive in the idols they made. The Jews were a people that were prepared for the coming of God amongst humans. They were formed. They were taught that there is only one God, a God with no beginning and no end; a Supreme Being who existed outside of creation. Humans could not trap God into one of their created idols. God cannot fit into any idol because he is greater than all of creation; beyond the imagination and thoughts of humans. Even the whole of creation could not contain or hold God captive; not the sun, moon, stars, mountains, hills, rivers, or oceans; nothing created by God or humans.

The Jews were taught that God's glory, the Holy Spirit, through God's initiative, could rest upon the Law. His glory could lead them and guide them, and be with them in the arc of the covenant and the temple. His Spirit could rest upon kings, prophets, and priests, through his anointing. His Spirit could come upon the waters, healing many. His Spirit could come to them in the form of clouds, which would lead them through the desert; and through various signs and wonders; all at the initiative of God. They knew that humans could never lay a trap for God. Humans could not go up to heaven and bring heaven down to earth, or unite God with humans. Humans could not control or manipulate God.

Before Jesus was born, the Jews awaited the coming of a Messiah, a new Moses and deliverer, because God had *promised* this through the prophets. They could not really conceive of God becoming human, because there was only one God, and if God became human, he would no longer be God. They could only conceive of a man being filled with the glory of God, like the prophets. They could not yet understand the concept of three persons in one God, the concept of the Trinity. How could God be three and one at the same time? This was beyond their reason and comprehension. It was a mystery. Even though they could conceive of the Holy Spirit as being God, the Holy Spirit was not a *being* to them, or a person. God was one Supreme Being. Jesus had to perform great signs and miracles, beyond anything known to humans, to prove to them that he was God, that he is Lord of all creation, that he came from heaven, and that he and the Father, and the Holy Spirit, are one.

If Jesus came as a Gentile or a pagan, he would have been perceived as one of many gods becoming man. He would be a Zeus or Jupiter, or one of the many Greek and Roman gods that they believed in; or, he might even be perceived as a *Buddha,* or a superman. He would be limited in what he could do, and have many competitors. The gods were very competitive. The Gentiles would not be able to recognize Jesus as the source of all life and eternal life. They would never have been able to recognize him as the only Son of God, or conceive of God as three persons in one God; the way was not prepared for them. Jesus came to the Jews first, because they were prepared for him. After the Resurrection and Pentecost, Jesus would send them out to the whole world to complete his mission. His mission was to fulfill the *promise* of God, going all the way back to the beginning of Genesis; to reveal God to humanity; to conquer Satan; to fulfill the words of the prophets; and to bring humanity back into union—relationship—with God. This was the revelation Jesus came to fulfill. There will always be more to come; that is the nature of *life*. Jesus said: "I have yet many things to say to you, but you cannot bear them now." (ICSB Jn 16:12)

I often hear nonbelievers ask questions like: Why would God choose the Jews, of all the nations of the world, to be his people? Why does the *revelation* of God come from the Jews and not from other nations and peoples? To begin with, God called Abraham, not the Jews, and Abraham responded! God wanted to form a people that would listen to his voice and be his voice to the world. God has no favorites. From the beginning of time, God wanted to save the whole world. The earth and everything in it belongs to God. God wanted to form a people for a particular mission to the world. The Jews were not a people, not a nation, when God first called Abraham. They did not become a people and nation, with a particular mission, until God formed them. He formed a people from Abraham because Abraham believed in the promise made to him. The mission of this people would be to *prepare the way of the Lord*. So, the real question is, "Why did God call Abraham?"

God has communicated with people in every time and place since the beginning of the world; with anyone and everyone that would hear his voice and respond. Abraham had *ears to hear and eyes to see*. He listened when God spoke to him. Among all the descendants of Adam and Noah that God could choose from, Abraham had exceptional faith and trust in God. When God called him to leave his family, country, and his father's house for a land that he would show him, Abraham followed. He took his wife, Sarah, with him and left everything, not knowing where he was going. God promised to make Abraham the father of a great nation, through his own blood line; even though he was old and his wife was barren. Abraham believed, and the *people of God* were formed. Perhaps, another reason that God chose Abraham rather than an already formed nation, was because Abraham was raw material, like a wild stallion that has not been broken; like the *tethered colt that no one has yet ridden*; upon which Jesus rode into Jerusalem (JB Mk 11:2). God wanted to start from scratch, like he did with Noah; to form and mold a new people who would worship the *one God*, and no other gods. A third reason is that God chooses the lowly when he wants to reveal his glory. Abraham was completely dependent on God because he had nothing of his own. St. Paul reminds us:

> No, it was to shame the wise that God chose what is foolish by human reckoning, and to shame what is strong that he chose what is weak by human reckoning; those whom the world thinks common and contemptible are the ones that God has chosen— those who are nothing at all to show up those who are everything. (JB 1 Cor 1:27—28)

Every great nation and people on earth has recorded their histories in their chronicles. But none of these histories reveal an unbroken succession of leaders, from the time of their inception, who were in relationship with the one God. None of these histories reveal the unbroken relationship between God and humankind. In contrast, the whole of the Old Testament is focused on God forming a people; God in relationship with his people. It is the only recorded revelation of its kind. Israel did not even begin to comprehend what God was doing in their lives, or what he was revealing to them, until they begin to write down their story. God revealed himself to them a little bit at a time. The revelation of God continued to evolve until the time of its fulfillment in the Messiah. In contrast, the revelation of God amongst the pagans continued to devolve, and people were blinded by a false image of God; fragmented into a thousand little gods with no integrity.

Jesus is a descendent of Abraham, with an unbroken genealogy from Abraham to Mary and Joseph. No other nation can make such a claim. Abraham can trace his genealogy all the way back to Noah, and Noah, back to Adam, the first man. This genealogy is so important that it was included in the New Testament (Mt1:1 — 17). Some people consider this passage to be the most boring passage in the New Testament, and wonder why it was necessary. This genealogy shows that Jesus is not only a descendant of Abraham, but also a direct descendant of David, fulfilling the prophecy and promise given to David. Jesus is the new Israel, the transformed Israel, prefigured by Jacob, the first Israel. The twelve apostles are prefigured by the twelve sons of Jacob, the twelve tribes of Israel.

In the first covenant, God formed a family and people of God from the blood line of Abraham. Although Jesus is not the natural son of Joseph, the Jews believe that children of adoption receive the same rights and inheritance as natural born children. This is significant because, through Jesus, all believers become adopted sons of God. However, there is a tradition that Mary was also a descendant of David, as well as Joseph, which makes Jesus a natural descendent of David as well as a descendent by adoption. There is a saying that *blood is thicker than water.* Natural blood line seems to play a major role under the old covenant. Under the new covenant, those who are related through the Spirit have an even more significant role. Jesus is the new covenant, and under this new covenant, water represents the Spirit, the means of regeneration; baptism, new life in the Spirit. In the new covenant, God is forming a universal family and people of God through the blood of his only Son: "This cup is the new covenant in my blood which will be poured out for you." (JB Lk 22:20)

The New Testament is the fulfillment of the Old Testament, the fulfillment of the promise. God has formed a people and has come to live amongst them; to unite all of humankind with God. In Jesus, Israel is made new and becomes the sacrament of God's presence in the world for all time; as the Church. The Church is a *kingdom of priests* formed to continue the mission of Jesus Christ. This new Israel, Jesus Christ, is the full revelation of God, who has come to draw all people back to union with him. He has come to form the whole world into the people of God; to form one *people of God* out of many nations, through a rebirth in the Spirit.

The *revelation* of God is complete in Jesus, the only Son of God; fully man and fully God. No further revelation is necessary. Jesus is the perfect image and likeness of God. As Christians, we are the Church, sent to proclaim God's Word to the world; to be God's voice, ears, eyes, hands, feet, mind, and heart. In Jesus, we become the new people of God, formed in his image and likeness; a people destined to incorporate all of humanity: "And when I am lifted up from the earth, I shall draw all men to myself." (JB Jn 12:32)

The apostles were privileged to be eye-witnesses to all that Jesus said and did. They believed because they saw. They were taught by the Holy Spirit, as well, to understand the fullness of the truth they had received. After Pentecost, under the guidance and direction of the Holy Spirit, they were commissioned to teach and write down all that they had witnessed and understood. The Holy Spirit quickened their memory so that what they wrote would be the whole truth, and nothing but the truth, no more and no less, necessary for the salvation of the world.

All that has come down to us from the councils of the Church, including Vatican II, all that we know today, and all the apparitions of Mary, are not new revelations. They are all hidden within the Gospels, like a buried treasure, waiting to be rediscovered. All believers, today, believe because we have faith, not because we have seen. None of us were eye-witnesses, or privileged to see what the apostles and early disciples saw. We believe because of their testimony.

So, how is it that some people think they have more insight into words and deeds and events of the life of Jesus than the apostles did? How is it that they think their knowledge and intelligence makes them an authority on Jesus and the apostles, understanding their intentions better than the apostles understood their own intentions? It seems to me that good theology *confirms* revelation, and brings it into the context of our present times. It does not presume to add on to the revelation of God. Revelation is Jesus revealing God to us; revealing the Father in relationship to the Son, through the Holy Spirit, in and with the Holy Spirit. Revelation is Jesus revealing the Father to us.

Some people refuse to believe that Jesus actually performed miracles, that he actually multiplied the fish and the loaves, or walked on water. These same people claim to believe in the Eucharist. How can someone who cannot or will not believe in the miracle of the fish and loaves, possibly believe in the miracle of the Eucharist? They can't! They do not believe in the Eucharist as the body, blood, soul, and divinity of Jesus; they only believe in the bread and wine, and call it Eucharist. They thank God for the bread and the wine.

Some people cannot believe that John's Gospel actually relates the words of Jesus, word for word, especially in the long discourses of Jesus. Oh, what little faith! There are non-believers who possess a natural gift of a photographic memory. They can memorize a page, or even a whole book, just by flipping the pages. There are people who can memorize a long speech as they hear it. There are many Protestants who have memorized most of the Bible. Yet, even though Jesus promised the apostles that the Holy Spirit would bring to their remembrance, all that he said to them, some people still refuse to believe. There is so much unbelief in the world today! Once again, I think it is time to *prepare the way of the Lord!*

Part 2

Marriage between Jesus and his Church, Beginning with a Promise

10

Nothing is Impossible for God!

*U*nless we believe that *nothing is impossible for God*, we really cannot say that we believe in God. If Scripture can only tell us about what is possible for humans, what we can see and understand, then, it is not the *revelation of God*, but merely a story about humans. What concerns me most, today, is the secularization of the sacred Scriptures. Some people read the Scriptures as though they were reading sources for research into sociology or anthropology. Some people see Scripture as merely literature with various literary forms. Some see Scripture as a historical synopsis or summary, of the origin and journey of the Jewish People, from Abraham to Jesus. They are intent on proving that everything in the Scriptures, that was thought to be supernatural or of divine origin, was very ordinary and natural, and all under the control of humans. Many people, today, read the Scriptures as though they were reading the *Daily News* instead of the *Good News*. They do not see Scripture as the revelation of God, from God, but as nothing more than the opinions and experiences of humans about God.

This has caused me to reflect on what brought me to a conversion; to complete faith in Jesus Christ, and to a relationship with God. My experience of God began long before I discovered Jesus in the Scriptures. I learned about Jesus from the Church, the sacraments, family, prayer, and the witness of the lives of the saints; although, it was very limited.

I recall hearing about some of the saints when I was preparing for confirmation. The witness of the lives of saints throughout the past two thousand years to the present day, made the Gospel come alive for me. I wanted to be like them; to love God and everyone like they did; to do the things they did; and especially, to be loved by God like they were. God walked and talked with them! The hope that I could be like them filled me with joy and a desire to follow and serve Jesus. Of course, when it did not happen immediately, the fire of that conversion began to die down, somewhat.

Years later, I experienced a renewal of that conversion through the *baptism of the Holy Spirit.* I was immediately filled with a hunger for Scripture. My conversion enabled me to read the Scriptures as the *Word of God.* The Scriptures were like love letters from God to me. One short verse of Scripture could fill me with joy and excitement for hours. I read the Scriptures, seeking Jesus; to know him and become closer to him. The Scriptures were touch stones to God, for me. The Holy Spirit enabled me to see those touch stones and to understand the Scriptures.

I recall the first time I heard that the *creation story* of Adam and Eve was a myth. I cried and cried, like a child discovering that Santa Clause was not real. It wasn't so much, finding out that the story was not a literal event that upset me, it was the arrogance manifested by those who were intent on shattering my illusions and enlightening me with their truth. They seemed intent on showing Christians how childish and foolish faith is, but could not offer a better or more believable story about creation. They had their own agenda.

As a child, I heard the story about Adam and Eve, and had no reason to doubt it, but it wasn't anything I spent time thinking about. Before my conversion, it would have made no difference to me whether it was a literal story or a myth, because I wasn't in a place where I was interested in knowing. In fact, I probably would have welcomed this new knowledge. However, after I *fell in love* with God and Scripture, and was seeking understanding, I attended a class where the teacher had the intention to attack faith, rather than to teach the truth. The teacher, a self-proclaimed theologian, wanted to show that there was no such thing as *original sin*, and that the Church taught error. That was his agenda.

God works all things for good, however. After that, I was drawn to meditate and reflect on the creation story, asking the Lord to show me what he wanted me to learn from it. I saw that this story of creation, inspired by God, revealed the power and greatness of God who is the Creator of all that is. It does not matter whether it is a literal story, lacking some facts; a figurative or allegorical story; or an apocalyptic vision, conveying truth. The truth is that *nothing is impossible for God*—nothing. There are many truths that this story has to teach us. It teaches us that God created the universe: our galaxies, sun, moon, stars, earth, and all that inhabits the earth, out of *nothing*. He created one man to start with, and out of him, a woman, and out of them, he populated the earth. (There is nothing in the story to suggest that God did not repeat this creation process in several places). God created man from the earth and spirit;

breathing a living soul into dust from the earth. All of creation is connected, in its material form, and has its origin from God. Man (at least Adam and Eve) lived in a paradise because there was no sin, and everything was in harmony and order. God created the world in stages—*a day can be a thousand years for God.* God is outside of time and space, but he created humans in time and space.

Some people are so anxious and driven to find a natural explanation for everything, that they lose their faith in the process. Unless we believe that *nothing is impossible for God,* we really do not believe in God. It takes a *God* to do the impossible. It takes faith to believe in God. We need to ask ourselves, is it faith seeking understanding and truth that motivates our search? Or, is it a lack of faith; doubt and the need to have proof? Or, is it simply pride, the fear of being seen by others as foolish or ignorant, and the desire to know more than others? Jesus said: *"Amen I say to you, unless you turn and become like children, you will not enter the kingdom of heaven."* (NAB Mt 18:3)

Personally, I have no problem believing in a spiritual world of angels; angelic beings, principalities and powers, which were created by God before he created our world. *Nothing is impossible for God.* I have no problem believing that God walked and talked with Adam; he continues to do so, with all the saints. God is spirit, but I have no problem believing that he can speak his word to us through his messengers and the angels; or that these angels can come in the form of a man, animal, donkey, or snake. *Nothing is impossible for God.*

It is clear to me, from the creation story, that God is master over all of life. Everything that God made is good, but not everything was made for consumption. I have no problem believing that Adam and Eve, the first man and woman, were faced with a temptation, and that this temptation came to them in the form of a lower life form; a reptile that they could see with their physical eyes; a creature that crawled upon the earth. *Nothing is impossible for God.*

I have no problem believing that God created man in his own image and likeness; that he did nothing, randomly. God had a plan and a purpose for everything he created. I have no problem believing that God *rested* on the seventh day; not to abandon man, but to take delight in all that he created, especially man and woman. The seventh day was a day for God and man to come together in a personal and intimate relationship. God would speak his words of love to Adam and Eve, and they would respond by praising him with thanksgiving. God would prepare them, with his Spirit, to go forth in his name on the eighth day, to fulfill the purpose for which they were created.

I have no problem believing that the forbidden tree would bring death to Adam and Eve; literally and spiritually. Perhaps the fruit of this forbidden tree was something that could alter their minds, and the temptation it offered was supernatural powers, like the angels had, that promised independence from God and competition with God. Perhaps they believed that this fruit would make them masters, not only of the earth, but of heaven and the whole spiritual realm, as well. Perhaps they recognized that the serpent had supernatural powers and they envied him. There could be many interpretations of this deadly fruit, depending on the time we live in. I have no problem believing that the temptation presented by Satan was a lie. Adam and Eve were faced with the choice of believing the truth, the voice of God, or a lie, the voice of Satan. I have no problem believing that Adam and Eve's sin was terrible and grievous. They refused to believe and trust in the Creator, one who was greater than they were, and chose to believe a lie from someone who was nothing.

I have no problem believing that this *original sin* would change the face of the whole original earth; the original design of God. It would be stamped in the heart of man, even changing his DNA, and affect the hearts of every man and woman created out of Adam and Eve, for generations upon generations, until a Savior would come to deliver them and take their sin away. I have no problem believing that Satan would continue to follow on the heels of man, and bite him, until the Savior, and his mother—his helpmate and handmaid—would come and crush his head. I have no problem believing that the Savior would be both, God and man, two natures in one person. I have no problem believing that this Savior would be free of sin, original and personal; and that he would come through a woman who was also free of all sin, original and personal. I have no problem believing that together, they would crush the head of Satan; that they would be the New Adam and the new Eve. The Savior would have a helpmate, someone formed from his own side, his own heart.

I have no problem believing that once humans are freed from sin, this Savior would give them the tree of life; the Holy Spirit and eternal life. I have no problem believing that this tree of life would continue to exist in the world through baptism and the Eucharist. I have no problem believing that the Son of God can become manifest—body, blood, soul, and divinity—in ordinary bread and wine. *Nothing is impossible for God.* I have no problem believing that this Savior is Jesus, because of his words and deeds; that this Jesus was persecuted and died for our sake; that he rose from the dead on the third day, in a physical body of flesh and blood, and ascended to the right hand of the Father; and that he will come again in glory, in the same way that he ascended into heaven; that he will judge the living and the dead. *Nothing is impossible for God.* I have no problem believing that the Gospels contain the events, acts, and words of Jesus Christ, and that they are all true. I have no problem believing that the Holy Spirit reminded the disciples, the eye witnesses, of all that they heard and saw, and "taught them everything" (Jn 14:26) before commissioning them to write it down; that the Holy Spirit led them to the complete truth (Jn 16:13). *Nothing is impossible for God.*

This is only my opinion, but it seems to me that although the story of creation was not written down for thousands of years after it began, by men who were not eye witnesses; and not fulfilled for thousands of years after it was written down; it is neverthe-less, truly *revelation,* and inspired by the Holy Spirit, who was an eye witness. The creation story was handed down through many different cultures, in various forms, but the fullness of truth was revealed in the Genesis account; handed down through the ages, beginning with Adam, as well as the Holy Spirit. The Holy Spirit and Adam from the sixth day forward, were eye witnesses of creation. It seems to me that this story is a form of apocalyptic vision. Sacred Scripture begins and ends with an apocalypse; revelation in the form of prophetic symbolism, looking back in time or forward into the future.

11

The Promise of the Father

$\mathcal{A}$t the time of Pentecost, the disciples were all gathered together in the *Upper Room*, praying, and waiting in expectation for the promise to be fulfilled. Jesus had told them, "I am sending the promise of my Father upon you; but stay in the city until you are clothed with power from on high" (NAB Lk 24:49). Since that first Pentecost, God has seen fit to pour out many similar Pentecost events upon his people.

Clothed With Power from On High

In the Gospel of Mark, Jesus commissions his apostles to go forth and proclaim the Gospel of the kingdom of God, and describes some of the signs that will accompany all those who believe and are baptized (Mk 16:15 — 18). The message behind these signs is that they will be *clothed with power from on high*. People will know that God is with them, that what they do does not come from any ordinary human power or strength. These believers will heal people that medicine cannot heal; they will have a wisdom that none of the philosophers and great thinkers amongst mankind can obtain; they will have a knowledge beyond the knowledge of science; they will be able to communicate their message to people of different and various languages; they will speak in languages that they do not know; they will deliver people of demons that psychology cannot accomplish, no matter how great its knowledge of human behavior and the workings of the human mind; they will not be able to be destroyed by fire, poison, sword, beast, water, or any of the elements of nature and humankind—until, and unless, God allows it for his glory.

God often chooses the lowly, the illiterate, the common, the poor, the handicapped, mere children, and even zealous enemies of God like St. Paul, to be his disciples and to manifest his power in them; lest anyone should doubt that it is by the power of God. The world will know that God is with them; that they are *clothed with power from on high,* and that their works do not come from any natural powers of humankind.

> Take yourselves for instance, brothers, at the time
> when you were called: how many of you were wise
> in the ordinary sense of the word, how many were
> influential people, or came from noble families? No,
> it was to shame the wise that God chose what is
> foolish by human reckoning, and to shame what is
> strong that he chose what is weak by human reck-
> oning; those whom the world thinks common and
> contemptible are the ones that God has chosen—
> those who are nothing at all to show up those who
> are everything. The human race has nothing to boast

about to God, but you, God has made members of Christ Jesus and by God's doing he has become our wisdom, and our virtue, and our holiness, and our freedom. As scripture says: *if anyone wants to boast, let him boast about the Lord.* (JB 1 Cor 1:26—31)

The signs of the power of God are manifest in all of the lives of the saints; in various ways and to various degrees. The saints witness to the power of God and his presence in the world. All believers are called to be saints—to be *clothed with power from on high.* The prophet, Joel prophesied: "In the days to come—it is the Lord who speaks—I will pour out my spirit on all mankind. Their sons and daughters shall prophesy, your young men shall see visions, your old men shall dream dreams. Even on my slaves, men and women, in those days, I will pour out my spirit." (JB Acts 2:17)

The charismatic renewal, first, referred to as the Catholic Pentecostal movement, began in 1967. It was a unique experience in the life of the Church in our times; a new Pentecost, like the first Pentecost, experienced by the apostles. It was not the result of any kind of renewal program or organized movement of humans, but a phenomenon of the Holy Spirit, a gratuitous gift of God; and the result of the prayer of the Church. In 1962, Pope John XXIII, in preparation for the Second Vatican Council, prayed to God: *Renew your wonders in this our day, as by a new Pentecost....* This outpouring of the Holy Spirit, initially received in baptism and confirmation, continues to be poured out as long as we keep praying for it.

The spread of this renewal was largely attributed to the Pentecostal Church, because of their reputation and experience as a charismatic congregation, manifesting the gifts of the Holy Spirit.

The Holy Spirit was poured out on Christians of all denominations, including nominal and lapsed Christians. Some people experienced the baptism of the Holy Spirit while alone, in prayer, or at a time of crying out to God in despair. They had no idea what happened to them. They begin to search for others who had the same experience, and for spiritual books that could explain their experience to them. Many returned to their churches with a hunger to know more, and a deep hunger for more of God. Many were led to the Scriptures, and begin to recognize their experience there within the early Christian community.

The Holy Spirit was also poured out on groups of people who were praying together; on groups during a retreat; wherever there were two or more praying together. These people began to come together and to form prayer groups. They sought out other groups who had the same experience, especially the Pentecostal Church. They searched for books with teaching on this experience and on the charisms. They turned to the writings of the saints. All these spiritual writings began to be mass produced—so great was the hunger of the people.

As people came together to pray and share their experience, walls of division between different denominations began to crumble. The doors were closed to no one. Deep seated prejudices were dissolved. Suddenly, there was neither rich nor poor, Catholic or Protestant, young or old, black or white, American or immigrant, Jew or Gentile. All were brought together in the one Holy Spirit under the lordship of Jesus Christ. Everyone loved everyone, and this love was evident. Their theme song became, "They Will Know We Are Christians by Our Love."

Gradually, these people began prayer groups within their own churches and denominations. They grew in number, inviting others to join them. The greatest growth of this movement of the Holy Spirit was within the Catholic Church. At the prayer meetings, the gift of hospitality was extended to all new-comers. The prayer group became the means through which others came to experience the baptism of the Holy Spirit, through the *laying-on of hands*. Newcomers were encouraged to make a commitment to attend several prayer meetings, (setting aside their reservations, differences, and concerns) before making a decision to stop coming or to continue.

Baptism in the Holy Spirit

The *baptism of the Holy Spirit* is not something new for Christians. We are baptized in the Holy Spirit when we are baptized with water, and this is confirmed for us in the sacrament of confirmation (when we personally give our "yes" to God to follow Jesus Christ). The *early Christians* received baptism and confirmation together, along with reception of the Eucharist. This is why Catholics refer to these three sacraments as the sacraments of initiation. However, because of the lack of catechesis and the growing apostasy in the Church and the world, God, in his goodness and mercy has seen fit to renew the Church through a new Pentecost, in our times—an outpouring of the Holy Spirit.

The greatest fruit of this experience is the experience and awareness of God's love for us that dramatically changes our life. We enter into a personal relationship with God, in which we experience him, not only as transcendent (outside of us), but immanent (inside of us). We come to know God, through Jesus, as Father, brother, friend, teacher, healer, and Lord, through a personal and intimate relationship with him. This enables us to experience the same joy, peace, and love that the apostles experienced in their relationship with Jesus.

All of the gifts of the Spirit that we received in confirmation: wisdom, knowledge, understanding, counsel, fortitude, piety, and fear of the Lord, are renewed or increased by the Holy Spirit; and elevated to a new, or deeper supernatural level through the experience of the *baptism of the Holy Spirit*. People become more aware of the leading and prompting of the Holy Spirit, and more able to discern what comes from God, from our self or ego, and what comes from the evil one.

Through this experience, people are filled with a desire to pray, and praise and worship God from their heart, rather than from obligation. They are given a desire for holiness and growth in the virtues. They receive a love and understanding of Scripture that they never knew before, and are eager to meditate on Scripture daily. They have a new appreciation for the sacraments, and desire to receive them regularly, especially the Eucharist. They are drawn to read the lives of the saints. They receive a desire to serve the Church and to love everyone, even their enemies. They experience, at an affective level, the call of God to follow him and become his disciples.

This experience has been taking place through many renewal movements within the Church—especially through the charismatic renewal—because of the emphasis on the Holy Spirit, life in the Spirit seminars, prayer groups, and the reception of the charisms of the Holy Spirit (1 Cor 12:6—10). These charisms are given to disciples in order to empower them to evangelize and to build up the body of Christ. In other renewal movements, however, this experience is not referred to as the *baptism of the Holy Spirit*. Nor, has this conversion experience been as widespread within the other renewal movements. A whole theology of the gifts and charisms of the Holy Spirit has developed out of the charismatic renewal, which is not yet prevalent within most other renewal movements within the Church.

Even though some people are not called to be part of the charismatic renewal, every Christian needs to experience a *new Pentecost*—a release of the Holy Spirit that we received in baptism and confirmation. Every Christian needs to have a personal experience of Jesus; to know him as their Lord, and to have a personal relationship with the Holy Trinity. Every Christian needs to personally, respond to the call to discipleship; to follow Jesus.

One of the charisms of the Holy Spirit is the gift of prophecy. In March of 1978, the Lord gave me a prophecy for his people. I share part of the prophecy with you, now, because it seems to me to be even more relevant for our present times:

> My people, I am calling you to see my wounds amongst you. I am calling you to walk with me on the road to Calvary, to share one another's trials and to help each other with your crosses. I am calling you to walk together, to be one, to be bound together as I was bound to the column. I am calling you to weep out of compassion for one another, to have your hearts rent for one another. I am calling you to help the weary and downtrodden, to wipe each other's faces. I am calling you to feed the hungry, to give drink to those who are thirsty. Feed their

minds with my Word, the mind of Christ. Feed their spirits with the power of my Holy Spirit. Feed their bodies from your own table and the labor of your own hands. I am calling you to anoint each other's wounds, to heal each other, to lead each other to rest—to my rest, and to eternal life. I am calling you to clothe each other with my armor, to build each other up. I am calling you to remain at each other's side, waiting patiently for resurrection, for new life to come forth in one another. Look around you, my people, look at my wounded body. Let your hearts be stirred to action. There are some members of my body that are lonely, that feel like strangers. They feel deserted. They cry out for community, for relationship, not just once a week, but daily. If you have a living relationship with me, you must have a living relationship with each other. There are those amongst you who have no one to celebrate special feasts with, and so they eat alone. I am calling you to a radical commitment to one another. Your brother's problems are your problems. You must care for one another as you would your own body. I am calling you to stretch out your hands and to reveal your wounds to each other. Let no one hide himself from his brother. I am calling you to bring your children to me. I want to prepare a place for them within my body where they can be nurtured and come to know the voice of their Shepherd. Do not leave them outside or they will be attacked and carried off by wolves. My heart cries out for my little ones. Bring them to me. Let me bless them. My Church is not a haven for adults. It is a home for all ages.

Listen, my people, I have not come to condemn you. I have come to prepare you. I want you to be ready for what is to come. In the past you have celebrated the Lenten season by choosing your own deserts, your own sacrifices and fasts. But, a Lenten season is coming upon the world of which no man has any control. I am leading you into a desert that you did not choose. I am preparing you for a time of glory, for victory. Trust me! Follow me! If you love me and love one another, the desert cannot hurt you. You will be victorious and through you I will save the world. I have warned you that days of darkness are coming upon the world, days of trial and tribulation. A great light will soon go out in Rome. When that happens, greater darkness will come upon the earth. Do not rely on any of the supports you have had in the past. I am going to strip you of everything you depend on now so that you will depend only on me. For my power is strongest in weakness. I will pour out all the gifts of my Spirit and when you are completely empty you will be able to fully yield to my Spirit and my power will be manifest in you and through you. Be prepared to lose everything for my sake and you will gain everything. You will have to suffer for a little while but your sorrow will be turned into joy. Nature will cry out in birth pangs and there will be famines and floods and earthquakes. But, I will renew the face of the earth. Trust in me. Many people will be given over to evil, rejecting God and hating all that is good and holy. You will be hated and persecuted, and some will even be martyrs for my name. I have told you all this so that your faith will not be shaken. Band yourselves together in me, for I will triumph and my glory will be seen upon the earth. A new day is coming and when that day comes your joy will be great. In that day you will have everything. But, you must let me prepare you. From now on a man's household will extend to his community, his brothers and sisters in Christ. It has been said, *a woman's place is in the home*. From now on a woman's home extends to the community. It has been said, *put your house in order*. But, I say to you, *put your community in order*. If you do not want your love to diminish, then keep my commandments.

- Do not let the sun go down on your anger. Make up with one another while you still have time. You must seek to heal all wounds of division and strife. Humble yourself before one another. If you really want to, you can make peace without compromising the truth.

- Do not resent you brother's every offense and never act in a fit of passion. Pray first, and let go of your anger before acting. I have no favorites. If you are angry when you correct your brother, you are as guilty as he is, unless it is righteous anger, which is seen only in the perfect.

- Do not find fault before making a thorough inquiry; first, reflect and pray, then give a reprimand.

- Jealously guard one another's reputation and good name. Do not allow anyone to speak against your brother. What they say about your brother they say about you, too, because you are one. Remember, your enemy will pile up false accusations against you to turn you against each other. Do not be quick to listen to all you hear. Do not be gossip mongers.

- Listen before you answer and do not interrupt a speech in the middle. Do not argue about something that does not concern you. Support one another; do not knock each other down.

- Do not put on airs when you are in difficulties. Do not be afraid or ashamed to let your brother see your vulnerability. Your vulnerability is precious to me and moves my heart to compassion. Be honest with yourselves and with one another. Do not repress your feelings. If your brother has offended you, then go to him, humbly, and make it known to him. You may discover that it was unintended, that your hurt was in vain.

- Make each other's needs your own. Suffer with those who are suffering, rejoice with those who are rejoicing. Be patient with one another and allow for each other's mistakes and weaknesses. Do not criticize or rashly judge one another. Your vision is limited and you do not see the whole of a man's heart. Teach one another. Build each other up in my love. Be gentle when you need to correct.

- Do not make comparisons, comparing one person with another or one group with another. Do not take sides, one against another. Have nothing to do with factions. Do not judge a man by his outward appearance, or whether he is rich or poor, young or old, black or white, educated or uneducated, Protestant or Catholic, layman or clergy. My choice has nothing to do with these things. I choose whom I will.

- Show your love for me by accepting all that I allow to happen to you with joy and thanksgiving. Do not grumble or complain. Trust in me. Praise me in adversity, in trials, in suffering, in tribulation.

My people, the world will not be changed until they can say, *blessed is he who comes in the name of the Lord*. You are my servants and I send you forth in my name. If you remain in my name, you shall truly be blessed and the world will come to acknowledge this as they proclaim, *blessed is he who comes in the name of the Lord*. You also must say to your brother, *blessed is he who comes in the name of the Lord*. Acknowledge one another as the image of God and see me in your brother and sister. Through you, and my Spirit living in you, all of mankind shall be recreated in the image and likeness of God and my glory will fill all the earth.

Several years ago, I reflected again about what the Lord was saying to the Church: What is the Lord doing in the Church today? What word has he been speaking to the Church for the past many decades? God is purifying his Church and calling us to be holy. He has been saying that he will not tolerate the evil that is going on among us. During this great time of mercy, the Lord's tolerance is *zero* when it comes to the greatest evil, the harm we do to our children; including the unborn. He is saying that we must recognize and acknowledge that sexual molestation of children is a grievous sin, a great evil, regardless of culpability. It must be rooted out and stopped, no *buts*. He is saying that his priests must be beyond reproach. He wants a holy priesthood who are able to discern good from evil and hold fast to his word. He is saying that we must remember this so that if the rest of the world accepts and condones sexual molestation of children tomorrow, we are not to follow them. He is saying more, this is only the beginning. He is saying that sexual molestation by a priest, of anyone—man, woman, youth, child—regardless of whether they consent or not, is evil and must be rooted out. The Catholic Church, especially her priests, is being singled out in regards to sexual molestation because more is expected from them. *Those to whom more is given, more is expected.* The Catechism of the Catholic Church tells us:

> Scandal takes on a particular gravity by reason of the authority of those who cause it or the weakness of those who are scandalized. It prompted our Lord to utter this curse: "Whoever causes one of these little ones who believe in me to sin, it would be better for him to have a great millstone fastened

round his neck and to be drowned in the depth of the sea" (Mt 18:6). Scandal is grave when given by those who by nature or office are obliged to teach and educate others. Jesus reproaches the scribes and Pharisees on this account: he likens them to wolves in sheep's clothing (Mt 7:15). (CCC 2285)

The Lord is saying that all sexual behavior outside of marriage is sin and evil—sexual molestation—with or without consent, for priests and laity. All sex outside of the sanctity of marriage is sexual abuse and must be stopped. He is saying, "Get busy, and decide what you can do to stop it. Get rid of your false teachers and prophets; rely on the word of God, not the experts." If we fail to listen to him we will be consumed by the purifying fire that is rising up, instead of purified. Fire either destroys or purifies and a fire is blazing across the earth. This is only the beginning. This is only the first of many sins that we need to be purged from. We must not only heal our children of the effects of sexual molestation but we must heal their minds, hearts, and souls from sexual abuse in all its forms. We must teach them the purpose and value of chastity. They will not recognize sexual abuse unless they come to accept that all sexual contact outside of marriage is sexual abuse; not only of their bodies and souls, but also of sex, itself. What is the Lord saying to the secular world? He is saying:

There is filth in the Church, as Pope Emeritus Benedict XVI has remarked, and it must be purged. However, there are many people in the world who attack the Church for malicious reasons, not because of a concern for those who have been abused by the Church. *They are hypocrites who have a plank in their own eye, while they attempt to remove a splinter in the eyes of their neighbor* (Mt 7:5). They attack popes and priests, while they shield and condone their own behavior and that of the rich, powerful, and prominent, in the secular world.

The majority of sexual abuse of children is within the secular world; in organizations, clubs, schools, and families; especially from boyfriends of divorced mothers. The Catholic Church, led by faithful priests and holy popes, has done more to protect, defend, and heal children than any other Church or organization in the world. *Let he who is without sin cast the first stone* (Jn 8:7). What is the Lord saying to the bishops? He is saying:

Repent and reform your lives so that you will have the integrity to call the people to repent. Trust in God, not in man. Get rid of your false prophets and teachers among you; turn back to the Gospel you are called to proclaim; turn back to the authentic teaching of the Church that you are called to defend. Be united as brothers—*be united in your convictions and united in your love, with a common purpose and a common mind* (Phil 2:2). Be true fathers of your priests and good models for them to follow. Do not support those who would destroy the Church and corrupt the message of the Gospels in the name of reform. Be on your guard.

I have continued to pray about what the Lord is saying to the Church, today. I have wondered about what happened to the charismatic renewal that began in the late sixties. It seems that only a remnant is left. Most of the prayer groups have become charismatic rosary groups, or charismatic Scripture sharing groups. I received this prophecy:

> My people have been mourning the leaving of the bridegroom, but the bridegroom is returning soon (Mt. 9:14—15). My people have been sustained and held together through this time of dryness and mourning through my mother and the rosary. A second wave is coming, greater than the first one. It has been mounting and will soon cover the earth. You have heard this prophesied many times. My word will not return to me void. You will see many great miracles in its wake. You have all worked hard, with great effort to plant seeds in the desert. But now it is time for those seeds to grow. They can only grow in praise and worship. The time is now. Gather together in praise and worship. The time is now for solid teaching. Prepare the way of the Lord!

I reflected on the meaning of all this. What is this *second wave,* and will it be like the first one in 1967? Once again, I feel the Lord is calling us to *wait in Jerusalem until we are clothed with power from on high.* I was reminded about the vision of the tunnel that I wrote about. It seems to me that *Jerusalem* represents the Church. We need to follow the Church, to remain faithful to her, to stay together, with one mind and heart. We need to stay close to Mary, who also represents the Church, *Jerusalem*. We are going through a time of great darkness, and it will become even darker. We cannot *see* on our own. *Jerusalem* also represents community. The Lord is calling families to be reconciled and to pray together, regularly. He is calling parishes to be reconciled and to come together to pray, regularly. He is calling every denomination to come together with their communities, to be reconciled and to pray together, regularly— to *wait in Jerusalem*. The Lord is saying that it does not matter how we pray communally, but that we pray together; whether we pray the rosary, Lectio Divina, the Divine Office, centering prayer, charismatic prayer, or Eucharistic adoration. He is calling everyone to gather together in community to pray as often as we can; and especially to receive the Eucharist. We are to keep our eyes on Jesus, to pray in the one Holy Spirit, and to expect a *new Pentecost*.

I believe that this *second wave* will be different than the first wave. We will receive many supernatural gifts, but they will be different. We need to let go of the past and be open to something completely new. As an illustration, let me share with you a story: Several years ago, I had a large grapefruit tree in my front yard. It was a beautiful tree and gave a lot of shade, which is very much needed here in the desert; this was its major asset. I was really not that interested in the fruit; it drew a lot of ants and flies. Nevertheless, I loved that tree. The tree became infected with some kind of blight that was fatal. I had it trimmed down, but it did not seem to help. More and more branches had to be removed from the tree. Finally, all that was left was the stump. I did not want to let that tree die, so the stump was pretty tall. I prayed that it would come back to life, and new leaves began to grow out of the stump.

At the same time, I noticed a tiny palm tree that came up out of the ground, right next to the grapefruit tree. I wondered, "Where did that come from?"

The new leaves on the stump of my grapefruit tree did not last long. They died, as well. I was still reluctant to have the stump removed. Finally, I had it removed. As soon as I did, the palm tree shot up. Almost overnight, it grew into a huge, full tree, giving great shade to my desert home. This palm tree represents, to me, what this new Pentecost will be. The Lord is going to do something completely new.

We need to receive "new wineskins" so that we can receive the "new wine" that the Lord wants to give us (Lk 5:37—39). We need to die to our old self and become new again—die to what was done in the past; our own understanding, expectations, and concepts of God. This does not mean we are to receive a new Gospel, or new covenant, but a renewal of our covenant with God. We are to receive a new manifestation of the power of the Holy Spirit in our times. The Lord wants to *clothe us with power from on high!*

12

A New Pentecost

$\mathcal{A}$ s the world crossed the threshold of the third millennium, the prayers of the Church for a *new Evangelization* and a *new Pentecost* increased and became stronger and stronger. The Church was well aware of all the problems that had surfaced, in the world and among the people of God; apostasy among Christians, individualism, relativism, and the lack of faith and spiritual life among Catholics were at the top of the list. It was apparent to all the leaders of the Church that the world needed a fresh out-pouring of the Holy Spirit, and a new zeal to evangelize, not only non-Christians, but those who left the Church and those who were still in the Church. It was apparent that Christians needed to return to God; to hear the Word of the Lord, to enter into a personal rela-tionship with Jesus, and to be baptized in the Holy Spirit and fire. The last three popes preached and prayed constantly for a *new Evangelization* and *new Pentecost*. Many of the faithful responded to this call to prayer, and turned their attention to evangelization and the Holy Spirit.

Catholic charismatics were encouraged and excited as prophecies came forth announcing the coming of another *new Pentecost*. The prophecies continued, and by the year 2012, expectations were high for a *new Pentecost*, a second wave, to be poured out any day. The prophecies said that God was doing something new, not to rely on our experiences of the past. We said, "Yes, Lord, yes, yes, yes!" But, deep down we still hoped for an explosion of religious experiences; for great signs and wonders, miraculous healings and miracles; for the rise of prayer groups and mass conversions over all the earth; for conferences and stadiums filled with people praising God and filled with zeal, enthusiasm, and joy. We waited, and waited, and waited. We began to see some signs in poor countries and countries where the Church appeared to no longer exist, but nothing like we saw in the past. We complained, "Where is this *new Pentecost*, Lord? You said you were going to raise up an *army of saints*; where are they?"

A New Pentecost: *The Second Wave*

What will this *new Pentecost* bring to the world? What is the need of the world and the Church, today? As with the first wave, many were filled with an expectation and hope for a divine intervention from God; another outpouring of the Holy Spirit that would renew the earth, change the world, and change our lives. These were our greatest needs and hopes; evidenced by our attraction to Marian apparitions, the "secrets" of Fatima, and the prophecies of Medjugorje.

It seems to me that this second wave will be different from the first. Unlike the first wave, I believe that this wave will be a *baptism of fire* (Lk 3:16), in order to purify the Church and raise up an *army of saints*. It should be noted, however, that saints are not canonized because of the spiritual favors they receive or the miracles and signs associated with them. They are canonized because of their extraordinary virtue, holiness, charity, and love of God and neighbor. They are canonized because they followed Jesus and embraced the cross; they died with Jesus. The signs that followed them were redemptive suffering and martyrdom. We need only look at the lives of all the saints that have been canonized in recent years to know the kind of saints that will make up the *army of saints* that the Lord is raising up.

Suffering and death are part of life in this world. No one can escape from it. Much of our suffering is due to our own sins, and we deserve it because of the choices we made in life; much of our suffering, however, is due to the sins of others, and to original sin; we did nothing to deserve it. This is true for believers and unbelievers, alike; for good and evil people, alike. Whether we deserve it or not, suffering and loss can be used to transform us; to build character and virtue in us, if we are able to accept it. Suffering either leads us to God and transformation, or it leads us to darkness, despair, and death.

Acceptance of suffering does not mean that we do not seek healing. It means that we accept it when it appears that we are not healed; after we have done all we can to be healed, and after we have asked God to heal us. We surrender to whatever God chooses to give us, or not to give us. We abandon ourselves to the will of God, trusting in his mercy and goodness. God always wills our greater good. He always wants to heal us. However, God's healing comes in two forms. He either removes our infirmity or he gives us the grace to accept it without complaining; without anger, bitterness, and resentment; without striking back at life, God, and others. We can only do that through the grace of God. When we can rejoice in the midst of suffering and loss, we have not only been healed, but transformed.

Those who embrace the cross for the sake of the kingdom of God, who suffer because they are followers of Jesus and choose to embrace the Gospel, are saints. They transform the world and have a share in the redemptive suffering of Jesus. The martyrs were only able to accept suffering and death with joy, because of the grace of God. Martyrdom is a charism, a gift of the Holy Spirit.

I believe that this *new Pentecost,* which has already begun, will take us beyond the prayer meetings. Pentecost is not something that happens on a given day or in a given place; it can continue for years. This *baptism of fire* will expand our understanding of the variety and meaning of the charisms of the Holy Spirit. We need to read *the signs of the times.* The Holy Spirit gives us the gifts and charisms that are most needed in our particular day. This *new Pentecost* will enable the Church to separate the wheat from the chaff. The charisms that will dominate will be wisdom and discernment; trust, fortitude, perseverance, and sacrificial love—martyrdom. Healing will consist more of reparation, repairing the damage of the past; reconciliation, and the power to turn away from addictions and sin. This *new Pentecost* will show the world the difference between good and evil; what sin is. It will deliver people from their denial and remove their false defenses. There will be charisms for obedience, humility, and trust in God; fidelity, fortitude, prudence, courage, chastity, and true charity. There will be a return to reason, common sense, and natural law. There will be great apologists, defenders of the faith, evangelists, and doctors of the Church who will be raised up as saints; many at the cost of martyrdom. The *new Evangelization* will reach out to those who have left the Church; to the *prodigal* sons and daughters of the Church. The call of the Church, today, is to be a *breach-mender*, a *restorer of ruined houses*. (Is 58:12)

The Lord is calling people to prepare for this *new Pentecost* with prayer, fasting, and almsgiving. Praying the rosary, daily, is good preparation. The fasting that the Lord wants is reconciliation. He wants us to be reconciled with everyone we are estranged from; spouses, children, parents, relatives, friends, neighbors, enemies; the Church, priests and nuns, bishops, and other denominations. He wants us to forgive everyone and to stop judging others. We need to make amends, where possible, and repair the damage to all our relationships. He wants us to show mercy and compassion to those who need it. We need to do all that we can to bridge the gap between other ministries, apostolates, and factions within the Church. The Lord wants us to give alms to the poor in our midst; those among our own families, parish, diocese, ministries, communities, and streets; to all those who ask and all those we are responsible for. We need to take the first step; the graces received from the *new Pentecost* will enable us to go all the way.

The Lord is calling us to help prepare others for this *new Pentecost,* as well. Every Christian should pray for everyone who has ever touched their life in any way: family, relatives, friends, acquaintances, neighbors, co-workers, and even our enemies; those who have hurt us, knowingly or unknowingly, in thought, word, or deed, throughout our whole life; all those that we minister to or serve, and all those who minister to and serve us. We should present them to the Lord, and consecrate them to his most Sacred Heart, his most holy will, his divine mercy and divine providence, and to the Immaculate Heart of Mary, his mother.

Priests will need to focus on the sacrament of penance; how to be good confessors, to be instruments of reconciliation and truth; to know how to confront with love; to deliver people from bondage to sin and evil. They will need to know how to afflict the comfortable, with love, and how to comfort the afflicted, with truth. They should not be afraid to ask people if there is anyone in their life who has something against them, and to pray with them for reconciliation and healing. They should not be afraid to ask a penitent what they are most afraid of; what is their greatest loss or wound; if they are in pain; or to ask them what their relationships are like.

Every priest needs to be a *breach-mender* and a *restorer of ruined houses*. The Lord is calling people to reconnect with all their relationships; to forgive, and to repair all their relationships. Those who are divorced should pray for their former spouses every day, and forgive everything. They need the grace to heal all wounds of the past; their wounds and the wounds they have inflicted on others. Priests need to use the confessional to help people to do this. They should be on the alert for broken relationships. Priests also need to be reconciled and to forgive their brother priests, their communities, and their bishops. Priests need to recognize the power that they have been given as confessors. They need to trust their anointing. They need to be assertive; firm, but gentle. They need to be like Jesus was with the Samaritan woman. He humbled himself, first, asking for a drink; treating her like a person with equal worth and dignity. Then, he gave her good news, a promise of new life. Then, he confronted her with the truth. He did not wait for her to confess. He confronted her gently and lovingly, without judgment.

This *baptism of fire* is a holy fire, for those who turn to the Lord; not something that destroys, but something that purifies. It will heal people of spiritual blindness and set prisoners of sin free; especially those suffering from addictions. It is an experience of enlightenment, a revelation from God, of God. People will know there is a God. It is a Spirit of truth, and gives grace. Those who are distressed by all the evil going on in the world around them will rejoice. It is a second chance for those who hate evil and desire goodness, peace, and justice on the earth; to receive faith, hope, and love. It is not a punishment. It is not the *Second Coming*. It will precede persecution and holocaust.

The *baptism of fire* is for the *army of saints* that God is raising up. Through this *army of saints,* God will purify the earth. The *baptism of fire* is like a "Tau" marking the inhabitants of the earth who hate evil. They will be untouched by the increase in evil and darkness that envelops the earth. As the darkness increases, those given over to evil will become more evil, and the just will become holier and holier. (Ezek 9:4—6)

Conferences should include teaching on the need to forgive and be reconciled with everyone; and how to be reconciled. They should include teaching on common sense, natural law, and the gift of reason. They should include teaching on the gift and value of suffering; sacrificial love; martyrdom; the Beatitudes; the gifts of the Holy Spirit, especially wisdom, discernment, fortitude, and true devotion. They should include teaching on the virtues and vices, especially: honor, humility, integrity, and justice.

Conferences should draw in speakers from other apostolates, outside the charismatic renewal, such as: apologists, moral theologians, Scripture scholars; spiritual directors, theologians; and various ministries to women, men, and children. The people now need to be fed with meat instead of milk. They need teaching that will enable them to use the new charisms of this *new Pentecost*.

Conferences should reach across denominational lines. They should be a welcoming place for non-Catholics and those who have left the Church, as well as those who are marginalized Catholics. Anointed speakers from other denominations, who are not anti-Catholic and who will not speak against the faith, should be invited to speak. We will find them if we look for them. *The family, who prays together, stays together;* even when they disagree. Christians, who pray together, stay together. Believers, who pray together, stay together.

The Church must go through many deaths and resurrections; sharing in the passion of Jesus. The followers of Jesus will not only be baptized with the Holy Spirit, they will be *baptized with fire*—the *passion* of Jesus (Mt 5:11—12). "In this way we are all to come to unity in our faith and in our knowledge of the Son of God, until we become the perfect Man, fully mature with the fullness of Christ himself" (JB Eph. 4:13). For a little while, it will seem to the world that the Church, instituted by Christ, is dead. But, she will merely be asleep, like Adam was in the beginning. Then, the new Eve will emerge from his side, and the two shall become one flesh.

The *new Pentecost* is a clarion call to the world to return to God. It has already begun. The *new Pentecost* is a wave that is building and mounting, a blazing fire that is growing and increasing; until it peaks and becomes a great sign given to the world by God, which no one can deny. Then, a time of glory will begin; a new day; a time of harvest.

> Then the King will say to those on his right hand, "Come, you whom my Father has blessed, take for your heritage the kingdom prepared for you since the foundation of the world. For I was hungry and you gave me food; I was thirsty and you gave me drink; I was a stranger and you made me welcome; naked and you clothed me, sick and you visited me, in prison and you came to see me." Then the virtuous will say to him in reply, "Lord, when did we see you hungry and feed you; or thirsty and give you drink? When did we see you a stranger and make you welcome; naked and clothe you; sick or in prison and go to see you?" And the King will answer, "I tell you solemnly, in so far as you did this to one of the least of these brothers of mine, you did it to me." (JB Mt 25:34—40)

No one knows the day or the hour when Jesus will return in glory; but the *signs of the times* suggest that we can expect a *type* of the Second Coming—an event that prefigures the Second Coming. This has already happened many times throughout the history of salvation. We can also expect that many of the saints in heaven will come to our aid, to intercede for us, especially Mary.

13

Every Life is a Gift
We are Loved Into Life by God

*After a traumatic experience of "date rape," rob-
bing me of my virginity, when I was 18 years old,
I discovered I was pregnant. Devastated and confused, I turned to God in prayer for understanding.
The Lord came to me in a dream. When I awoke,
I knew that the child within me was a gift, not a
punishment. I knew that every life is a gift, and
every person is loved into life by God. I was filled
with joy and fell in love with the child growing
within my womb.*

When I was a young girl preparing for my confirmation, I
was introduced to some of the lives of the saints. I seemed
to hear them say that the Lord was calling everyone to be a saint,
and that all we had to do was to say "yes" and God would do the
rest. I can remember how excited I got. I was filled with joy, as
though I had just discovered a hidden treasure. I wanted to love
God with that same kind of love I saw in the saints, and to be

loved by God as they were. I ran off by myself to pray, and said, "Here I am, Lord, make me a saint. I want to belong to you and to serve you."

Later, I reflected, "Well, if it was that easy, then why does not everyone want to be a saint?" I concluded that, perhaps, I have to become worthy first, before I could be a servant of God. I asked the Lord, "Does this mean that I have to become a Nun, because I want to be a mother and have twelve children?" After trying and failing to attain instant holiness, I soon gave up believing that God was calling me to be a saint. Instead, I decided I would prepare myself to be the perfect wife and mother. I would be a virgin, a pure and untouched gift for the man I would marry (I was very idealistic at that time, and my ideals were somewhat superficial).

When I was 18, I started dating a man who was an amateur actor, and became pregnant as a result of *date rape*. In my distress, I turned to God for help. I prayed, "Lord, how did this happen? Did I, somehow, bring this on myself? Is this pregnancy a punishment? What do you want to teach me through this? What is your will for me?" God heard my prayer and came to me in a dream.

I dreamt that I was traveling across country in a car on the way to my birthplace—Ohio. We were in the middle of the desert. My father was driving and I was sitting in the back seat. Suddenly, parts of the car began to lift off and float away—the doors, roof, hood, windows—until all that was left was the foundation of the car. Then, a shower of beautiful, indescribable jewels began to fall out of the sky into my lap; they were as light as feathers. I was filled with joy and awe. I said, "Daddy, stop the car! I have to see where these are coming from." I got out of the car and found myself in a beautiful crystal city of white sparkling gems. I cannot express the joy and wonder I felt. There are no words to describe it. I had an apron around my waist and began picking up loose gems from the ground and putting them into my apron. Suddenly, I heard voices behind me. I turned to look; I was looking out across a foreign country. I saw people running towards me but they could not see me. They were dressed in biblical clothing. Their faces were filled with fear and they were shouting, "Jeremiah is coming, Jeremiah is coming!" I looked behind them and saw a huge mountain. On the top of the mountain, stood a man dressed in a long white robe, sandals on his feet, with long hair and a staff in his hands. I blinked my eyes, and suddenly, the man disappeared and the mountain was split in two, from east to west, with a wide valley running between. I found myself wondering what happened—what happened to the man and how did the one mountain become two? I blinked my eyes again, and just as suddenly, one half of the mountain began to withdraw and spread out to the north; the other half of the mountain spread out moving to the south. The valley that ran through the mountain was filled in by the shift, leaving no outlet. Again, I was puzzled, trying to understand how this happened. It was almost like looking at still snap-shots of each change.

I woke up, trembling and filled with awe. I knew this was no ordinary dream—that I had experienced God, face to face. I felt a strange fear, wondering, "Why me? Who am I that I should be given such an awesome gift?" I tried to tell my mother the dream; trembling, with tears flooding my eyes. My mother said, "Why are you crying?" I replied, "I don't know! What does it mean? Who is Jeremiah?" My mother said she thought he was a prophet in the bible, and that I should look in the bible. I did, but did not know where to look or what I was looking for.

Then, I realized that the dream had changed me. Suddenly, I knew that the child in my womb was not a punishment, but a gift—that all life is a gift—no matter what the circumstances. God loves us into life. I began to rejoice and thank God for this child growing within me. I was filled with love for this child and was healed of many of the effects that normally are associated with rape. I had no anger or bitterness towards the man who did this to me, only pity and sorrow for him, and I began to pray for him. I had not lost my virginity in vain. I began to prepare myself for motherhood. Somehow, I knew I was going to have a son. I had two names picked out: Michael and Daniel.

I recall that a month before I was due to give birth, my doctor asked me if I had thought about giving the baby up for adoption, because he knew a couple that would be happy to adopt him. I was in shock and began to cry. I could not believe that he would think I could do that. I said to him: "I could never give up my baby." I mention this because the doctor actually saved my baby's life. I think that once he saw how much I wanted this baby he was very diligent in his care for me and for my baby.

When the time came for me to give birth, on the way to the hospital I asked the Lord, "What shall I call him?" Then, I saw a sign that said, "Vote for Danny Thomas," so I decided to name him Daniel. The doctor suspected there was a problem because it seemed the baby had been ready to literally "fall out" of the womb for weeks—he was so low—and I was three weeks early as it was. Earlier that day, when my doctor examined me, he told me to call him and go to the hospital if anything at all happened. Later, I had a slight showing as a result of the examination, but no labor. Nothing happened after I got to the hospital. After several hours the doctor decided to induce labor. As soon as he broke my water, the labor became so intense that I was delirious with pain. I said, "Push the baby back—I can't go on—I will come back tomorrow and try again." I was so weak that I could not even clench my fist or scream out. But, there was no turning back! There was not even time for the medication to take effect. The doctor had to remove my son with forceps because the cord was wrapped around his neck. He was blue and bruised, but by the next day, fully recovered. I believe that if I had waited any longer, my baby would have strangled to death.

Even after this experience, however, I still did not have a personal relationship with Jesus. My faith was more of an *Old Testament* faith. When my son was two years old, I married a man who became a career AF officer. While he was in Vietnam, I once again, turned my attention to God, seeking his will with all my heart. Again, the Lord came to my aid and revealed his love to me. I began to reflect that all my life I went to God when I needed something, but what did God want from me? I realized that if anyone asked me why I was a Christian, why I believed or loved God, who Jesus is for me, I would not know what to say. I felt like I knew him in my heart, but I did not know him with my mind or understanding.

My husband returned from Vietnam after a year and we were sent to England. I went to the priest to see if he had an adult catechism class. I wanted to learn all I could about Jesus and about the Church. The priest said, "No," but he needed catechism teachers and said that I could learn while I taught. And, I did. My search continued, however. Eventually, it led me to a prayer group of non-Catholics. It was the beginning of the charismatic renewal in all the Churches. These women challenged many of my beliefs and introduced me to scripture. This challenge was a painful, difficult struggle, because it called me to change and to grow. I had to let go of my preconceived ideas about God and become as a little child again. Finally, not wanting to resist the Holy Spirit in any way, I prayed, "Jesus, I want you to be Lord of my life, I want only your will, and I want to serve you. If I need this *baptism of the Holy Spirit* in order to serve you, then let it be done." Then, in the presence of these women, I was unexpectedly baptized in the Holy Spirit.

I literally fell in love with Jesus, and delighted in reading scripture. I saw the Word of God as love letters from God, and read it as though it was written to me, personally. One day, as I was reading scripture, I came across a passage from the book of Zechariah:

> That day his feet shall rest upon the Mount of Olives, which is opposite Jerusalem to the east. The Mount of Olives shall be cleft in two from east to west by a very deep valley, and half of the mountain shall move to the north and half of it to the south. And the valley of the Lord's mountain shall be filled up when the valley of those two mountains reaches its edge; it shall be filled up as it was filled up by the earthquake in the days of King Uzziah of Judah. Then the Lord, my God, shall come, and all his holy ones with him. (NAB Zec 14:4—5)

This was my dream! I could not believe it! I still did not know what it meant, but that wasn't important. Scripture brought me even closer to my own Catholic Church, and I turned to the lives of the saints for inspiration. I was so full that I had to empty myself to make room for more. I began writing letters to God, to Jesus, pouring out my soul to him—my thoughts, feelings, life experiences, loves, dreams, desires, insights, questions, beliefs and so forth. Jesus became the center of my life, the Lord of my life.

All I wanted to do was to pray, read Scripture, and care for my family, but I soon discovered that the Lord does not give his gifts for us alone. I did not want to be a leader and was terrified of speaking to a group of people, but even more afraid to resist the Holy Spirit. Many doors began to open for me to witness to the Lord. Time and time again, I found myself having to step out in faith, doing things that had been unthinkable or impossible for me before, trusting in the Holy Spirit to be my power and strength. Once again, I discovered that God really is calling everyone to be a saint, and he does not wait for us to become holy or perfect, first. He calls us while we are sinners, and transforms us as he uses us. This was only the beginning of a long journey that has led to many deaths and resurrections in my life—to joy and sorrow, to loss and gifts, and to failures and successes.

After high school, my son attended a charismatic conference in Steubenville, Ohio. He heard the Lord call him while some people were praying with him, and one of them read the call of Jeremiah from scripture. Nevertheless, most of his life was like a pendulum, swinging back and forth between the kingdom of God and the kingdom of the world. Daniel eventually joined the Benedictines and they gave him a new name—Brother Jeremiah. After a few years, he left them and went back into the *world,* only to return again and join the Franciscans. Again, he became Br. Jeremiah. One day as I was praying, I reflected on the dream I had when I was pregnant with him and wondered what the name, *Jeremiah,* means. So, I looked it up in Webster's Dictionary. It means, literally, "Saved from the womb; loosed from the cord." I began to rejoice and shared my story with my son. He wept, thanking God. Then, after eight years as a friar, just before his final vows, Jeremiah met a young woman and fell in love. He left the friars, and decided to get married. His marriage ended in divorce, however, but also with a son; the love of his life. For the past eighteen years, his son has been the voice of God for him, constantly calling him back to the kingdom of God.

Jeremiah has gone through many desert experiences, many upheavals and falls, and many rebirths and infillings of the Holy Spirit since that time. Today, he lives with me and is in recovery from the wounds of the past, shedding his old skin; like a caterpillar enclosed in a cocoon, waiting to discover God's plan for his life to unfold. Please pray for him!

Much of the prophetic dream that I had has already been revealed; much of it is still not clear to me, and may not even be revealed in my lifetime. I just know that it was a divine revelation. Even though it took many years for me to recognize it, I know that through it, the Lord called me to be one of his *handmaids.* He made a covenant with me, inviting me into a personal and intimate relationship with him. He promised me a share in his kingdom. He gave me a blessing, the gift of the Holy Spirit. He also promised that it would not end with me but that I will pass it on to others—to my son and my three daughters, and to their children.

When I had the dream I was in a *wilderness* experience, desolate and broken. This is symbolized by the drive through the desert. I was on my way to my birthplace. This symbolizes my pregnancy, as well as a journey of re-birth, for me. The car is symbolic of my life; of me. My father was driving; I was still but a child, living under my father's roof. The collapse of the car—all the outer parts ripped away—was the collapse of my ideals, dreams, and hopes for the future. The foundation that remained was faith, hope and love. The jewels falling into my lap from the sky were gifts and graces from God—healing, mercy, compassion, hope, gifts of the Holy Spirit—completely gratuitous gifts and graces from God. The desire to find the source of these gifts was a call from God. The crystal city was the kingdom of God—a foretaste of heaven. The apron I wore was symbolic of a servant, and ministry; of a call from God. The jewels I picked up and put into my apron were gifts of the Spirit that I chose or acquired through service. The coming of Jeremiah was the announcement of the son I was carrying. God called him from my womb, to be a prophet—a servant of God—as he did me. The man on top of the mountain was Jesus, preparing me for his coming more fully into my life; and perhaps reminding me that his final coming could be at any time—to be ready. The rest of the dream has not been revealed. I do know that between each of those stages of change in the mountain, it could be a day, a thousand days, or a thousand years. It did not happen all at once; at least it did not seem so in my dream.

I do not know why God has chosen me, why he would give me such extraordinary blessings. I just know that it did not have anything to do with me, and all to do with him. Until he comes again, I believe that the Lord will continue to give prophetic dreams, along with all the other charisms of the Holy Spirit to all those who seek him and want to serve him.

Looking back over my spiritual journey, I have to believe that it started with my confirmation; that time in a Catholic's life when we are prepared to answer the call to follow Jesus, to be a witness; a call to holiness and to become saints; a call to receive the Holy Spirit in a fuller way, empowering us with the gifts of the Holy Spirit. The seed of God's call was planted within my heart when I responded with my "yes."

The first stage of my call was my experience of rape and pregnancy. I have to believe that God was very pleased with my *yes* to accepting my son as a gift. He blessed me with the knowledge that every life is a gift. There are no mistakes. Every person is loved into life by God. He gave me a prophetic dream that would eventually lead me to search for him, and through the *baptism of the Holy Spirit*, he brought fulfillment to that dream. He showed me that the baptism of the Holy Spirit is a baptism in his love, and for everyone who desires to follow and serve him. He showed me that he is raising up an army of saints, and that everyone is called to holiness; to be a saint. All life is a gift from God, and meant to be given away in love to others.

In baptism, we are born anew of the Holy Spirit into the family of God. In baptism, we are consecrated prophet, king, and priest— servants and heralds of God. In baptism, we are reborn as children of God, and come to experience the unconditional love of God. Finally, in baptism, we receive the assurance that nothing can ever separate us from God. As Scripture says, "For I am certain of this: neither death nor life, no angel, no prince, nothing that exists, nothing still to come, not any power, or height or depth, nor any created thing, can ever come between us and the love of God made visible in Christ Jesus our Lord" (JB Rom 8:38—39).

I believe that God fell in love with us the moment we were conceived within our mother's womb. From that moment, God was in a relationship with us, and we belonged to him. We were not conscious of that relationship, however. Baptism brought us into a more intimate relationship with God. We were no longer simply his creation—his creatures. In Christ, we became his adopted sons and daughters. For most of us, however, we were still not consciously aware of our relationship with God. Our whole life, we have been experiencing God's love, through the Holy Spirit; but, again, we were never consciously aware of these experiences, and so, we could not fully respond to them.

A newborn baby is loved by its parents, but the baby is not conscious of that love or of its relationship to the parents. The baptism of the Holy Spirit, an adult renewal of our baptism, is an experience where we become consciously aware of God's love for us, and of our relationship to him. We are then able to respond to that love through an adult conversion. As an illustration, imagine a young couple who meet and see each other from time to time. On an unconscious level, they fall in love, but they do not yet know they are in love. Finally, one day one of them realizes it, and tells the other, who upon hearing this profession, realizes it is mutual. From that moment on, their relationship is changed. It becomes intimate and personal. They make each other the center of their life. Adult conversion is like falling in love with God, entering into a personal relationship with God. This is followed by the baptism of the Holy Spirit, a baptism in God's love.

This is my story, my experience of conversion and the baptism of the Holy Spirit; which is on-going, from the time of my baptism until the moment I enter into heaven; leaving this life on earth. The crowning moment of my spiritual journey was my experience of the baptism of the Holy Spirit, when I became fully conscious of who Jesus is, and of God's love for me.

Before I end this story, I want to say something about the gift of faith. As Catholics, we know that in baptism, we were given the gift of faith, hope, and love. This gift of faith was implanted within our souls as a tiny seed that never goes away. It can never be lost. But, this tiny seed is destined to grow into a mighty tree that gives shelter to all creatures of the world. However, it needs to be nurtured in order to grow. That growth can happen over a lifetime, or overnight. Nothing is impossible for God. I think that is why there are so many deathbed conversions; preparing for death has a way of also preparing us for new life. This is also the experience of the baptism of the Holy Spirit. That tiny seed burst forth through the ground and becomes a mighty tree, giving shelter to everyone who comes into our lives.

This growth is different for everyone who experiences the baptism of the Holy Spirit. This growth can be gradual, coming in spurts, or instantaneous, reaching its full capacity in a day. It depends on our response to the gifts God offers us. It also depends on how we nurture that little plant that has become visible. Every time we make an act of faith, every time we exercise our faith, that little plant grows larger and larger. That little plant represents our relationship with Jesus. It is nurtured by reading Scripture, by prayer, and by frequently receiving the sacraments of confession and Eucharist. It is nurtured by our stepping out in faith, witnessing to others, and exercising the charisms we receive. It is nurtured by our communion with others who share our faith; attending Mass and prayer meetings, and by the testimonies of the saints. If we stop these things, the tree stops growing and remains dormant until we return to these spiritual practices. The tree can even die and return to the soil (our souls) as a seed. But, the seed never dies and can burst through the soil again and again, as a little plant ready to conquer the world. It is never too late, even for those who lose their faith and become atheists. We never can lose the gift of our baptism. We can never lose our place in the family of God. God is forever, our Father. Mary is forever, our Mother. Jesus is forever, our Lord and Savior. We are forever a part of the body of Christ, and of the Church. The Holy Spirit is forever our Advocate and life-support.

Make a decision today! Become like a little child. Take a leap of faith. Call on Jesus and ask him to come into your life, to be your Lord and Savior, and to fill you with the Holy Spirit. Do not be afraid to turn your life and will over to God; because God is love, and he loves us as he loves his own self. His will and plan for your life can only lead to perfect happiness; to perfect joy and peace.

14

Spiritual Warfare

Who could have ever guessed how widespread witchcraft, Wicca, occultism, magic, Satanism, vampirism, and demonic activity would become in the last fifty years. It would seem that the charismatic renewal, which also began fifty years ago, is especially providential for our time in history. The battle that we are fighting is a spiritual warfare, calling for spiritual weapons to defend and conquer the enemies of God and the Church. The wisdom gained through this renewal has taught us a lot about discernment; about how and when to use the charisms of the Holy Spirit, and how not to use them; about the discernment of spirits—what comes from God, what comes from ourselves and what comes from the evil one.

When the charismatic renewal first began, most people were excited about the charisms of tongues, interpretation of tongues, healing, miracles, and the prophetic gifts. The gift of discernment of spirits and exorcism did not appeal to most people; perhaps because we really were not sure about the existence of Satan and evil spirits. Discernment for most people had to do with prudence and right judgment—making right choices and discerning between true and false, right and wrong, good and bad, God and self. We were sub-jects of *psychology* and the existence of Satan and evil spirits was considered to be superstition. Demons were seen as personal defects of character, or merely temptations—not supernatural, intellectual beings that could have any effect on us. Some people, however, saw demons everywhere; denying any personal responsibility for sin or evil—this was the domain of *superstition*.

Of course, the lack of experience and discernment led to many abuses in the early days of the renewal. Today, most charismatic Christians have grown in discernment and wisdom, and recognize that we are in the midst of a very real spiritual warfare. But, the stakes are higher today, and we need even more discernment. The evil spirits of today are much more subtle—*angels of light*—and very good counterfeits of the charisms of the Holy Spirit. We do not stand a chance against the evil one if we deny the existence of Satan and evil spirits.

Why is it that so many Christians are reluctant to accept the reality of Satan and evil spirits? Throughout the Old and New Testaments, God warns us of the *fallen angels* and the power of Satan in the world. Yet, even among Christians who cling to the Word of God as their sole authority, there are so many who just cannot accept this reality. There is so much evidence, today, that supports the warnings of God; so much evidence of supernatural, demonic powers in our world. Still, we refuse to accept it. Why? We prefer to file all this evidence under the category of magic, fan-tasy, or science fiction. Perhaps we deny reality because of fear. We cannot face our fears. Fear is Satan's greatest weapon against us. Scripture tells us that all unreasonable fear comes from the evil one. The only antidote for fear is faith in God; faith in the power of the Holy Spirit to conquer evil, faith in God's love for us, and trust that he will not abandon us. But, humans are so slow to believe, that Jesus had this to say: "But, when the Son of Man comes, will he find any faith on earth?" (NAB Lk 18:8)

What we need today is a spiritual awakening. Every Christian needs to wake up from their sleep—to repent and be *baptized in the Holy Spirit*—to experience a *new Pentecost*. We need the spiritual gifts, the charisms of the Holy Spirit, in order to remain faithful until the end. We need these gifts in order to evangelize the world and to fight against the *powers of darkness*.

As I reflect on my own spiritual awakening, I can see seven steps that led me to a full spiritual awakening and the *baptism of the Holy Spirit*. This, I think, is necessary before we can really develop *spiritual discernment*. St. Paul tells us: "The unspiritual man does not receive the gifts of the Spirit of God, for they are folly to him, and he is not able to understand them because they are spiritually discerned" (RSV 1 Cor 2:14). We need to become spiritual, to awaken to the spiritual life in order to receive the fullness of the Holy Spirit. Then, we will be able to discern the truth about the things of God. The eight steps that I experienced are:

- **Repentance**
- **Recognition that I did not really know Jesus**
- **Search to know God—Father, Son, and Holy Spirit**
- **Awareness of the power of Satan and evil spirits**
- **Awareness of the power of God**
- **Desire for the truth**
- **Asked for the Baptism of the Holy Spirit**
- **Received the baptism of the Holy Spirit**

Looking back to when I was a child, I recall that I had brief and scattered awakenings leading up to when I received the sacrament of confirmation. My confirmation was a more profound experience than my previous experiences of God, but it still lacked maturity and consistency. My real conversion came when I was an adult; when I discovered what "sin" is, that I was a sinner, that I could not save myself or atone for my sins; when I discovered that I needed a Savior and turned to Jesus to save me. This is when I understood the meaning of Calvary.

I really do not think we can comprehend what sin is until we discover what love is. Repentance does not seem to go very deep when we think that the only people our sins have hurt are strangers. Repentance that leads to salvation requires that we come to the realization that we cannot save ourselves; we need a Savior. It requires that we realize that we cannot undo what we did; we cannot atone for it; we cannot take away the pain that we have caused those we love; and we cannot be reconciled with them. This was the condition that Mary Magdalen was in when she met Jesus, her Messiah. She received hope when she learned that he had the power to forgive her and set her free from her anguish and her sins. She was forgiven much because she loved much. The more we love, the more we become aware of what sin can do. The more we have been hurt by sin, the more we know what sin can do to others. If we do not love, we do not really care about what we have done to others. We do not even recognize sin. We are all sinners, but we just do not know it.

St. Peter called upon Jesus to save him many times, and each time, his faith increased. Conversion, however, is something that radically changes us; we become a new person. I think that St.

Peter's total conversion was preceded by his denial of Jesus. When we betray a friend or someone we love, trust, and believe in, it can cause us great anguish. When we betray someone who loves us, believes in us, and trusts us, it can be devastating. How do we even face them? How do we forgive ourselves? This was Peter's state of being. Peter knew that Jesus loved him, trusted him, and believed in him. After he betrayed him, he experienced Jesus' love and forgiveness, in an even deeper way. Jesus continued to love Peter, believe in him, and trust him even though Peter betrayed him. Jesus reconciled Peter to himself and did not take back his promise, or his choice of Peter. Scripture says: "what proves that God loves us is that he died for us while we were yet sinners" (JB Rom 5:7). Conversion begins with repentance, but is made complete in experiencing the love of God—his mercy and forgiveness; his embrace. We are made new again; the past is forgotten. We are restored to new life.

When I came into the experience of Jesus as my Lord and Savior, when I experienced his mercy, forgiveness, and love, I felt like a new person, and was full of joy. I began to reflect that all my life, I turned to God whenever I had any problems or had to make any major choices, but I had to ask myself, what did God want from me? Was there something I could do for him? Did he have some kind of plan or purpose for my life? What was his will for me and for my life? I thought about Jesus, and realized if anyone asked me who Jesus is, I would not know what to say. I knew all the usual things about Jesus that everyone knows. But, who is he, really? Who is he for me? I felt like I knew him in my heart, but I could not really witness with my words, who he is. I always believed that God is love, but how do you describe or define what love is? I realized that I really knew very little about my faith, about Jesus, and about the Church. I knew nothing about the Bible, except how to open it.

Suddenly, I had such a hunger to know God. I wanted to know everything I could possibly know about Jesus. We were preparing to move to England, at the time, and I made a firm resolution that as soon as we got settled, I would go to the priest and ask him to teach me. And, I did. I went to the priest and asked if he had an adult catechism class. My priest decided that we needed a Women's study group in the chapel, and put me in charge. I did not know any more than any of the other women, but my hunger for God made them hungry. We looked for inspiration from the lives of the saints.

I discovered that as soon as someone begins to seriously seek the Lord, Satan is hot on their trail. One neighbor wanted me to read his books on Edgar Casey. Another neighbor wanted me to read about Jeanne Dixon, and "automatic writing." A man in my bible study class wanted me to read his books on Lobsang Rampa, and Eastern mysticism. I quickly became aware that I needed discernment. I did not know how to discern spiritual things; between what was from God and what was from evil spirits. I really did not know what *idolatry* was. I prayed continually for discernment. My desire to know and do God's will, increased. My fear of being deceived and led away from God also increased. The people in the books I was reading appeared to be really good and compassionate people, but I felt waves of nausea and fear as I read. I prayed more and more for discernment. I would beg the Lord, with many tears, to give me wisdom and not allow me to be deceived. The desire for God's will became almost an obsession for me, because I was so aware of my ignorance of Scripture and authentic spirituality. I did not know where to go to find the truth. I was like a defenseless lamb among wolves. However, as I read those books, I recall saying to God: "Lord, if these things are of the devil, and counterfeits of your power, then, your power is so much greater than I ever imagined! It never occurred to me how great your power is, or that nothing, absolutely nothing, is impossible for you!" I realized that some of the things I was reading about were supernatural, beyond the powers of mere humans. If these things were counterfeits, then the real thing had to be greater than I ever imagined.

During this time, it seemed that the Lord was really protecting me from evil, even though I remained ignorant. One day, my neighbor invited me over. She had a Ouija Board, and a few friends also joined her. I had never heard of a Ouija Board before. I watched as they asked questions and the answers were spelled out on the board by some invisible force moving the pointer. Inwardly, I kept praying for discernment because my stomach was nauseous. My friend asked me to ask a question, but the board went wild and spelled out: "We do not like your friend. Tell her to go home." So, I did! I became more and more concerned about my friend, and started praying for her daily. I was concerned that if these were evil spirits and she continued to communicate with them, she would become possessed. I still did not know if they were evil spirits. Shortly after that, she did become possessed; but was also delivered by Jesus.

These things all took place almost fifty years ago. It was the beginning of the *new age movement*, as well as the charismatic renewal. The Church did not teach a lot about divination and the occult sciences because it was not that visible in our culture, before this time. Suddenly, however, everyone was talking about *extra sensory perception* (ESP), and the Church was waiting, watching, and discerning.

I think I always knew that astrology and fortune tellers were a "no, no." But, that was the extent of my knowledge about the occult. I did not know why they were not approved of or what was wrong with them; or if the Church still condemned these practices. Almost over- night, astrology and psychics made their way into Church circles. Jeanne Dixon was a Catholic and a daily communicant, as well as being an astrologist and fortune teller with a crystal ball. Edgar Casey had made many predictions in his time, that came true, and he was known as a *healer*. He predicted great earth-quakes in California, to happen in our time. I was so confused!

My neighbor introduced me to another way that you could get answers about the future; by putting some thread through a ring and holding it over a glass. As you ask questions, some kind of force or energy begins to move the ring either back and forth, like a pendulum, or around in a circle, giving you yes or no answers to your questions. It occurred to me that I might be able to find out exactly when this great earth-quake would happen by asking questions with a yes and no answer. Very soon, I began to feel queasy in the pit of my stomach again, and wondered what God thought about all this. I began to pray, "Lord, I do not know how to tell if this is good or evil. Show me your will and help me to discern between what comes from you and what comes from the devil." I then, went to my priest to ask him about this. I told him what I was doing and the results. I asked him if this was evil or a sin. He just responded that the Church was looking into this whole area of ESP. I still felt confused when I got home and prayed earnestly for the Lord to show me his will.

Shortly after this, I had a dream. I was in a darkened room, or space in the sky, by myself. Suddenly, a light came towards me, and beckoned me to follow. It had no features but the shape was in a form of a person. The light spoke to me and said, "God wants to speak to you." I began to tremble, and thought to myself, "God? What does he want with me?" I followed the light and was led into another room. As soon as I entered the room, I became as a little child, about six or seven. All fear left me. There was an elderly man sitting on a chair in the middle of the room. The man was smiling and looked at me with such love. We did not need words to communicate. He knew my thoughts and I could understand his heart. I thought to myself, "Oh good, now I can ask him about that *ring thing*." Immediately, I heard him in my heart, say, "It is not necessary." But, I thought, that still does not answer my question. I want to know if it is right or wrong, good or evil—if it is a sin. Then, I heard him ask me, in my heart, "Why do you want to see California destroyed?" I wanted to defend myself. That is not what I want, I thought to myself. But, he is God. He knows me better than I know myself. I fell to my knees and began to cry, saying from my heart, "Lord, is that what I want?" He responded in my heart: "When you heard about that earth-quake, what did you do? Did you fall to your knees in tears, and plead with me to grant them mercy, and to stop the earth-quakes? No, instead, your curiosity took hold of you. You were more interested in finding out the day and time. You put your faith in that prophecy, instead of me, which works toward making it happen. It does not have to happen! People choose to make it happen, before its time. Everything that leads you away from God—away from love—comes from the evil one. Everything that leads you to God—to love more deeply—comes from me." I have since learned that when the Lord foretells future events, it is

152

always for our good: to prepare us, to draw us close to him, to lead us to repentance, to save us, or to give us hope.

I have no doubt that this dream was a revelation and gift to me from God. It was unexpected and came as a total surprise. It gave me wisdom that I did not have before. It drew me closer to God and showed me what love is. It increased my love for God. It delivered me from the wiles of the evil one. Shortly after this dream, I was invited to join a group of women down the street for a prayer meeting. They were very devout Christians, but I was the only Catholic. They introduced me to the Scriptures. I began to read the New Testament daily. They also began to talk about the *baptism of the Holy Spirit* and the charisms of the Holy Spirit. I had never heard about this before and became afraid of being deceived and falling into heresy. I did not feel nauseous at all, but I cried a lot and prayed a lot for understanding. I thought that if it was really from God, the Church would have told me about it.

The more I read Scripture, the more I saw that what they said was true. The charisms were active in the lives of the saints, but I did not know of any ordinary Catholics who had any of these charisms. Nevertheless, I wanted to know God—to know his will and to be holy—to be a saint, and to serve the Lord. I began to realize that I needed to be *baptized in the Holy Spirit* in order to do these things. So, I prayed, "Lord, if I need to be baptized in the Holy Spirit in order to serve you then, baptize me in the Holy Spirit." This was the point when I let go of all resistance and abandoned myself to the Lord in faith and trust.

The next day, I was with my friends, listening to a tape on the testimony of a man who talked about his experience of the Holy Spirit. As I listened, I prayed inwardly, "Oh Lord, if the *baptism of the Holy Spirit* can do that, baptize my mother with the Holy Spirit, so she will know she is loved by you, and be healed of her depression." Without warning, as soon as I finished this prayer, I was baptized in the Spirit, manifested by uncontrollable weeping for about ten or fifteen minutes. I cried buckets of tears, and from then on, I had the *gift of tears*. When I opened my eyes, my friends were all smiling and praising God for baptizing me with the Holy Spirit. Joy began to bubble up within me. By the time I got back home, I could barely contain the joy. I wanted to call everyone I knew and tell them what I experienced. Prudence prevented me from doing that, but I did call one friend. I could not stop praising the Lord, and continued to pray in private. I wanted to sing but did not know any songs. So, I just began to sing in *tongues*. When I started to doubt this gift, I heard the words of Scripture, "If you then, who are evil, know how to give good gifts to your children, how much more will the heavenly Father give the Holy Spirit to those who ask him!" (ICSB Luke 11:13). Then, I felt a bolt of electricity go through my whole body, from head to toe, and I never doubted it again.

This experience radically changed my life—not that I did not have to cope with all the normal problems of life; or even that I did not fall back into sin. But, looking back, I hate to think what my life would have been like—what I would be like—if I had not received this wonderful gift of the Holy Spirit. Without the Holy Spirit, the gift of faith, hope, and love can easily dry up, or go to seed. The Lord told one of the saints, (I forget which one) "You have two choices. You can either become a saint, or go insane." I think that is pretty much true for everyone, especially in our present age. Of course, in the eyes of the world, the saints often appear to be insane. The *judgment* of God will reveal the truth. This experience produced many wonderful affects in me. Scripture came alive, and I was suddenly able to understand it. I fell in love with Jesus, and entered into a personal relationship with the Holy Trinity. I fell in love with the Church, as well, and all the saints. I was filled with love for everyone. My prayer life deepened and I was able to pray without ceasing. My desire for the Eucharist increased. I became a *witness*, and more and more opportunities to witness and to serve the Lord were opened to me. I grew in knowledge, wisdom, and discernment.

I never asked for any particular charisms of the Holy Spirit, but I prayed that I would never resist the Holy Spirit. This resulted in the manifestation of many different charisms, at different times and places, in accordance with the needs of others and the designs of God. The charism that has been the most consistent in my life is that of prophetic teaching and writing. It seemed to me that this charism was confirmed for me through the vision of an angel. One night, I was listening to a tape by an evangelist. It was on "The Scope and Magnitude of God's Love." I prayed inwardly, praising God, as I listened to the tape. My eyes suddenly got very heavy, so I closed them. As soon as I did, I seemed to go right through a port hole. Before me, stood a youthful angel, with a pageboy hair style, dressed in a white cassock, with a red chasuble or blouse over it. He was holding a pointer stick in his hand, and pointing to a blank blackboard. The words that came out of his mouth were the words on the tape: "Nothing can touch you unless it is first screened by the Father's love." I knew that this is the truth, even if I would be tested by Satan, like Job was.

I do recall saying to the Lord, "Lord, I do not ever want to resist your Holy Spirit, but I hope you will never ask me to deliver anyone from an evil spirit." It seemed to me that it would be embarrassing or humiliating for people. I could understand why this gift, like confession, would be designated for only priests. In fact, in most cases those who are oppressed by evil spirits can be delivered through the sacrament of confession. Nevertheless, there have been occasions where I was put in a position of having to bind or cast out demons in the name of Jesus, or be attacked, myself. Among Catholics, cases of actual possession needing exorcism have been rare, but lately are becoming more common. This is because of all the occultism, witchcraft, and Satanism that is so rampant today. Sometimes I think it might be a good thing if every Christian could witness the manifestation of evil spirits, so that they would not deny their existence, or be taken unawares. The greatest weapon of Satan is to make us believe that he does not exist. I think that every Christian will experience some spiritual warfare, but we need not be afraid if we put on the armor of God, and keep our eyes on Jesus.

> Put on the whole armor of God that you may be able to stand against the wiles of the devil. For we are not contending against flesh and blood, but against the principalities, against the powers, against the world rulers of this present darkness, against the spiritual hosts of wickedness in the heavenly places. Therefore take the whole armor of God that you may be able to withstand in the evil day, and having done all, to stand. Stand therefore, having fastened the belt of truth around your waist, and having put on the breastplate of righteousness, and having shod your feet with the equipment of the gospel of peace;

besides all these, taking the shield of faith, with which you can quench all the flaming darts of the Evil One. And take the helmet of salvation, and the sword of the Spirit, which is the word of God. Pray at all times in the Spirit, with all prayer and supplication. (ICSB Eph 6:10—18)

15

Pray Without Ceasing

$\mathcal{S}$t. Paul exhorts us to "pray without ceasing" (1 Thes 5:17). The only way we can do that is to make our whole life a prayer; to glorify God in all that we think, feel, say, and do. Prayer is living a life in the Spirit, doing all for the glory of God. It is nothing more than *loving God with all our heart, soul, mind, and strength; and our neighbor as our self.* Prayer is not so much what we do, but how we live. It is a life lived in union with Jesus. (Mk 12:30—31)

One evening, many years ago, I was in a group meeting with my parish priest. The priest said: "Everyone seems to be asking how to pray. What do you tell people when they ask that question?" The priest was not really expecting an answer, he was just thinking out loud. Nevertheless, I could not stop thinking about it, and when I got home, I asked the Lord about it, in prayer. I said, "Lord, I think I know how to pray, but I would not know how to teach someone else how to pray. How do you teach people to pray?"

I felt a certainty within me that the Lord was going to answer me, and I was content to wait for his answer. The next day, I received a call from a woman in my prayer group. Her husband was the Baptist chaplain on base. She was involved with the Protestant Women of the Chapel (PWOC). She proceeded to tell me that the PWOC were planning a day of prayer, and the theme for the day was: "How to Pray." I immediately began to rejoice within my heart. I knew that I was supposed to be there, that this was the answer to my prayer. I knew the Lord was in this. I was so absorbed in this that when she asked me to be the speaker, to give the talk on prayer, I said "Yes" without realizing what she was asking. I thought I was saying yes to going. Afterwards, I prayed, "Lord, what did I do? I do not even know the answer, yet, and I have never given a public talk to any group. I will be terrified, and I do not even know what to say. What if nothing comes out of my mouth?" After I prayed, I knew with conviction that the Lord was asking me to do this, that it was God's will for me, even if nothing came out of my mouth. My fear and anxiety left me, and I thought to myself, if nothing comes out of my mouth, than I need the humility that this experience would give me. I saw it as a gift. I had nothing to lose. But, I told the Lord, "That is not really fair to those women, they are coming to be fed."

I turned to Scripture and reflected on the passage where the disciples said to Jesus, "Lord, teach us to pray," and Jesus taught them the "Our Father." I became a part of that event, and watched and listened as Jesus turned to the Father and began to pray to the Father in behalf of his disciples, like the Old Testament prophets who interceded for the people.

I continued to pray and meditate as the days went by, but no clear thoughts came to me, having to do with instruction on prayer. I was, however, led to reflect on some writing that I had done, previously; witnessing to my relationship with Jesus, and my faith journey. When I wrote it, I had no particular reason for writing it, except that I was compelled to write in order to get it out of my head. It was a form of journaling for me. At the time, I told the Lord that I did not know why I wrote it, but if he wanted to use it, he could have it.

When the day arrived for me to speak on prayer, I still had no clear idea of what to say. So, I grabbed my essay and went on my way. When the chaplain's wife introduced me, she said she had to share a story first. She said that when she was asked to find a speaker, she went home and prayed, asking the Lord who she should ask. Immediately, she heard my name and gasped, "That must be from Satan, she is a Catholic." She said, "Lord, that can't be right, she is a Catholic, and this is a Protestant women's group." She decided she would seek a confirmation from her husband. When her husband came home, she told him she needed to find a speaker on prayer and asked him if he could suggest anyone. Immediately, he suggested me. This little introduction gave me great confidence and assurance that the Holy Spirit was with me.

I started out by sharing my own experience of fear and why and how I accepted the invitation. I also shared my lack of experience as a speaker. I began to read the essay I had brought with me, but once I got going, I forgot about myself and spoke from my heart. It was not until I was almost finished that I discovered the answer to my prayer. I told them that prayer is a personal relationship with Jesus. Although there are some common expressions of prayer that we can all share, real prayer is unique to each person. I told them that no one can really teach another person to pray, except for Jesus. All we can do is witness to our relationship with Jesus, our faith journey, and how we pray. We can then, encourage them to go to Jesus to ask him to teach them to pray.

The women were deeply moved by what I had to share. So was I! The strange thing was that I only met the chaplain once, by accident. I had a very dramatic mystical experience one day, beyond my control, in the presence of a group of women. I believed that the experience was from God, but later, thought I should speak to a priest about it. I did not want to be deceived. I went to the chapel and asked for a priest. The Baptist chaplain greeted me. Both priests were out of the office. The chaplain asked if he could be of help. I thanked him but said no, and started to walk away. Then, I stopped and said, "Well, maybe you can." I told him about my whole experience. The chaplain happened to be "baptized in the Holy Spirit" and very familiar with the writings of St. Teresa of Avila. He affirmed me in my experience and referred to St. Teresa's writings. That is why he thought of me when his wife mentioned a speaker on prayer. Mystical prayer, however, is not something we can teach to another, or something we can learn. Contemplation and mystical experiences are totally a gift from God, not something we can earn or attain on our own. It is not what we do, but what God does. Contemplation takes us out of our self and into God. It is an experience of union of a part or all of our soul with God. It is God who lifts us up and draws us to himself. All we can do is be open and receptive to God's love.

One day I was with a group of charismatic women at a prayer luncheon in someone's home. Two of the women began to argue. One of them was very susceptible to false teaching, going from one philosophy or speculation to another. The other woman reacted in anger, saying, "Not my Jesus!" I asked the women if we could stop and pray. I was sitting down with my elbows on my knees and my head in my hands. From the depth of my soul, with my whole heart, I prayed out loud, "Jesus, please help us all to keep our eyes fixed on you." Suddenly, my whole body began to tremble, my head went up, and my arms went up in praise. I could not hold my arms down. I felt my soul shoot out of my body like a rocket (that was the sensations I felt). It seemed as though God was drawing my soul right up to him, out of this world; as though he were a huge magnet. The thought flashed across my mind, "in a moment I will be dead, unless the Lord changes his mind." I had no power to resist, even if I wanted to. Then, suddenly, it was over and I was back to myself. A peace and calm came over me, and I just praised the Lord, silently. Everyone saw what happened and knew it was the Lord. Peace came back into the group, and everyone had their eyes fixed on Jesus, in prayer. The "speculator" became silent, and the "angry one" became peaceful. Later, on the way home, the "speculator" suggested that maybe what I experienced was from the devil and not Jesus. So, I decided to see a priest to confirm it.

For me, the purpose and goal of prayer is union with God—union with Jesus Christ; union with the will of God; to be one with Jesus Christ as a husband and wife are called to be one—in good times and in bad, for richer or poorer, in sickness and in health, for all eternity. Whatever form or method of prayer that can prepare us to enter into this union with God, and his will, is the highest form of prayer for us. There is not one form or method of prayer, but many. What makes these methods of prayer authentic is that we pray *in the spirit*—with attention and intention—we are in a personal relationship with God. Relationship involves many ways of communication. It involves our whole being and life.

There are many ways in which we express our love for God, and many ways in which we can receive his love. To love is to give our self away—to surrender to God. We love with our bodies, our intellect, reason, understanding, will, feelings, emotions, senses, imagination, memory, and spirit—with all that we do, think, and say. We love God through all the experiences of our life. To me, love and prayer are synonymous. Prayer opens us up to the whole life of Jesus—everything he experienced. To be *in the spirit* is to know when to speak, when to be silent, when to mourn, when to rejoice, when to give and when to receive.

In any personal relationship, we communicate and relate in many different ways, depending on the person, or kind of relation-ship; our stage of growth; and the events and circumstances of our life. We express ourselves and communicate with those we love through our bodies; through gestures, touch, tears, smiles, laughter, words, singing, dancing, writing, silence, stillness; through our very presence. We pour out our hearts and express our minds; our thoughts, feelings, and desires. We listen to, acknowledge, accept and receive the one we are with, and what they have to give us. We use words of praise, thanksgiving, and affection. We also share our fears, doubts, struggles, failures, guilt and pain. We ask for help and counsel when we need it, as well as for their prayers and inter-cession. We seek to know and understand those we love through our questions, dialogue, requests, and constant companionship. We show our love through service, acts of love, work, suffering, gifts, prayer, peace, joy, and respect for others. We can do this when we are at rest, at play, at work, at study, and at meals; when we are walking, running, sitting, standing, kneeling, and lying down. In all these sundry ways of communicating, however, two things are necessary to make it truly personal: it must come from the heart and be motivated by love. This is what makes it a life of unceasing prayer.

There are numerous devotions and religious practices that are pathways into prayer; however, it seems to me that if we want to pray as Jesus prayed, we need to enter into his Sacred Heart—his sacred humanity—just as he entered into our humanity, our human condition. Jesus, through his own humanity, suffered every aspect of the human condition known to men. He knew hunger and thirst—physically, mentally, emotionally, and spiritually. He experienced every natural desire and appetite that every man experiences. He probably experienced the need and desire for the love of a woman, for sexual intimacy, for marriage, and to father a child. He denied himself the fulfillment of these desires for the sake of the kingdom of God. Nevertheless, Jesus knew the power of the flesh, the desire for pleasure and self-gratification, and the pain of self-denial. He knew the challenge of love, and the suffering that accompanies authentic, eternal love.

When I contemplate the Sacred Heart of Jesus, this is what I see: Jesus prayed alone and with others. He prayed the Scriptures. He wept over Jerusalem. He wept over Lazarus. He wept over the loss of Joseph. He interceded for his disciples. He cried tears of blood. He entered into the closet of his heart. He ate with his disciples. He ritualized his prayers and experiences. He prayed and taught the *Our Father*. He shared his Father with others. He lived the mysteries of the rosary. He shared his mother with others. He loved his mother. He honored his mother. He loved his disciples. He had close friends. He listened to others. He was touched by others. He touched others. He received from others. He gave to others. He walked with others. He was baptized. He fasted. He partied with others. He worked for others. He revealed himself to others. He spoke with women. He respected and honored women. He witnessed to the Father. He did the will of the Father. He trusted in the Father. He imparted the Holy Spirit. He walked on water. He performed miracles. He healed the sick. He delivered people from evil spirits. He forgave sins. He taught others. He gave himself to others. He fed others. He looked at others with love. He was present to others. He served others. He was humble. He was meek. He was vulnerable. He kissed others. He let others kiss him. He trusted in others. He believed in others. He rejoiced in God and in others. He was firm with others. He was righteous. He was angry. He corrected others. He was passionate. He was emotional. He was intelligent. He was wise. He was a mystic. He was discerning. He was silent. He shouted. He used his imagination. He was creative. He was sensitive—physically, emotionally, and spiritually. He was loved. He loved his enemies. He loved the poor. He loved sinners. He was followed. He was believed in. He was worshipped. He was honored. He was respected. He was listened to. He took the lowest place. He accepted the first place. He was a Jew. He loved the Jews. He loved the Samaritans. He loved the Romans. He loved the Gentiles. He loved children. He loved women. He went to the Temple. He loved the Temple. He taught in the Temple. He was thrown out of the Temple. He went into the desert. He submitted to testing. He was cold. He was rejected. He was lonely. He experienced darkness, not knowing, not understanding, blind faith. He was abandoned. He was judged. He was persecuted. He was taken for a criminal and heretic. He was scourged. He was mocked. He felt pain, anxiety, and anguish. He bled for others. He fell down many times. He was misunderstood. He was ridiculed. He carried the cross. He was crucified. He died for others. He rose from the dead. He ministered to the dead. He interceded for the souls in purgatory. He ascended to the Father. He will come again.

Jesus taught that *true worshippers will worship the Father in Spirit and truth*; (JB Jn 4:24). To me, this means to worship with a new heart—the heart of Jesus (truth) and the love that comes from the Holy Spirit. It is only through the heart of Jesus that we can enter into a personal relationship with the Father. It is only through the Holy Spirit that we can call God *Abba, Father.*

People were praying long before the Incarnation of Jesus. They fasted and gave alms and made sacrifices to God. They followed the Commandments, repented of sin, and prayed the psalms. They reverenced God and the Scriptures. They worshipped God, alone, and in community—in the temple. Their relationship with God, however, was that of a servant to his master; not an intimate, personal, or familial relationship with God.

When the disciples asked Jesus to teach them how to pray, it was not because they never prayed or did not know how to pray. They recognized something different in the way that Jesus prayed. Jesus prayed in union with God, with power and love. He prayed with all of his mind, all his heart, and all his soul. He prayed to the Father in *spirit and truth.*

If we want to know how to pray, we should look at how Jesus prayed; and ponder what Jesus taught about prayer. Jesus taught his disciples to pray to the Father, in the name of the Son; through, with, and in the Holy Spirit. He said: *So you should pray like this: Our Father in heaven, may your name be held Holy, your kingdom come, your will be done, on earth as in heaven* (JB Mt 6:9—10).

Jesus prayed to the Father, *I have made your name known to them and will continue to make it known, so that the love with which you loved me may be in them, and so that I may be in them* (JB Jn 17:26). Jesus taught the disciples: *I tell you solemnly, anything you ask for from the Father he will grant in my name.* (JB John 16:23)

Jesus taught his disciples what to pray for: *Give us this today our daily bread. And forgive us our debts, as we have forgiven those who are in debt to us. And do not put us to the test, but save us from the evil one* (JB Mt 6:11—13). He said again and again, *Pray not to be put to the test... .Get up and pray not to be put to the test* (JB Lk 22:40, 46). Jesus taught his disciples to bring their offerings to the altar with a pure heart; to be reconciled with everyone by making amends; to forgive everyone; and to pray for their enemies (JB Mt 5:23—24, 44; 6:14—15). He also taught his disciples to fast and to give alms, but in secret (JB Mt 6:2—4, 16—18). Jesus taught his disciples not to give up, but to persevere in prayer: *Ask, and it will be given to you; search, and you will find; knock, and the door will be opened to you* (JB Lk.11:9). We need the Spirit to know what to ask for, where to search, and to be able to recognize it when we find it.

Jesus prayed for all those whom the Father gave to him—his mother, family, friends; the apostles and all his disciples; and all those who would come to believe in him. As Lord of heaven and earth, every human being has been given to Jesus, and he prays for them all. He said: *And when I am lifted up from the earth, I will draw everyone to myself* (NAB Jn 12:32). Jesus calls us to pray for everyone God has given us—everyone who has ever touched our life in any way, including our enemies. We are to pray for the whole Church, and all of humanity, as well. Jesus taught his disciples to pray with each other and for each other; to ask each other for prayer and to intercede for each other. Likewise, St. Paul urges us to: *Never get tired of staying awake to pray for all the saints;* (Eph 6:18).

Jesus taught his disciples to pray with words and without words; through teaching and by example. He taught them to pray alone and with others. He said: *But when you pray, go to your private room and, when you have shut your door, pray to your Father who is in that secret place* (JB Mt 6:6). He also said, *if two of you on earth agree to ask anything at all, it will be granted to you by my Father in heaven. For where two or three meet in my name, I shall be there with them.* (JB Mt 18:19—20)

Jesus continues to make himself known to us, through the Holy Spirit, and through Mary, his mother. We cannot worship the Father without the Holy Spirit. Jesus taught, *But the hour will come—in fact it is here already—when true worshippers will worship the Father in spirit and truth...God is spirit, and those who worship must worship in spirit and truth* (JB Jn 4:23—24). Jesus said, further: *But when the Spirit of truth comes he will lead you to the complete truth, since he will not be speaking as from himself, but will say only what he learnt; and he will tell you of the things to come.* (JB Jn 16:13)

St. Paul taught Christians: *Pray all the time, asking for what you need, praying in the Spirit on every possible occasion* (JB Eph 6:18). Paul insisted that Christians should pray with the mind as well as in the Spirit (*tongues*). He said: *Surely, I should pray not only with the spirit but with the mind as well? And sing praises not only with the spirit but with the mind as well?* (JB 1 Cor 14:15). Praying *in the spirit* is contemplative prayer—not what we do but what God does—in, with, and through us: *The Spirit too comes to help us in our weakness. For when we cannot choose words in order to pray properly, the Spirit himself expresses our plea in a way that could never be put into words, and God who knows everything in our hearts knows perfectly well what he means, and that the pleas of the saints expressed by the Spirit are according to the mind of God* (JB Rom 8:26—27). The Rosary—repetitive and mental prayer— affective prayer (prayer of the heart), meditation (praying with the mind), and praying in *tongues* (praying in the spirit) are all gifts that can lead us to contemplation (union with God).

There is no end of ways in which we can pray. Fasting, alms- giving, and sacrificial acts of penance are also forms of prayer. We pray by giving thanks to God—alone and with others—and by praising God—alone and with others. We worship God and honor the Lord's Day by celebrating the Eucharist. We can do this on a daily basis, as well. We can worship God through Eucharistic Adoration—alone and with others. We pray whenever we receive any of the sacraments. We pray when we read and meditate on the Scriptures, and other spiritual writings. We can pray the Liturgy of the Hours, the Rosary, or other devotions, such as novenas and chaplets.

We can pray in song or in dance, in writing and in preaching, and in creative art. Whenever we practice a virtue, we are praying. Everything we do, think, and say can be a prayer, if it is in Christ, and united to his Sacred Heart; if it is rooted in the love of God. The greatest prayer is suffering and laying down our life out of love for others, and for the kingdom of God. Everyone has suffering—a cross in their life. When we take up that cross, without bitterness, and unite it to the suffering of Jesus, we are praying and working for the salvation of the world.

Jesus taught his disciples to consecrate their lives in truth—to hear the word of God and do it—to be abandoned to the will of God. Jesus prayed to the Father, *As you sent me into the world, I have sent them into the world, and for their sake I consecrate myself so that they too may be consecrated in truth* (Jn 17:18—19). The highest form of consecration takes place in Holy Orders. Every Christian, however, is consecrated to God through baptism and confirmation. In addition, there are many other kinds of consecration, as well: consecration to the Sacred Heart, consecration to the Immaculate Heart of Mary, consecration to the religious life through the evangelical counsels, and consecration to family life through the sacrament of marriage, to name a few. To be consecrated is to be set apart for a particular purpose or mission.

We cannot truly pray without faith in God and in eternal life. We can never pray the *Our Father* in *spirit and truth,* unless we have a personal relationship with God as our Father; and unless we believe in the Communion of Saints, the resurrection of the body, eternal life, and the kingdom of heaven. For anyone who does not believe in life after death, it makes no sense to even believe in God. If there is no resurrection, and life is only temporary, faith in God would be meaningless. Life would be merely vanity, lacking purpose and meaning, and end in futility.

Our relationship with God is reflected in our personal relationships with our brothers and sisters—all humanity. This is the only way we can truly know if we love God. We love God as much as we do our worst enemy. Prayer is the way in which we manifest our love for God and humanity. We cannot love God without loving our neighbor, and we cannot truly love our neighbor without also loving God. Whenever we love our neighbor, selflessly, we are praying. Whenever we pray to God, we are also manifesting love for our neighbor. The woman who wept over the feet of Jesus, revealed that she was forgiven—in right relationship with God—by the way in which she loved Jesus (Lk.7:36—50). She loved him with abandon, and no concern for herself or what others thought of her. She openly wept tears over the feet of Jesus, wiping them with her hair. She anointed his feet with oil, with no concern of the cost. She spared nothing. This is prayer. To pray without ceasing is to love without ceasing. This is the only kind of life worth living.

16

The Breakdown of the Family

$\mathcal{F}$amily life, as well as the Church family, has undergone a severe breakdown in recent times. As I reflect on the Church as "family," it seems to me that the Church is a family of persons who, if separated from Jesus Christ, would be a very dysfunctional family. Every member of this family is limited in their understanding and their faith, as well as in their love and trust in God, in spite of the fact that the Church has been given the *fullness of truth*. The Church, as a family, always has to consider the *common good* over the individual. The Church is like a mother, with a shepherd's heart, always seeking out the lost and the broken, and leading them back into the fold. She has to do this while making sure that the rest of the *fold* are safe and secure, first.

It is impossible to separate Jesus from the Church. As Scripture says: "What therefore God has joined together, let no man put asunder" (ICSB Mt 19:6). There can only be one Church because there is only one *bride*. Jesus only has one *bride*, not many. Even though we are unfaithful, God is always faithful and will never divorce us. This marriage is a public, visible, and sacramental sign;

made actual at Pentecost. The Church is a divine institution, not simply a mystical body of believers. It is divine because Jesus established it, and has given it authority and the Holy Spirit. The Church was born of the Holy Spirit. Nevertheless, her members will always consist of saints and sinners.

The Catholic Church is as vital to the new covenant, and to Christianity, as Judaism was to the old covenant. There would not be an old covenant without Judaism, without Israel. There would also not be a new covenant without the new Israel, the Catholic Church. The Church is as vital to Christianity as Mary was to the Incarnation. The Church is also vital to the Bible, the Word of God. We would not have the Bible if it were not for the Church. The Bible would not have any authority, unless the Church that gave it to us, also had the same authority; given by Jesus Christ. All baptized Christians are members of the Catholic Church, even those who are separated from her and do not know her. There is only one Church. The Catholic Church considers all baptized non-Catholics to be part of the Church, and refers to them as *separated brethren,* because there is only *one, holy, catholic, and apostolic Church.* (CCC 865)

The division between Catholic and Protestant Christians reminds me of the Jews during the diaspora, who were dispersed and separated from the authority of the throne and chair of David, the Temple, and Jerusalem. How disheartening this must have been for them! To me, the Catholic Church is like Jerusalem. She is also like the father in the parable of the *Prodigal Son,* watching and waiting for all her children to come home (Lk 15:11—32). The Church longs for all her children to come home again, that we may all be one; that we may all share Eucharist together. Any mother who has had a child leave home and become estranged from the rest of the family understands this kind of love, and sorrow. The division in the Church is the greatest sorrow of the *breakdown of the family*. The *bride* will not be made ready for the marriage feast until we are all reunited and made one.

The Catholic Church was the only Church founded by Jesus Christ. All other denominations have been founded by men; good men who have *stepped into the breach*, but they were not Christ. The meaning of Church is very different for Catholics than it is for non-Catholics. For most non-Catholics, a Church is simply a community of the faithful, a gathering of Christians. If you are Roman Catholic, that is not enough. We recognize the value and gift of the Mass, the teaching authority, the magisterium, the sacraments, Church tradition, and apostolic succession, which make it possible to live out our faith and to become holy. For Catholics, the Church is the bride of Christ, and the mother of Christians in the world.

The Church encourages all Christians to grow in their faith and their knowledge and understanding of God. She encourages the study of religions, philosophy, and the natural sciences. She encourages Christians to meditate, to reflect, and even to question and speculate. This is all part of the learning process. However, she also cautions them to hold fast to the teaching of the Church and Scripture, and to have good guides, teachers, and spiritual directors for their faith journey, in order to be able to withstand the confusion, doubts, distractions, and false teaching that often accompany the study of religion. Most people are aware of the importance of a balanced diet to the health of our bodies. We know that not everything we can consume is good; some things are poisonous, or can cause an allergic reaction. We know that diet is dependent on age, growth, and development; small babies can only be fed milk. We know that too much of a good thing is bad, and can lead to obesity. If diet is so important to the health of our bodies, we should be even more concerned about what we feed our minds, souls, and spirits.

It seems to me that the Church gives a lot of license to theologians, for speculation and theories when it comes to the study of religion, because she knows that it takes time to *flesh out* meaning and understanding. However, the Church does not give theologians permission or authority to teach their speculations and theories to the faithful, as truth, when they contradict the teaching of the Church; of Scripture or Tradition. Nevertheless, the Church has been flooded with false teaching and erroneous theories in recent times.

When it comes to sin, the Church teaches what is *objective mortal sin*. But, that does not mean that she presumes to judge any individual of being in a *subjective state of mortal sin*, which involves their conscience and personal relationship with God. The Church judges actions and behavior, but cannot judge the state of a person's soul. In order to be a *mortal sin*, a person must know it is a sin, think about it, and deliberately choose to do it anyway, knowing that they are rejecting God, intentionally. There is malice involved in mortal sin. People today, have had their minds and consciences formed, or at least highly influenced, by the secular culture. Their understanding of sin is not the same as the *teaching of the Church*. Everyone is influenced by the secular culture to some degree. Most people today, have an aversion to the word, *sin*. For them, sin represents: shame, rejection, judgment, condemnation, and hell.

Jesus really does make a difference in the lives of Christians. He came to give us new life, the fullness of life. This new life is a *personal relationship* with the indwelling Holy Trinity, making us an intimate member of the family of God, the household of God; the kingdom of God. Through our union with the Holy Trinity, we have access to *sanctifying grace,* which can transform us into saints. This is what we lose through *mortal sin* and by leaving the Church. It seems to me that a person, who is actually spiritually dead due to conscious sin, is incapable of really loving God or anyone else. This is often evidenced by malice, hatred, violence, rebellion, and a lack of virtues. The person cannot even repent on their own volition. It takes grace coming from outside of them to bring about repentance and conversion; someone to prepare the way of the Lord; the Word of God; the sacraments; miracles; prophecy; and healing. This is the mission of the Church.

Some people practice immoral behavior and they know they are doing wrong. But, there are others who really do not believe that what they are doing is immoral or a sin. Some examples from the past are: slavery, the Crusades, religious intolerance, racial bigotry, and injustice to women and children. Present day examples might be: abortion, euthanasia, homosexual practices, sex outside of marriage, divorce, religious indifference, and relativism. The human conscience has been corrupted. Unless the conscience is reformed by the *Truth*, we cannot expect others to live according to the *Truth*. As Christians, we must strive to inform the conscience of others, through love. I think that, in some cases, it is useless, and maybe even harmful, to try to change our behavior, without first changing our conscience and what we believe. These people have not yet come to a full conversion, a moral conversion. Full conversion is abandonment to the will of God, and is necessary in order for us to put on the *mind of Christ*, and change our behavior.

Some Christians have seemingly rejected the morality and teaching of the Church, no longer having anything in common with the Church; and some even believe that the Church is corrupt or evil. Although these persons have separated themselves from the Church, the visible *body of Christ* on earth, it is possible that they may not have separated themselves from the Spirit, the *mystical body of Christ*. They may only be rejecting certain members of the Church, rather than the Church, at large; or certain teachings of the Church. They may be acting out of a distorted or corrupt conscience. Some people are close to God, subjectively, but not objectively through the Church. God meets every person where they are at, and will never abandon anyone. There is always a danger, however, that a person will lose their subjective or personal relationship with God, if they consistently reject an objective relationship with God through the visible Church; or do not live in fidelity to natural law. Only God can judge a soul, but the Church can and must judge the objective behavior (actions) of her children according to the teachings she has received. We have to experience a conversion to the *Word of God*, made known to us through the Scriptures, oral and written, and the authority of the Church, given by Jesus Christ; *the teaching authority of the Church.*

We forget the seriousness of the *original sin* of Adam and Eve. This sin infected all of humanity, even though humanity was not held accountable for it. The only antidote is salvation through Jesus Christ. Sin, whether we know it is sin or not, leads to death. We suffer the consequences of sin in this life and the next, even if we do not choose to sin; even if we are not held accountable for the sin, or are not culpable for it. The Church will be held accountable if she does not teach us what sin is, as well as the consequences of sin; if she does not strive to form our conscience according to God's law.

There is much diversity among the people of God because we are all unique individuals, with unique gifts, talents, and virtues; as well as faults, vices, and limitations. Diversity is not the same as division, however: "There is one Lord, one faith, one baptism, and one God who is Father of all, over all, through all and within all" (JB Eph 4:5—6). St. Paul exhorts us: "be united in your convictions and united in your love, with a common purpose and a common mind" (JB Phil 2:2). The universality of the Church, the common good, and the *communion of saints*, cannot be replaced with individualism and pluralism, or the Church will be fragmented. Unity does not mean that we are all at the same place in our spiritual growth, or that we all have the same understanding. It means that we are a family and continue to love each other and stay together; to pray together. We respect each other even when we disagree. Diversity builds up the Church; division tears it down. Without love, sacrifice, and prayer, diversity will lead to division and separation.

Abuse of authority is a major cause of division in the Church. Abuse of authority is not only the misuse of authority, but the attack against authority and the usurping of authority by those who have not been given authority; such as when children govern their parents, and when individuals try to govern the magisterium. Unless we reverence lawful authority, we cannot reverence God; and we will always be divided and at war with everyone, including ourselves.

Some people would say that the reason we have so much division and disunity in the Church, and in the world, is due to a lack of communication and dialogue. Yet, never before has there been a time where communication skills have been so advanced, and opportunities for dialogue so plentiful. So, what is the real problem? It seems to me that one of the real problems is the lack of understanding. Everyone is talking to each other, but no one is listening; we all seem to speak a different language, and there is no one to interpret what we hear and say. Our skills of understanding and interpretation are so limited that we only hear half of what is really being said, and what we hear is usually distorted or taken out of context. We do not know how to really listen or be present to each other. In spite of all our advanced communications, we are in the same world state as the people of Babel were.

In spite of heresy, error, false speculation and teaching, as well as all the division and apostasy in the Church, we should not be fearful or surprised. Jesus tells us: *Be not afraid!* Like Jesus, the Church must take up her cross and follow in the footsteps of Jesus. From the cross, she must cry out, '*Father, forgive them; they do not what they are doing*' (JB Lk 23:34). This is also what every parent prays for their children. The temptation is to resist the cross, and instead, resort to violence and hatred. The Church as the mystical body of Christ will never die, but the Church as a divine institution will go through many deaths and resurrections; her visible form and structure is always changing. Through these deaths, she is purified.

My heart longs for the day when all Christians will be reunited and reconciled as one Catholic Church; sharing Eucharist together at the table of the Lord; and *being of the same mind, having the same love, being in full accord and of one mind* (ICSB Phil 2:2).

The Church family is so intrinsically connected to domestic family life that it is hard to know if the *breakdown* began with the Church or with family life. All the priests and ministers of the Church come from families. Family life has never been perfect, before or after Christ, but today, we are experiencing a massive breakdown and destruction of family life throughout the world. Families, the Church, and the secular culture are all to blame; but as we know, blaming others is useless and only escalates the problems. Instead, we need to give our attention to how we can heal family life, the Church, and society. We are at a point where only a miracle from God can save us. We have to acknowledge our powerlessness and need for God to heal our land and our people. As a people, we have lost our faith and trust in God. Without faith, there is no authentic love, only counterfeit love. We have to repent as a nation. Those with faith have to pray for the conversion of the world, and be ready to fast and make sacrifices; even if it requires our life. Mental illness is on the rise, and seems to have replaced cancer as the number one killer of humans. The only hope is for us to put on the *mind of Christ*. We will either have to become saints or become insane.

17

The Crisis in the Church

*T*was just reflecting that throughout the past two thousand years, the earth has suffered many cataclysmic times; times when the pendulum swings wide. So far, these times have always led to a re-birth of the earth and humanity. These are times of great upheaval, affecting not only humankind, but nature, as well. These are times of famines, earthquakes, and all manner of natural disasters. It is almost as though nature is at war with humans, rebelling against her abuse. These are times of wars, violence, divisions, and factions; times of great moral corruption in the Church and society; times of heresies and heretics; and times of apostasy — rejection of God, Christ, Christianity, and the institutional Church. But, the pendulum swings in both directions. These are also times of great awakenings, revivals, renewals, and the emergence of many great saints. The period of the *Enlightenment* was just such a time. The twenty-first century is just such a time. It was just such a time when God chose to send his Son, Jesus, into the world to redeem it. It will be just such a time when Jesus returns, in order to gather the faithful and judge the world. In the meantime, the battle goes on between good and evil, truth and lies, sanctity and infamy, light and darkness, and life and death.

As I reflect back over the history of Christian theology and religion, it is no surprise that we are experiencing a crisis in the Church today. The seeds of all the problems of today, as well as our growth and redemption, were planted centuries ago. Not only were they planted centuries ago, even going back to the beginning of creation, these seeds have undergone many, many harvests, producing a harvest of good and of evil. Every age or generation passes on new seed for posterity, with its potential for both, good and evil. The pendulum swings back and forth in every generation. Every discovery, true or false, has an adversary; and is met with a response from all sides, within the Church and within the world. It is also evident that since the time of Jesus, there have been no new revelations, and no new heresies, just new ways of seeing old things. The same truths and lies come back again and again, with a face-lift or a new outfit.

For many people, the very word "crisis" conjures up a negative image of doom and hopelessness, but that is not the meaning of the word. According to Webster's Dictionary, the word *crisis* means: *turning point; the decisive moment; a crucial time in which a decisive change is impending.* A crisis is a call to action or reform. A crisis can lead to good or bad depending on the decisions that are made or not made. A crisis cannot be ignored; it does not just go away by itself, it demands attention. A crisis is analogous to a pot of stew that comes to a boil; the flame has to be turned off or down to a simmer. If the stew is left to boil, it will boil over or burn up. As Christians we know what the final outcome will be, from the promises of Christ; that the Holy Spirit will be with the

Church until the end; that the gates of hell will not prevail over the Church; that Jesus came to establish his kingdom upon the earth; and that God can bring good out of evil. Nevertheless, if we do not act responsibly, there will be needless and prolonged suffering for all humanity.

I believe that the recent crisis affecting the Church, today—sexual abuse of minors by priests—is not simply an issue of morality and justice. This crisis effects, not only Catholics but, all Christians, and ultimately, the whole world. It is a *wake-up call* to all Christians to return to the Lord, and to see how far we have drifted away from the teachings of the Gospel; the ways in which we have embraced the beliefs and practices of an atheistic humanism. Every Church doctrine, every Christian belief, is on trial. Even natural law, as revealed by God and confirmed by science, and as we have known it from the beginning of creation, is on trial. For the Church, there is no conflict between natural law and divine law because God is the author of both, not society. Nevertheless, it seems that both natural and divine law, are quickly becoming counter-cultural to our present society, which makes the Church and all Christians counter-cultural, as well.

The crisis at hand affects doctrinal issues such as sin, conversion, mercy, forgiveness, and judgment by God. These beliefs are counter-cultural to the beliefs of society, at large. We are no longer a predominantly Christian society. Our present culture is an atheistic, humanistic society. Much of our society does not believe in eternal life, the resurrection of the dead, or a final judgment—where Jesus Christ is the judge. These differences may seem inconsequential to many Christians, but they are central to the problems that Christians face today. The crisis in the Church today, is not just about persecution from non-Christians or non-Catholics, it is also an internal struggle and persecution. Persecution from non-Christians actually forces Christians to unite and to become stronger. However, internal persecution and rebellion is a tearing down instead of a building up, and very destructive. There are many forces at work, inside and outside the Church, that are determined to bring down the Catholic Church. I think that what is happening in the Catholic Church will also happen in every Christian Church, as well. This is really just the beginning. Then again, perhaps it is necessary to separate the wheat from the chaff; to purify us and reform us into the *body of Christ* we are supposed to represent. We can only deserve the name Christian if we have put on the *mind of Christ* and believe, profess, and live the teachings of Jesus Christ.

It seems to me that the crisis in the Church today reveals many problems: the failure of Church ministers to proclaim the Gospel, the teachings of Jesus Christ and of the Church; the lack of trust and reverence for God, the hierarchy, the priesthood, parents, and basically, all authentic authority; a lack of understanding of the role of priests, how it differs from that of the laity and protestant ministers; a lack of belief in the *paschal mystery*—the power of the cross and of suffering, and the death and resurrection of Jesus Christ; a lack of a recognition of the presence of Jesus Christ in the sacraments, the priests, the Church and in all the people of God; a loss of faith, hope, and love among believers; a lack of an awareness of sin and need for repentance; an inability to distinguish good from evil; the failure of the Church to heal the wounds of those who suffered abuse by priests, ignoring the seriousness of these sins; the increase of false teachings and teachers within the Church and within society; and the failure of Christians to affirm and live out the "creed" that they profess with their lips—*The Nicene Creed.*

Our present society is centered on this life only, except as it relates to heredity and the evolution of man. Some believe in reincarnation, which is not the same as resurrection, and in fact, is radically opposed to it. Whereas, Christians believe that man does not have the right to judge another person, only their actions, atheists believe that every person is responsible to judge every other person; God is not our judge, because there is no God. Christians believe that this life is a journey, or pilgrimage to the next life; atheists believe that this life is the end of the line. Therefore, suicide, euthanasia, abortion, and war make sense to atheists; our culture is a culture of death, not life. Atheists do not believe in the forgiveness of sins; the need for salvation and redemption by God. They do not believe in *sin,* or that all humans are *sinners.* They believe that humans are either functional (productive and whole) or dysfunctional (sick and unproductive). They believe that a person is judged by his behavior; he is either good or evil, according to the standards set by society. They also do not believe in the need to forgive others or to receive forgiveness from others; it serves no real purpose. Christians believe they are called to love their enemies, and to see everyone as their brother. This is ludicrous and even evil, for the atheist. Christians believe that God can bring good out of evil; atheists do not, they do not believe in God. Atheists believe that "the end justifies the means," and therefore, humans can bring good out of evil, or do evil in order to obtain good.

There is a great difference between human love and divine love. Humans may deplore evil, violence, injustice, and also have compassion and concern for the poor, but without Christ, their love is a condescending love; a love that sees the poor as needy, as *nobodies;* and one's self, as *savior.* Christians are called to love with the love that comes from God. Divine love enables us to see the poor, those in need of a Savior and deliverer, as equal to ourselves, with equal dignity and worth; and to see Jesus as the only Savior. Divine love enabled Mother Teresa of Calcutta to look into the faces of the poor, of sinners, of the least in the world, and see Jesus. She saw the poor as better than herself, and loved them without condescension. Christians believe in the virtue of humility, that we are called to serve, and to take the lowest place. Atheists believe that humility is dependence and passivity; evil. They believe that serving others is slavery. An atheistic society is bent on success, winning, being first; competition. Christians believe that God can redeem suffering, that there is value in suffering. Atheists believe that the *cross* is folly; no one who is *free* would choose to be a victim. They believe that most people are either abusers or victims; only those who are nei- ther, abusers or victims, are free. They see everyone who submits to others, who accept suffering, who is humble, as a victim. In every relationship where one is a victim, the other is presumed to be an abuser, so atheists gradually move away from all relationships in order to be free and *whole.*

I really think that abuse is a part of life that we cannot escape from; the effects of original sin, our fallen nature. We abuse each other every day, knowingly or unknowingly. We will never find an ideal relationship where we are never abused or never abuse the other. This is why the grace of forgiveness is so important, espe- cially in marriages and families. Marriages fail more often from the refusal to forgive, than from abuse.

Christians believe that wholeness is an effect or consequence of holiness; we cannot be whole without becoming holy, first. Jesus is our holiness, and it is only in union with him that we are made holy. Christians believe that all people are basically good, that God dwells in every person; but, everyone is also vulnerable to weakness and sin, and always in need of God's grace. Christians also believe in the power and presence of evil in people and in the world, due to sin.

Who and what is the Church? In addition to being an institution, the Church is the people, *the body of Christ*; not only the laity, not only the hierarchy but, both. I recall that America was built on the ideology of Republicanism. The Church is not a republic, not a democracy, not a corporation or a business, not an ideology. The Church belongs to Jesus, not to the people. Jesus set the model for his Church, the model of a family and of a bride. He gave authority, not to the children, not to all his followers, but to the parents—the apostles and those called to succeed them. He gave authority to the clergy and the magisterium; those consecrated for this mission. It seems to me that a Church without apostles is not apostolic, and has no mission or authority. A family that is controlled by the children is a dysfunctional family, without balance and order. A Church that is controlled by the laity, without authority and leaders, is a dysfunctional Church.

The words that Jesus quotes in the gospel, "I will strike the shepherd, and the sheep of the flock will be scattered" (ICSB Mt 26:31), are significant for the Church, today. The world is attempting to strike down the shepherd, the priesthood, in the hope that the flock will scatter. The more atheistic our society becomes, the more the Church will be a sign of contradiction. Atheism is not compatible with Christianity. The Church, especially the Roman Catholic

Church, is a formidable opponent to the philosophy and goals of atheism for a global one-world government. The pope still has a powerful voice, and his stand on contraception, abortion, euthanasia, same-sex marriage, natural law, and the Gospel is an obstacle that atheism cannot tolerate. The hatred of atheists for the Church and the Gospel is growing each day. Jesus said: *He who is not with me is against me, and he who does not gather with me scatters.* (ICSB Mt 12:30)

I think that probably every age asks the question: "Is this the grand finale, the end of the world, or is there another re-birth beyond the horizon?" We need to be prepared for both. How do we prepare for both? Perhaps, this is our greatest challenge, today. How do we love the world, love life, and yet, not cling to it, but be open to: "*What no eye has seen, nor ear heard, nor the heart of man conceived, what God has prepared for those who love him,*" (ICSB 1 Cor 2: 9).

In the final analysis, will the atheists of the world succeed in their mission to crush the Church, Christianity, and all religion? What can humans do, what *must* humans do, in order to defeat the mission of Anti-Christ? It seems to me that the only answer is that we *must* wake-up from our sleep, return to the Lord and listen to his voice, and do what he commands: "*You shall love the Lord your God with all your heart, and with all your soul, and with all your mind... You shall love your neighbor as yourself*" (ICSB Mt 22: 37, 39).

All in all, looking back over the history of the Church, I find myself less anxious about the future, or the present. I am reminded that *all things work for good for those who trust in the Lord* (Rom 8: 28). The Lord holds everything in balance. History reveals, from the beginning of time, that the real *Anti-Christ* is unbelief. If we judge by human standards we would be quick to condemn all those who hold beliefs and views different from our own. But, thank God, we have a God who is a God of mercy; a God who does not leave us to ourselves; a God who looks into the heart and mind of every person and knows how it was formed; a God who is the only true judge and giver of the final verdict; a God who is the only one who can *crush the head of the serpent,* through Jesus and Mary, the New Adam and the new Eve.

18

Attachments and Addictions

I have been thinking about all the people in the world today that are suffering from attachments and addictions, including myself, and wondering what word the Lord would want to give them. Jesus came to set prisoners free, and it seems to me that all attachments and addictions are prisons of the soul. Most of us will not be completely free until death—or, will we?

Some people are quick to judge those who suffer from addictions. They do not seem to believe that these people will go to heaven. They believe that they will, at least, have to go to purgatory, if not hell. I have read this in some of the revelations from people who claim they have visited purgatory and hell. When I think about God's mercy, however, I find this hard to believe. It seems to me that we are our own judges. We condemn ourselves. We choose purgatory because we judge others, and so, must judge ourselves, as well. If only we could let go of our need to judge others and demand retribution, we would be able to receive the fullness of mercy and be transformed by love.

I am reminded of a vision that the prophet, Zechariah, had about Joshua. This is what I think will happen to most people, who trust in the Lord's mercy at the time of judgment or death.

> Then he showed me Joshua the high priest standing before the angel of the Lord, while Satan stood at his right hand to accuse him. And the angel of the Lord said to Satan, "May the Lord rebuke you, Satan; may the Lord who has chosen Jerusalem rebuke you! Is not this man a brand snatched from the fire?"
>
> Now Joshua was standing before the angel, clad in filthy garments. He spoke and said to those who were standing before him, "Take off his filthy garments, and clothe him in festal garments." He also said, "Put a clean miter on his head." And they put a clean miter on his head and clothed him with the garments. Then the angel of the Lord, standing, said, "See, I have taken away your guilt." (NAB Zec 3:1—5)

I believe that when we get to heaven, we will neither want, nor need those things that we are addicted to. The desire for them will just fall away like dirty garments. It seems to me, that addictions can be something outside our control or will; something that we have to depend on medicine or grace to be set free. Most people suffering from serious addictions know they are prisoners and long to be set free. They struggle all their lives, without much success. If these people look to God's mercy, I do not think they will have to suffer purgatory for their addictions, after death. God's grace can deliver them, but God does not always give it, or they are not able to receive it, while in their body. While those who judge people with addictions, and have no compassion or forgiveness may have to spend a lot of time in purgatory, where they may even have to endure what those who are addicted have to endure: *"Stop judging and you will not be judged. Stop condemning and you will not be condemned. Forgive and you will be forgiven"* (NAB Lk 6:37).

I have the sense that God and everyone in heaven has no problem being around sinners. They would have no problem with being in a room full of cigarette smoke. We sinners, however, have a problem being around God because we feel unclean in his presence, and in the presence of saints. God could sanctify any one of us, including the most hardened criminal, in the twinkling of an eye. However, we need to have the humility and confidence in his love and mercy, in order to want him to sanctify us. Judging ourselves and others comes from pride and prevents us from choosing heaven, from the enjoyment of heaven. Heaven is not a place of isolation for the holy, and hell is not a place of quarantine for sinners. Darkness is not darkness for God; but for those who are *at home* in darkness, the presence of God is unbearable. So, God in his mercy hides his light from them. God will not force his presence on anyone because he is love, and love is free. At least, that is how I see it.

Jesus prayed for Peter, and did not judge him, knowing that Peter would deny him (Lk 22:31—32). He did not condemn the woman caught in adultery, but instead gave her hope and encouragement to change (Jn 8:3—11). He did not condemn or judge Mary Magdalene, even though she was a sinner, but instead acknowledged her great love, and defended her before her accusers (Lk 7:36—50). He did not condemn the Samaritan woman for her sins or heresy, but instead, gave her *truth* and *living water* (Jn 4:1—26). He did not judge or condemn the thief on the cross, but instead, took him immediately to heaven, without stopping in purgatory (NAB Lk 23:39—43). Jesus forgave everyone from the cross, saying, *"Father, forgive them, they know not what they do."* (Lk 23:34)

It seems to me that all of the saints possessed the virtue of *detachment*, to some degree; to a high degree. What does it mean to be detached? I do not think it means that we become angels and deny our humanity, including our weaknesses, frailties, and limitations. I think it means, first of all, becoming very little, like a child. Children get away with murder! It means to abandon ourselves to the will of God; to become totally dependent on God, possessing nothing of our own, living as though we do not even possess our own lives. It means clinging to nothing; our reputation, possessions, gifts, talents, virtues, family, friends, health, work, ministry, and life itself. Even our weaknesses and limitations do not belong to us; they are on loan, whether we like it or not. We give up being Lord over our own body, soul, mind, and spirit. We can only do this if we are very humble and have absolute trust and confidence in God's love and mercy. We give up trying to become holy, and allow God to make us holy, through love, in his time and manner.

I think we are mistaken if we think that we can attain holiness by systematically giving up all our attachments and addictions. We are still attached, more attached, to pride and perfectionism. Those who are holy are detached through humility. They are stripped of their attachments and addictions by Jesus, who replaces them with virtue and love. Holiness is not the same as perfection, as we understand perfection. The Lord does not remove all our weaknesses, imperfections, and attachments; only those that he calls us to let go of, and only those that prevent us from receiving his love; those that prevent us from loving others or cause our love to become lukewarm. Our weaknesses and attachments dispose us to need and receive God's love, as well as to have compassion and understanding for others. All that is necessary is that we want to be holy, we will to be holy, and we ask the Lord to make us holy. Then, if we fix our attention on loving others, every act of love breaks us free from our attachments — *love covers over a multitude of sins* (1 Pet 4:8).

Mary, our mother, was so holy, without sin, and "full of grace" (Lk 1:28)) that she was completely selfless. She only had eyes for God and others; for love. Self-knowledge, for Mary, was her awareness of who God is and who she was; that she was poor, meek, little, and nothing without God; totally dependent on God for everything. Grace allowed her to know this without having to learn it through experience, through sin. Most of us become aware of our need for God and our dependence upon God through our experience of the loss or lack of grace, through failure to love, through our vulnerability to sin, and through our limitations. God did not create the rest of us *full of grace*, as he did Mary. Christians spend so much time and energy on trying to become holy through their own efforts; trying to rid themselves of all their attachments. If we, by chance, happen to succeed, we are most unfortunate, because pride and vanity are knocking at the door.

As an illustration, when my children were little, I was a meticulous housekeeper. It was more for me, than for anyone else. My family could really care less. In fact, they suffered for it. I liked the feeling of cleaning my house immaculately, and then sitting back to enjoy and admire my work. It was exhausting. My children were right on my heels, making a mess as I cleaned. I had a wool carpet that showed every footprint right after vacuuming, so I was reluctant to let anyone walk on it. Finally, I thought, if I could just get my home cleaned, perfectly, and had five minutes to enjoy it, that would be enough. Then, the children could come in and have their way. How ridiculous is that? It was futile and such a waste of time and energy, when I could have been using my energy and time to love my children. Every mother knows this kind of futility. No matter how hard we work, it does not even last a day. It is the same when we try to make ourselves holy, by attempting to get rid of all our attachments. They come right back, just like weeds.

I do not mean to make light of attachments and addictions. There is a reason why Jesus taught so much about them. I think that attachments and addictions are pretty much the same in the eyes of God. Although, those who suffer from addictions are usually prisoners of something in the make-up of their bodies that prevent their will from being completely free; making them less culpable. Unfortunately, those who suffer from addictions usually have many attachments, as well. Attachments are anything that prevents us from hearing and responding to God, to love; and anything that causes us to sin. Attachments are things we cling to, while addictions are things that cling to us.

Attachments and addictions control and possess us. They can make us possessive of other people and things; they can cause us to attempt to control others—the free will of others. We can become attached to our own will and wants; our own way of thinking, feeling, believing, and seeing. Attachments prevent us from being open to anyone or anything that opposes us.

Attachments and addictions can lead to lying, stealing, cheating; to self-deception and deceiving others; to greed, envy, possessiveness, abuse, and even to violence and murder. They can cause us to become spiritually blind, and prevent us from hearing the call of the Lord and God's will for us. They can prevent us from being able to really love others or respond to the needs of others. Our attachments and addictions have all our attention and energy.

The Pharisees were so attached to their own authority and power that they could not be open to a higher authority and power; to God. Some were attached to their own vision, understanding, beliefs, and concepts of what they wanted Scripture to say, and so they could not be open to Jesus; to hear or recognize him.

One of Jesus' disciples said to him, *"Lord, let me go first and bury my father." But Jesus answered him, "Follow me, and let the dead bury their dead"* (NAB Mt 8:21). Jesus was not opposed to burying the dead; the Law required this. Jesus was not talking about going to a funeral, but about waiting until another person is no longer with us, which could be too late. It all depends on *who* is calling us, and what our priorities are. Some *calls* require an immediate response. Jesus is the *Word;* the voice of God, and of love. If we are overly attached or controlled by our parents, we will not be free to answer his call.

If a mother is overly attached to one of her children, she cannot leave the side of that child for anyone or anything else. If that child is sick, she will not move from the child's bed. If one of her other children suddenly needs her help or love, she will not respond to them. All her time and energy is given over to the child she is attached to. When God is not first, all our other loves become disordered:

> Whoever loves father or mother more than me is not
> worthy of me, and whoever loves son or daughter

more than me is not worthy of me; and whoever does not take up his cross and follow after me is not worthy of me. Whoever finds his life will lose it, and whoever loses his life for my sake will find it. (NAB Mt 10:37 — 39)

Jesus said: *It is not what enters one's mouth that defiles that person; but what comes out of the mouth is what defiles one* (NAB Mt 15:11). He is not saying that it does not matter what we ingest into our bodies. There is nothing evil about cigarettes, alcohol, or drugs, but these things can or may lead us to sinful actions. If we are inebriated or drugged, we cannot respond to others. We cannot hear God. If a mother is drunk, and her child becomes sick during the night, she cannot care for that child or protect them from harm. If a person drives under the influence of drugs or alcohol, they endanger their own life as well as everyone else on the road or in the car with them. If our mind is altered, our will is asleep; and we may be abusive to others or indulge in sinful practices. If someone is attached to smoking, they may resist going anywhere where smoking is not allowed. They resist a call to prayer, a call to love, and a call to relationship because of their addiction. They may endanger the health of others who are allergic or do not have a developed immune system, as well as their own health. They cannot respond immediately to God or anyone else. They have to finish or have a cigarette, first.

Jesus said: *And if your right hand causes you to sin, cut it off and throw it away. It is better for you to lose one of your members than to have your whole body go into Gehenna* (NAB Mt 5:30). Jesus is not speaking literally, but figuratively. The *right hand* can

197

be something good, but also an *attachment* that we need to be cut free from, because it prevents us from loving God or our neighbor; from receiving God's love or the love of others. It controls us and takes first priority over our life. The *right hand* could also refer to an illicit relationship, or a codependent relationship.

We can be attached to people, places, and things; work, sports, possessions, money, power, authority, status, television, and even religious practices. Attachments prevent us from being able to respond immediately to the call of God, or to love, without hesitation. If we wait, it may be too late. Scripture tells us: *Gird your loins and light your lamps and be like servants who await their master's return from a wedding, ready to open immediately when he comes and knocks* (NAB Lk 12:35—36). If we are completely free to respond to God immediately, we will react like the "Good Samaritan" (Lk 10:29—37), not worrying whether we will be late for another appointment, or whether we might be in danger, or whether we can afford it. If we are completely free to respond to God, we will be mystics.

Our generation has made people aware of some of the destructive consequences that come from people who attempt to control others and the lives of others, as well as their own selves. This kind of control is humanity's greatest attachment. It is a vice that has always been rooted in the makeup of humans; but in the past, it was often seen as something good and even virtuous. Humans did not recognize that it was a cancer of the soul, having deadly consequences. Therefore, it has always existed in culture and in the Church. The only place that it does not exist is in the truly humble and fearless, like Mary. Humility drives out all fear. Perfectionism and fear are at the root of this particular vice; fear of failure, fear of loss, fear of pain and suffering, fear of the unknown, and even fear of death and hell. The only cure for perfectionism is abandonment to the will of God, and the love of God.

Self-control is a "fruit of the Spirit" (Gal 5:23). It does not come from the self, from us; it comes from the Spirit, from grace. Our only control is to say "yes" to God, to will it; to will to love; to will and desire holiness. Saying yes to God, requires that we have patience; that we are willing to wait for God. We say yes to the moment of grace, moment by moment. We need to abandon ourselves to God, to love, not to our attachments or addictions; we need to avoid our attachments and addictions and use whatever means are in our power to leave them, without taking our eyes off of Jesus. We do not need to defend them or rationalize them as good. We await our deliverance from God. We hold them out to God, like someone holding out their hands with chains around their wrist, waiting expectantly, for God to cut them. We do not follow where our addictions try to lead us—to sin—but instead follow the path to love. We stay in the garden with Jesus, praying, *My Father, if it is possible, let this cup pass from me; yet, not as I will, but as you will* (NAB Mt 26: 39). We give our attention to the Lord, not to our chains.

Our choice is not between giving in to our addictions and not giving in to them. Our choice is not between love and our addictions. Our choice is recognizing a call to love and saying yes or no to it. Attachments and addictions are not sin; sin is where they lead us, what they cause us to do, and what they prevent us from doing.

In practical terms, the more time and energy we give to our relationship with God, to prayer and reflection, the less time and energy we have to give to our addictions and attachments, and the more we are able to recognize the presence of God and hear his voice. The more time and energy we give to our vocation and relationships with others, fulfilling our duties and responsibilities, the less time we have for our attachments and addictions, and the more we are able to love others. The more time and energy we give to serving those who have less than we do, the less time and energy we have to give to attachments and addictions, and the more we grow in holiness and become like Jesus.

Many years ago, just before I experienced the *baptism of the Holy Spirit*, I was surrounded by various cults and *New Age* practitioners. In prayer one night, I realized that God's will was my perfect good. I was filled with the desire for union with God and to abandon myself to his will. Nothing was more important to me in that moment than God's will, including my husband, children, and my own life. At the same time, I became aware of what could happen to me if I lived outside of the will of God. I was suddenly filled with a fear of rejecting God, and of being led astray by heresy and false teaching. I cried out to God, "Lord, if there is any chance that I would reject you or be led astray, let me die now. I would rather die than leave you." I meant it with all my being and I even expected to die at that moment. However, I did not die. The Lord was not as fearful as I was. I believe that if I had died in that moment, I would have gone right to heaven.

Shortly after this experience, I had a dream. In this dream, I saw a huge silver bell hanging in space. So huge was this bell, that next to it I was the size of an ant. Suddenly, the bell changed into a golden chalice, turned upside down, as though its contents were being poured out. The chalice was the same shape as the bell. I was hanging onto the lip of the chalice, suspended in space. I clung tightly to the lip of the chalice until I could no longer hang on, and my fingers gave way. In that moment, I realized that the chalice was holding onto me and I did not fall. In fact, I was fused onto the lip of the chalice. The bell, I came to realize, was the Lord calling me. The chalice was Jesus. He was holding onto me, while I thought I was holding onto him. It was a promise of salvation to me, and removed my fear of falling away from Jesus. I may deny him many times, like Peter, but he will not let me go. In fact, I have denied him, and I would not have been able to return to him on my own. The Lord never left me, and he brought me back to where he wanted me to be.

19

Proclaim Liberty to the Captives

When will the Lord come to set the captives free, in our present age? It seems to me that a whole generation has been hit by a plague that has touched every family on the earth. This plague seems to have caused an obsessive-compulsive disorder in the mind and emotions of all the children of God. Everywhere I look, mothers are weeping for their children. It does not seem to matter if these children come from religious families or non-believers; from affluent and educated families or poor and uneducated families; from healthy and stable families or dysfunctional and divided families; from families who have everything and families who have nothing; from families in free countries and families from countries dominated by tyrants; from families who are citizens and families who are emigrants.

This mental disorder manifests itself in many ways: an obsession for materialism and pleasure; for power and control; and for an escape from suffering and death. It manifests itself in addictions to relationships, romance, sex, pleasure, idols, gambling, drugs, alcohol, food, sports, money, shopping, knowledge—the list is endless. It is a disorder because it has become an obsession and compulsion that negates the will and deepest desire of the captives and victims. The captives soon become obsessed with the desire to escape from their obsession, after experiencing the pain and emptiness that their obsessions have caused them. They go from one addiction and obsession to another, in order to escape from their former addiction. It is no wonder that Jesus told the women, on his way to Calvary, "Daughters of Jerusalem, do not weep for me, but weep for yourselves and for your children" (ICSB Lk 25:28).

Alcoholism and drug addiction are disorders of the mind and emotions. They are an obsession and a compulsion for the one who is addicted, and cannot be conquered by the will alone. No matter how much they want to over-come this obsession and compulsion, they are powerless to do so without help. It is just as hard for them to give up their addiction and compulsion as it is for a homosexual person to give up his or her behavior and inordinate desires. They are all captives and prisoners, and only the grace of God can really set them free.

Of those who go through recovery programs, the number of those who actually stay in recovery is very small; and most of those who persevere will have periodic "slips." In spite of these *slips*, they manage to stay in the process of recovery, taking two steps forward and one step backwards. Those who are successful and continue to *work a program*, usually have a personal relationship with Jesus or a strong faith and trust in God, and a lot of family support and encouragement. If they do not believe in a God who can and wants to help them, they will not be able to persevere. God works through people and love, however, so if they do not have strong support from family and friends, they will not be able to persevere. If their family and friends abandon them, their only hope is an extraordinary miracle of God.

If friends and family do not have faith in their loved one, and in God, that he or she will recover and be healed, they will not be of any support or encouragement and instead, will only discourage their loved one. Friends and family who have the same disorder will often enable and condemn, at the same time, the one who is in recovery. Family and friends of someone in recovery need to be healed from wounds of the past before they can be of any support and encouragement. If family members are not healed as well, the person in recovery will have to be separated from them, or risk a slip. There needs to be forgiveness and compassion for healing to take place. Otherwise, they will see their recovering loved one through the same lenses that they had when he or she first started using. Neither the addicted person nor the family members are the same persons that they were in the past—whether they are using or not—especially if they started using at a very young age. Our personalities are always in the process of being shaped and formed throughout our whole lives. They are formed by what we learn and experience, by the choices we make and do not make, by the opportunities and events of our lives, and by all the people and relationships we have throughout our lives. Some personalities get better with age, and others get worse. It is a false assumption that an addict or alcoholic stops developing mentally and emotionally, from the time that he or she starts using; or that there is any such thing as a fixed or set personality—especially an alcoholic personality, or an addictive personality.

It seems to me that forgiveness is not really enough, in order to be healed and fully reconciled with others. We also have to let go of our former negative projections, assumptions, expectations, and perceptions of others. Everything that a person does or says—whether it is a question or comment—can be perceived negatively or positively, depending on what we expect from them or how we perceive them. For instance, years ago I wrote a letter to my aunt. My feelings for her were deep affection and love. I ended the letter saying that she was in my prayers. At the time, however, there was some enmity between my mother and my aunt. Therefore, my aunt interpreted my words as insinuating that something was wrong with her and that she was really in need of my prayers. She was deeply hurt and angry at me.

Simple comments, and even words of affection, can be perceived as criticism or abuse, and deeply wound us when our expectations are skewed. We need to let go of expecting someone to act in a certain way, or the way they did in the past—expecting the worst from them. We need to let go of our assumptions, assuming that someone will never change and that we really know them. We need to let go of our perception that someone does not like us, or rejects us. If we are not healed of past wounds, or if we still have unresolved issues with anyone, we will probably project them and our feelings onto other people, as well. I think that this is true for everyone.

Family members of anyone recovering from alcohol or drugs need to be set free of their fears and expectations for their loved one and be able to trust in God, not forgetting what a major step it was for their loved one to even enter into recovery. They have to believe that this step has placed him or her on the road to recovery for the rest of his or her life, no matter how many times they fall. It is the road to Calvary and resurrection, not death. If family members are not healed of their fears, they will expect instant change and transformation (which may never come), and panic at the least sign of regression. They will panic at every step backwards and miss the two steps forward.

It seems to me that the primary difference between an alcoholic and a drug addict is that alcohol is legal and drugs are not, and of course, drug use involves breaking the law. They are both lethal to one who is addicted, and sometimes, to those in relationship with them, as well. Drug use is usually a much faster road to death, however, and causes damage to the brain and one's perception, much sooner than alcohol. Drugs and alcohol, both, can cause memory loss, blackouts, amnesia, and hallucinations. Nevertheless, morally, there is no difference between the drug addict and alcoholic, the homosexual person, the sex addict, and anyone else who suffers from an addiction. The difference is in the consequences. They are all obsessions and compulsions. They all make us slaves to sin and hold us captive. They are all affected by a disorder in the brain and emotions. At least, this is my understanding according to what I have studied, observed, and experienced.

Does this mean that those who suffer from these disorders do not have any personal responsibility for sin? Certainly not! All disorders begin with the consent to sin, and we have to make reparation for all harm that we do to others and ourselves. We are still accountable for all our actions, whether they are intentional or not. We can make reparation through acts of charity and virtue; by doing some form of penance; and by making daily sacrifices of our ego.

We are all born with an inclination to sin, and a weakened will, due to the original sin of Adam and Eve—some more so than others. When does sin, freely chosen, become a disorder of obsession and compulsion? How many times does a person need to give consent to sin before it becomes an obsession that makes them a captive? I think that the answers to these questions are different for every person. All obsessions begin with our consent, but the power of desire is stronger in some people than in others. Some people are born with a stronger inclination towards particular sins than others—an inclination that is almost an obsession from the start. Some people only have to give consent to a particular sin a few times before their will is no longer in control and they are powerless to say "no." Sometimes we sin through ignorance and immaturity, because we do not know what sin is. We have been evangelized by a culture that calls good, evil, and evil, good. Sometimes sin is pre-empted by emotional wounds and scars, or from some deprivation of basic human needs. Sin begins in the mind and is influenced by our beliefs. In some cases, an evil spirit is waiting for our consent to sin, and enters as soon as we give our consent, making us captive to sin.

I think I have a very different interpretation of the Gospels when it comes to addiction, especially from some advocates of Alcoholics Anonymous. I believe that Jesus teaches us to judge only behavior, not persons. Scripture tells us not to lie for anyone who is captive to sin or any addiction—not to call good, evil, and evil good. It tells us not to tempt others by our actions or our words—not to be an occasion of sin for anyone; not to encourage others to sin by condoning and excusing their behavior, especially to them. Scripture tells us to confront the sinner, in love; encouraging them to make their own decision, to turn away from their addiction and to get help. It tells us to pray for them, and to continue to love them and support their efforts to change. It does not say that we are enabling their addiction by showing them mercy or by helping them with the consequences—unless we have to lie or do evil in order to do so. If we love them, we endure the consequences with them—we help them carry their cross.

What is the answer to sin? What will set us free? I think that St. Paul gives us the answer to this dilemma in his letter to the Romans, chapters seven and eight. We need to read and meditate on every word in these two chapters. The only way to be set completely free is to become saints. A saint is one who is filled with the Spirit of God; one who cries out, *Abba Father;* one who suffers with Jesus in order that he may also be glorified with him (Rom 8:14—17). How do we become saints? I think the answer is, by following in the footsteps of Jesus, in union with his will. Jesus works through people, through the Church—his family of brothers and sisters. I think that this is how Jesus will deliver the world and set *captives free*. This is the mission of the Church—to lead people to Jesus in order to be filled with the Holy Spirit; to give them the *mind of Christ*. The mission of the Church is to be a family of saints to all the families of the world: leading them into recovery; supporting and encouraging them, and not abandoning them; and by laying down our lives for them as Jesus did. The canonized saints are models of what it means to be a saint. Unless our lives mirror theirs, we are still captives—judging one another and looking for the *speck in our brother's eye*. (Mt 7:3)

Deliverance from any kind of addiction or obsession is not instantaneous. It takes a lifetime. We can, however, enter into recovery; and when we fall or *slip*, get back up again by means of the sacraments of confession and Eucharist. Those who do not have access to this recovery program are deprived of a great grace, and we must pray for them. Saints pray for, and hope for, the mercy of God upon all the people of the world. They do penance and make sacrifices for them, as Jesus did. I believe that many captives will not be set free until the Lord returns in glory. Most of these captives are longing to be set free. The poor are truly blessed, because most of them want to be set free from the obsessions that control their lives. They are waiting to hear the good news. The world needs more saints to proclaim this good news.

Saints do not segregate themselves from the rest of humanity. They are not afraid of being made prisoners because they have died to themselves. Christians in recovery have to be more careful about who they associate with, so that they will not *slip*, themselves. Nevertheless, they cannot separate themselves from others completely or they will never become saints.

There are many kinds of physical illness; some are contagious and some are not, some are common and others are lethal. A person with a common cold does not usually shut himself or herself off from everyone and everything else, but merely takes some precautions. People with deadly diseases, that are not contagious, need a lot of support and attention from others. They cannot afford to be isolated. Those who are highly contagious need to be isolated and avoided by others, except those who are their caretakers.

It seems to me that obsessions work in the same way as these physical diseases. Serious obsessions, like drugs and alcohol, are only contagious if the behavior of these captives become abusive, or it they attempt to infect others by solicitation. They are contagious to others who are recovering from the same disease. They are contagious if they use in front of the young and impressionable. Some obsessions are only dangerous to the individual. Many obsessions, like sports, exercising, food, shopping, romance, people, and relationships, are like the common cold or flu; they need to be tended to and watched, lest they turn into something worse, but they are not usually deadly. Sexual obsessions, witchcraft, sorcery, false teaching, and idolatry are extremely dangerous and highly contagious, and their captives need to be avoided.

I do not think that the captives can be set free by anything less than the free gift of sacrificial love—Calvary love. It is not free for the one who loves, for the one who sets the captives free; it is very costly for him or her. There is no social program, therapy, or self-help method that will set the captives free; no singular religious experience or act of turning our lives over to God will set us free. Real freedom is a total life experience, an everyday event that is very costly. Only one who is God can give his life for everyone; for the totality of our lives. That one person is Jesus. Nevertheless, the captives have to receive the love of God from those who are part of his mystical body. This kind of love is a selfless love, a total and free sacrifice. It is more than a desire or act of the will. It is a love that will cause us to weep tears of blood—to weep as Jesus did when he wept over Jerusalem; and over Lazarus; and at the same time, able to wait for the right moment to act.

Selfless love, like a mother's love, allows the beloved to be totally free to make his or her own choices; without coercion or manipulation. It is a death to self-love, selfish love. It does not abandon the beloved or force him to leave the nest before he is ready. It does not push the beloved out of the nest to force him to fly. Selfish love seeks to possess the beloved, to control the beloved, to make the beloved into something they were not created to be. Selfless love changes others without intention, through charity and example. Selfless love models love for her young. Her young will watch her and follow her example when they are ready. In the same way, when a butterfly emerges from its cocoon, it must divest itself of the remnants of the cocoon clinging to its wings, before it can fly. If someone, out of selfish love, attempts to free its wings from the cocoon, the butterfly will die before it is even able to fly.

Selfless love always seeks to save and rescue those that really need to be saved and rescued. At the same time, it continues to love, unconditionally. Selfless love can distinguish between the strong and healthy and the weak and lame; between the rich and the poor; between those in need and those who are not in need—those who are able to help themselves. Of course, everyone needs help at various times throughout our lives. I do not mean to contradict myself, but I think there are exceptions to every rule. I think that there are instances when a "caretaker" needs to apply pressure or force to someone with a serious addiction or handicap, because these persons lack hope and motivation and cannot make an effort to help themselves, or change unless they are forced to. Nevertheless, great prudence and wisdom is necessary.

Jesus never refused anyone who came to him who was truly in need and asked for help. Selfless love is not invasive. It is gentle and free and does not force itself upon another. Selfless love sees others as they really are; loves them for who they really are—individual and unique persons of dignity and children of God.

I long for Jesus to come in glory. I weep for myself, my children, and all the children of the world. I long for all the captives to be set free—free of all the obsessions and compulsions that prevent us from being what we were created to be. I long to see, in our day, the fulfillment of Jesus words: *The Spirit of the Lord is upon me, because he has anointed me to preach good news to the poor. He has sent me to proclaim release to the captives and recovering of sight to the blind, to set at liberty those who are oppressed, to proclaim the acceptable year of the Lord.* (ICSB Lk 4:18—19)

20

Things are Not Always as They Appear to Be!

$\mathcal{W}$e only have to turn on the news or go to Facebook or Twitter to realize that *things are not always as they appear to be!* There is so much slander, gossip, calumny, lies, and fraud in the media today, as well as in our daily conversations, that it is no wonder so many people believe that there is no such thing as *truth*. It seems to me that one of the most destructive weapons of humans is that of judging our neighbor. Is this not what led to the crucifixion of our Lord? We do not even know ourselves and yet we think we can judge the hearts and intentions of others, as well as their character, based on something we see them do or hear them say, or something someone else says about them. This is especially dangerous for Christians who have little self-knowledge. Satan can even deceive us into believing that our rash judgments come from the Holy Spirit, and is a gift of *reading hearts*. This must be Satan's most powerful counterfeit, but the fruit reveals the truth: That *things are not always as they appear to be?*

In many cases, the faults we see in another person are merely the projection of our own faults. We judge them, and in judging them, we judge ourselves. We may harbor jealousy, envy, resentment, or anger against them, and want to bring them down. Sometimes, what we see in others is merely their shadow, or a mask. We see their unlived potential and mistake it for the person. We see them struggle with temptations, and mistake the temptations for actual sins or faults. We pass judgment on them, slander them, gossip about them, and try to warn others to avoid them or beware of them. Is this not what they did to Jesus? Often, we do need to be able to judge the *actions* of others and the *fruit* that comes from those actions—whether the actions and fruit are good or evil, wise or foolish, with or without outside influence; but we cannot judge the motives or intentions of the heart of another person. We cannot judge their character, whether they are good or evil, or their relationship with God. Neither can we know the culpability of another person. St. Francis de Sales has given some wise counsel in regards to judging and detraction:

> Our Crucified Savior, unable to excuse the sin of those who crucified him, minimized their malice by pleading their ignorance. So if we cannot excuse a sin, let us at least be compassionate, attributing it to such extenuating causes as ignorance or weakness. May we then never judge our neighbor? No, Philothea, never; even in a court of justice, it is God who is the judge; true, he makes uses of magistrates that his judgments may be heard, but they are only his spokesmen and interpreters and as such should pronounce only that judgment they have learned from him. If they act otherwise, following their own

feelings, then it is they alone who judge and who in consequence are judged, for it is forbidden for men, as such, to judge others. To see or know something is not to judge it; for judgment, in the sense used in the Scriptures, presupposes some difficulty great or small, true or apparent, which must be resolved; that is why we read: "The man who does not believe is already judged; there is no need of judgment for there is no doubt of their damnation."

We may, it is true, speak freely of infamous and notorious public sinners so long as we do so in a spirit of charity and mercy, avoiding arrogance and presumption and not taking pleasure in their misfortune, for this would mark us as mean and base. This does not apply, of course, to those who are openly enemies of God and of his Church, for we must denounce heretics, schismatics and their leaders to the best of our ability, charity bidding us cry wolf when the flock is in danger. (St. Francis De Sales 1962)

Few people are actually appointed, or have the authority, to judge anyone. King Solomon was given authority by God, through the office he held, to judge the people. When he had to judge between two mothers, as to who was the real mother of the child that they both claimed, God gave him the wisdom to know how to test them. They revealed their own hand, when put to the test, and Solomon did not need to accuse them or read their hearts in order to make a determination. (1 K 3:16—28)

Our Lady had the gift of *reading hearts* (Lk 2:35). Her heart was united to the heart of her son, and as his heart was pierced for love of us, so was her heart, enabling her to know the hearts of others. Some of the saints also had this gift in special circumstances, such as when they were called to give spiritual direction or counsel. I think that this is how our Lady used her gift. This gift is sometimes given to the priest in the sacrament of confession, when he represents Jesus, through his divine office. It enables the priest to set penitents free, bringing them into the truth. As with the other sacraments, especially the Eucharist, this gift is not dependent on the holiness of the priest. In fact, he could even be in a state of sin. Nevertheless, in the sacraments, he is not himself; he becomes "persona Christi." Padre Pio had this gift, and I pray that all priests will be open to receive this gift of reading hearts. (Pio 1999)

The gift of reading hearts is usually given to the *pure of heart*; to those who know how to use it for the good of others and the glory of God. It is given to those who do not seek it. It is not the same as the gift that psychics claim to have, which may be from an evil spirit. The pure of heart seek to know and understand others in order to love them more. The knowledge they receive does not cause them to expose those persons to others. It moves them to great compassion, as they see their own self in the other; their weaknesses and strengths. They are moved with compassion to intercede for them, never to judge or scorn them; or, they are moved to rejoice, and give glory to God for them. These persons can say with all their heart: *There go I, except for the grace of God;* or, *there go I, with the grace of God.*

This gift may convict someone of a serious sin that is an obstacle preventing them from turning to the Lord, or remind them of a sin that they have forgotten; enabling them to repent. It may reveal what kind of healing a person needs in order to lead them to be healed. It may reveal broken relationships that need to be reconciled. It may discern the presence of evil spirits trying to oppress a person or tempt them. It may reveal the presence of the Holy Spirit trying to get a person's attention. This gift is very similar to the gift of prophecy (1Cor 14:24—25).

Some people think they can see into the soul of another person and know them better than that person knows their own self. This often happens in marriages and friendships, where one thinks they know the other, completely, and there is no more to learn. It brings relationships to a standstill. We can never fully know our own self, let alone that of another person. Love deepens as we grow in our knowledge of others, but once we think we know them through and through, we have made an idol out of them and love dies.

Some people do not claim to have a gift of reading hearts, but they claim they have a gift of intuition, perception, or a psychic gift that enables them to see into the hearts and lives of others; causing them to make various assumptions and judgments. This is usually nothing more than the vice of suspicion, judging, prejudice, pride, or the work of demons. We can only know as much about another person as that person reveals to us, while understanding that people generally do not know themselves very well. Humans are very complex, and the heart has many layers. Every charism must be tested because the evil one tries to counterfeit all the charisms of the Holy Spirit. The counterfeit of this gift is "divination." The Church warns us:

> All forms of *divination* are to be rejected: recourse
> to Satan or demons, conjuring up the dead or other

practices falsely supposed to "unveil" the future. Consulting horoscopes, astrology, palm reading, interpretation of omens and lots, the phenomena of clairvoyance, and recourse to mediums all conceal a desire for power over time, history, and, in the last analysis, other human beings, as well as a wish to conciliate hidden powers. They contradict the honor, respect, and loving fear that we owe to God alone. (CCC 2116)

Allow me to share some personal stories that might bring clarity to what I am trying to relate. Years ago, I made an eight-day silent retreat that was one of the most memorable spiritual experiences of my life. I started reading St. Catherine of Sienna. As I read about the gift of reading hearts, I thought how wonderful it would be if every priest could have that gift. As I am aware of how often I can deceive myself, and be deceived by others, I would love to have the priest, in the sacrament of confession, make me aware of my deceptions; because I want only to know and do God's will.

I did not know anyone on the retreat, but I suddenly became aware that when I observed different people, it was as though I could see into their soul. I could see the weaknesses and temptations they were struggling with. I prayed, "Lord, if this is the gift of reading hearts, I do not like seeing other people's faults or weaknesses, I just want to see their strengths and virtues." I asked the Lord why he would give me this gift, and what the purpose was for it. I began to reflect that maybe it was from the evil one. I decided to reject everything that I saw and just say a prayer for each of the people.

When I spoke with my spiritual director, I told him all about this. He assured me that it was good discernment to reject those thoughts. He reminded me that the purpose of my retreat was not to intercede for others or to read the live of the Saints. My purpose was to grow in my knowledge of God and of myself in order to enter into union with God; to listen to the Lord and to hear what he wants to say to me; to deepen my relationship with God. He cautioned me to treat those thoughts as a distraction, and to keep my eyes on Jesus, staying only with the scriptures. This was very good advice and opened me to the experience of God's love in unimaginable ways.

St. Catharine of Sienna warns us that we need to take great care and discern carefully, if the Lord gives us insights about our neighbors. We need to ask why the Lord is giving us those insights. It may be that the Lord wants us to pray for them; that the Lord wants us to correct them or warn them of something—to give them counsel; or perhaps, the Lord wants us to wait for the right time to approach them in order to share the insight, if at all. These insights could be very helpful for spiritual directors with their directees; for priests, as shepherds and confessors; for those called to a healing ministry; and for those called to intercessory prayer. In all these situations, we need to have the authority to use this gift, and to be led by the Holy Spirit. It is also important to acknowledge the freedom of the recipient, whether they are ready or open to what the Lord wants to give them through us. This gift is never invasive and it does not violate the freedom and dignity of the recipient. It is up to the recipient to confirm the validity of the insight. Unless a relationship of trust has been established between the minister and the recipient, there will be no insights from God to give, or openness from the recipient to receive. (Martin 2003)

Great discernment is necessary because Satan can also give us insights about others, and some may even be true. We must be prepared to reject them. This is frequently the case when we seek insights about others, even in prayer. When the Lord wants to give us insights, he will give them without our seeking them, and when we least expect them. Insights that come from the Lord will humble us and deepen our compassion and love. We will see those insights as counsel for ourselves as well as others. The insights will greatly benefit those for whom they are given. They will lead them to healing and freedom. We should never seek insights or supernatural knowledge about others, unless the Holy Spirit is leading us to do so. This is an open invitation to Satan. The Lord never gives us insights in order to satisfy our curiosity or to have power over others. Insights about our neighbors will always have a purpose for good if they are from the Lord. Satan's purpose is to distract us from Jesus, and from love; to cause us to judge others, reject others, or to idolize others. He plants seeds of division, suspicion, and mistrust in us. He puffs us up with pride, making us think that we are better and holier than our neighbor. He leads us to gossip and detraction.

Some people are naturally very intuitive and can see the character, weaknesses and strengths, of various people, especially people they know. They must be very careful not to judge, or to make assumptions about others. They have to take these intuitions with a grain of salt and not cling to them. Instead, we should seek understanding and wisdom, in order to love and better understand others; as we do with our own children and loved ones.

Years ago, I had a chaplain that I found very challenging to love. I seemed to be a constant irritant to him, a *thorn in his side*. Other parishioners were complaining about his insensitivity and felt wounded by him. I was constantly battling with judgmental thoughts, and praying for the Lord to increase my love for him. I became overly concerned about his spiritual welfare and wondered if I should let him know what other people were saying. The more I thought about him and prayed for him, the more unsettled I felt. I genuinely loved him, but I was losing my peace, because of all my worry about him.

Then, in prayer, the Lord brought to my mind, an "Egg and Spoon Race" that I participated in a couple times. Every year in Hadley, England, the town holds an *Egg and Spoon Race*. Ten English women race against ten American Military Wives, down the main street of town. At the finish line, the Mayor of the town awaits the women and hands out the prizes. There is a first and second place winner, but everyone in the race receives a silver spoon in commemoration of the race. Each woman wears an apron and is given a long wooden spoon, to hold in her right hand. She must put her left hand behind her back throughout the race. At the start of the race, each woman is given a raw egg to carry on the wooden spoon. If she drops her egg, she can go back to the start and get another egg, as often as necessary. When the race is over, all the contestants and their families are invited to a feast at the local pub.

The first year I was in the race, I came in second, first of the Americans. An English woman came in first. I learned from that race that it was very important to keep my eyes fixed on that egg, looking neither to the right nor to the left, or even at the finish. If you took your eye off the egg, even for a moment, you would lose your balance and drop your egg. You could also lose your balance if you did not keep your left hand behind you, although that was not the purpose for doing so. The purpose was so you would not be tempted to hold the egg on the spoon with your left hand, if the egg started to fall. I also saw that it was important to walk down the middle of the road, away from the attention and cheering of the crowds lined up along both sides of the road.

The second year I was in the race, it was a little more difficult. I was seven months pregnant, so I stood out in the crowd. Since I was a winner the year before, many eyes were on me. My in-laws, visiting from America, were also watching me. However, I managed to focus my attention on the egg, blocking out all those who were watching me. I also walked down the middle of the road, avoiding the distractions of the crowd. Half way through the race, I could see in my peripheral vision, a woman walking along the edge of the road. She was ahead of me. Suddenly, a little boy standing on the edge of the road yelled out, "Boo!" This did not startle me at all, but, the next second, the woman dropped her egg. That caught my attention, and I gasped in concern for the woman. I took my eyes off my egg, and as I did so, I dropped my egg.

Even though the race was half over, I was undaunted and went back to the start to get another egg, and got back into the race. The crowds begin to cheer me on, but I stayed focused. Their cheers, instead of distracting me, encouraged me on. I did not win the race but I continued on to the finish, even after the race was over. The crowds treated me as though I had won the race, because of my perseverance.

In bringing this race to mind, the Holy Spirit began to counsel me through it, giving a spiritual significance to every symbol in the race. He reminded me of my purpose for being in that race. I was representing the Americans, and my purpose was to be single-minded and steadfast, and to race to the finish. It was not my place to be concerned about others in the race. At the same time, I realized that it was not my place to be concerned about the faults of the priest I was so concerned about, or any priest; and by looking at him, I would fall, as well.

I am called to keep my eyes fixed on Jesus (the egg); to be steadfast, single-minded, and single-hearted unto the Lord. The wooden spoon represents the Holy Spirit. The Holy Spirit holds up Jesus for me, and enables me to follow him. The apron signified that I am called, along with all the others, to be a servant of God; to serve God and others according to the purpose and will of God and the gifts he gives me. I can only serve others by keeping my eyes on Jesus. The Mayor represented the Father and the Kingdom of God. The road, Main Street, is holiness.

There is no competition in this race. We compete only with our own self, and it does not matter where we are along the road, as long as we stay in the race and continue on to the finish. If we fall, we need to get up and get right back in the race; we start over again, with Jesus. Our perseverance and fortitude witness to others, and gain for us the same reward as coming in first or second. To walk the way of holiness means that we keep our left hand behind us; *Do not let your left hand know what your right hand is doing*. We give without expecting anything in return. In keeping that hand behind us, we resist the temptation of pretense and hypocrisy. We *look neither to the right nor the left*, but keep our eyes on Jesus, judging no one. We do not take sides, forming prejudices, or get involved with factions. We walk in humility and prudence; walking down the middle of the road, and avoiding all attention and gratification from others. The silver spoon signifies transformation; growth in holiness through the Holy Spirit.

The Lord showed me through this reflection that it was not my place to correct, admonish, or save his priests. My place is to love, honor, obey, and pray for them. I need to keep my eyes on Jesus and trust the Lord to save his priests, because he loves them so much.

Another example of rash judgment that seems to be rampant today, even among Catholics, is rash judgment of the apostles and canonized saints. This grieves my spirit, because if we defame our heroes and models of holiness through detraction, we cut ourselves off from ever becoming saints.

The apostles and saints have already been tested and tried by the Church, and found to be extraordinary holy servants of God. Yet, people today think they are qualified to judge them. I frequently hear people hold up St. Paul as an example of a chauvinistic and prejudiced man who was proud, arrogant, egotistical, and boastful, while he consistently talked about humility and love. These people do not know St. Paul at all. They read bits and pieces from his letters, taking them out of context, in order to highlight *a splinter in his eye, and cover up the plank in their own eye* (Mt 7:3). They are quick to quote passages from Scripture as examples to prove their point. If they ever really read through all of St. Paul's letters in the spirit they were written in, they would know that St. Paul knew that he could do nothing on his own, that he was totally dependent on the grace of God for everything (1 Cor 2:1–5). He knew that he could never have endured the trials, persecutions, and sufferings that were a part of his Cross, without the Holy Spirit.

In some passages, St. Paul was forced to defend himself for the sake of the Christian community. Paul's reputation and authority as an apostle, sent by Christ, was at stake. He was forced to respond to the accusations and slander by some members of the Christian community who opposed him. He did not boast of personal achievements, but of the grace of God. The evidence he gave was the Cross; the fruit of the true disciple, manifesting the grace and power of the Holy Spirit. There was no other way he could have endured those things. His life belonged to God. Jesus said, "A servant is not greater than his master. If they persecuted me, they will persecute you;" (ICSB Jn 15:20). He also said, "If anyone wants to be a follower of mine, let him renounce himself and take up his cross and follow me" (JB Mt 16:24). There were also times when Jesus was forced to defend himself to the Pharisees. There is a time when we need to refrain from defending ourselves and let the Holy Spirit defend us, and times when justice demands that we defend ourselves; especially when our good name is necessary for the edification of others, as in St. Paul's case.

Scripture reminds us that within the hearts of all humans are two store-rooms. One is the kingdom of God, and the other is sin. Jesus said, "For a man's words flow out of what fills his heart. A good man draws good things from his store of goodness; a bad man draws bad things from his store of badness" (JB Mt 12:34—35). Maybe I am interpreting this passage incorrectly, but it reminds me of what St. Paul says, "In short, it is I who with my reason serve the Law of God, and no less I who serve in my unspiritual self the law of sin" (JB Rom7:25). St. Paul tells us that sin lives within us; in our unspiritual self. We are always battling between good and evil within our own hearts:

Let me put it like this: if you are guided by the Spirit
you will be in no danger of yielding to self-indulgence, since self-indulgence is the opposite of the
Spirit, the Spirit is totally against such a thing, and
it is precisely because the two are so opposed that
you do not always carry out your good intentions.
(JB Gal 5:16—17)

It seems to me that because of this struggle, we cannot judge
others. We do not see the secret intentions of men's hearts, or what
is hidden in the dark. *Things are not always as they appear to be.*
St. Paul tells us:

True, my conscience does not reproach me at all,
but that does not prove that I am acquitted: the Lord
alone is my judge. There must be no passing of pre-
mature judgment. Leave that until the Lord comes:
he will light up all that is hidden in the dark and
reveal the secret intentions of men's hearts. Then
will be the time for each one to have whatever
praise he deserves, from God. (JB 1 Cor 4:5)

There is such a thin line between perception (seeing) and rash
judgment, assuming to know. Seeing is not the same as knowing,
and perception can move very quickly into rash judgment; especially if we cling to being right, and are not open to the possibility that our perception is flawed, distorted, or incomplete. I am
reminded of an illustration I received from a theology class, the
"Johari Window," a four-paned window. One pane represents those

things that are evident to others about us, as well as God, but are not evident to us. It is believed that everyone has a *blind spot.* The second pane represents those things about us that are evident to others, to God, and to us. The third pane represents those things about us that are evident only to God and to us. The fourth pane represents those things about us that only God can see and know. Based on this theory, our perception of others has only a fifty per cent chance of being true.

We make judgments based on what we see and know, or what we think we see and know. Judgment is a faculty that we need in order to judge between good and evil, and to judge external behavior and actions. Judgment is also a part of discernment, which helps us to know ourselves. Jesus warns us, however, that this faculty was not intended for us to judge the hearts of other people — their will, motives, intentions, or whether they are good or evil.

Jesus is God, and knows men's hearts. Nothing is hidden from him. Never the less, when Jesus judged some of the Pharisees as being "white-washed sepulchers," it was because they already judged themselves. The words and judgments that came out of their mouths revealed their hypocrisy, as well as what was in their hearts. The Pharisees had a different standard of judgment for others than they had for themselves.

Christians should always desire to become holy, to become saints. When this desire comes from the kingdom of God within us, our motive is only because we want to glorify God and build up his kingdom on earth. When it comes from sin, we desire this in order to glorify ourselves. We seek to grow in self-esteem, and to be esteemed by others. When we desire the gifts of the Spirit in order to glorify God, to reveal his love to the world and to enable others to become holier than we are, this desire comes from the kingdom of God within us. When we desire the gifts of the Spirit in order to increase our power over ourselves and others, to save the world and become its Messiah, the desire comes from sin within us. The only cure is humility. "We must decrease, so that God can increase." (Jn 3:30)

21

The Source of Suffering

Where does suffering come from? There is no suffering in heaven, and Adam and Eve had no suffering before the *Fall*, before sin entered into their hearts. Yet, we are told that there can be no love without suffering, and we know that there is love in heaven. So, where does suffering come from—love or sin?

It seems to me, that there are two kinds of suffering. One comes from being less than whole; unfinished. The other comes from sacrifice; giving ourselves away to others. Suffering, in this life, usually comes from sin and the lack of perfect love. To love others means to give a part of ourselves away to them; to deny ourselves some good in order to give to another, motivated by love. In this world, because of sin, self-denial and self-donation are painful for us. Therefore, it seems to me that to love others is painful, in this world, because of sin; because we are not yet whole.

In order to give birth to new life, to give birth to a child, a woman must embrace labor. Actually, she is going to have labor whether she embraces it or not, but the more she resists the pain, the greater and more prolonged her pain will be. Because of sin in the world, it has become natural to give birth in great pain. If there was no sin in the world, child-birth would be painless. Child-birth, when accepted, is an act of love; with or without pain. The pain is not the act of love, but in order to love, the woman must also embrace the suffering. This is what Jesus did.

I have the sense that in heaven, self-denial and self-donation brings, not suffering but, ecstatic joy. We experience small doses of this joy, even in this world. Parents lay down their life for their children every day, in countless ways, with no thought of them-selves, or what it cost them, in order to do good to their children; in order to secure their well-being and happiness. They experience only joy in the giving because they are so surrendered to love, and detached from their own self; their own good. The joy of giving far transcends the loss to their self. They are oblivious to any suf-fering or pain.

The joy that we experience in giving, in this world, does not go too deep. It has to do with giving our time, talents, money, posses-sions, comfort, security, and superficial pleasure. When giving is really deep, it wounds the body, the soul, the heart, and the spirit; bringing great anguish, pain, and even death. To give one's body, soul, and heart is painful, like labor in childbirth. There is no other way to love, except through the cross.

This reminds me of when I was in labor with my first child. I was in so much pain that I did not even have the strength to scream, I could only moan, I could not even clench my fists. In my delirium, I said to the Doctor, "Please stop, and push the baby back, I will come back tomorrow and try again, I can't go on." This was a very problematic delivery. Then, I heard the words, in my head, "The greater the gift, the greater the pain." I accepted this word, and discovered a newfound strength to go on. Those words had a tremendous impact on my faith, ever since.

I believe that the cross—suffering and death—entered into the world through sin. In order to conquer sin completely, one must embrace the cross, motivated by love, and enter into the resurrection. In order to love selflessly, and have the power to embrace and endure our cross, we need to come to Jesus Christ, and receive the Holy Spirit.

Mary's *fiat* was a total *yes* to love, regardless of the cross that came with it. When she embraced love, the will of the Father, she also embraced her cross. She was willing to do whatever is necessary in order to give birth to love; and live out her life with love. Love, Jesus Christ, came to birth through the power of the Holy Spirit. God became one with us, taking on human nature, to take onto his self the original sin that brought the cross into the world. He embraced that cross; all that man could suffer, and has suffered, because of the sin of the world. The *original sin* of Adam and Eve gave birth to sin in a humanity that was innocent of that *original sin* and undeserving of the cross that came with it. Nevertheless, humanity has added to that sin and expanded that cross; giving birth to sin, of which they were not innocent. This, too, Jesus took upon himself and offered forgiveness of sin. He gave us his Holy Spirit after suffering for our sins, because without the Holy Spirit, we are incapable of not giving birth to sin; we are incapable of loving selflessly.

This same Holy Spirit was given to Mary at her conception, allowing her to be *full of grace* and to give her total *fiat* without hesitation, and of her own free will—because she never conceived sin or gave birth to sin. Before saying "yes" to God, she said "no" to sin. Mary, united with her son, suffered the Cross with Jesus, for love of us; according to Scripture, when it says, *and a sword will pierce through your own soul also* (Lk 2:35). She died with Jesus, and rose again with him. Later, after the death of her body, her body was resurrected and assumed into heaven with her soul, to reign with her son, forever.

Jesus never left us, however, and is still united with us. He still continues to suffer with us, along with Mary, through his com-passion; and we, with him, sharing his com-passion for all humanity. We unite our suffering with his upon the Cross; and our suffering is never in vain, just as a woman's labor before birth is not in vain. The labor is filled with hope. This suffering is gladly embraced because of the hope that it will give birth to. All our suffering, when we repent of sin, will give birth to new life.

In the normal cycle of nature, the human body begins to grow and develop from the time of conception until it reaches its peak in middle age. Then, the body begins to decline and to die a little each day. The life span of the mind is probably longer, if it is properly nourished and fed. Nevertheless, even the healthiest body is not perfect. Every human has its own handicaps to contend with—some more, some less—so that not everyone reaches their potential human growth cycle (in fact, no one). This same pattern of life can be seen in all of nature—in plants and animals.

Suffering is a part of all of life. We can attempt to resist it, which usually only increases our suffering. We can strive to overcome it, with help from God and others. We can also accept it and unite it to Jesus' sufferings for the sake of others. There are even some people who are able to absorb the suffering of others and unite it to the Cross; to the suffering of Jesus. We can choose to be victims and wallow in our suffering in order to get sympathy and attention from others. We can also bring on suffering by neglecting to care for and nourish our bodies, or by abusing our bodies. We can do the same with those who are placed in our care.

Jesus was not a victim. He freely chose to lay down his life out of love for others. He said: "No one takes it from me; I lay it down of my own free will" (JB Jn 10:18). Those who are truly innocent and pure of heart often become the target for abuse from others and from attacks of the evil one. They are the true victims, but they do not see themselves as victims. They choose to accept their suffering without bitterness or complaints; without blaming or judgment; without self-pity or retribution. This is the path that Jesus chose. This does not mean that we should not do what we can to avoid and resist pain and suffering, if we can do so without resorting to sin. Jesus could have avoided the Cross, but only by using his supernatural powers. He resisted that temptation. Whether suffering comes to us through nature, through abuse from others, through self-neglect and abuse, through attacks from the evil one, through vicarious suffering and compassion, or through freely laying down our life for the sake of the Gospel and others, it is our response to suffering that really counts. Our response can bear good fruit or bad fruit.

If we are sick, we should do as St. James recommends: "He should summon the presbyters of the Church, and they should pray over him and anoint him with oil in the name of the Lord, and the prayer of faith will save the sick person, and the Lord will raise him up. If he has committed any sins, he will be forgiven." James also says, "Is anyone among you suffering? He should pray. Is anyone in good spirits? He should sing praise." (NAB Jas 4:13—15)

If we are sick, we should also examine our life-style and make the necessary changes. We should seek medical attention, if available. When we are sick, we should pray for others who are suffering, and unite our suffering to the suffering of Jesus. We can also work for justice to set captives free, by offering our suffering as reparation for sin and showing mercy and compassion to others who are suffering. We should examine ourselves and repent of all sin. We should also look at the examples of others, who have suffered great infirmities and responded with courage, fortitude, perseverance, flexibility, and patience.

Many people who have been afflicted with great handicaps have developed new gifts, talents, and strengths, in place of their handicaps. Their handicaps did not prevent them from living full lives of service, creativity, and love for God and others. Some of our afflictions, whether they be caused by ourselves, by others, or Satan, are allowed by God in order to sanctify us, purify us, increase virtue within us, develop new gifts in us, or to protect us from pride and sin. St. Paul tells us:

> Therefore, that I might not become too elated, a thorn in the flesh was given to me, an angel of Satan to beat me, to keep me from being too elated. Three times I begged the Lord about this, that it might leave me, but he said to me, "My grace is sufficient for you, for power is made perfect in weakness." (NAB 2 Cor 12:7—9)

Paul gives us a good example to follow. After we do everything in our power to over-come suffering and illness, including praying to God, if we are not healed, we should thank God for the infirmity and unite our suffering to those of Jesus' on the Cross. In addition to physical infirmities and poverty, and loss of loved ones, there are also other kinds of suffering that some Christians may have to endure. Jesus said:

> Blessed are they who are persecuted for the sake of righteousness, for theirs is the kingdom of heaven. Blessed are you when they insult you and persecute you and utter every kind of evil against you [falsely] because of me. Rejoice and be glad, for your reward will be great in heaven. Thus they persecuted the prophets who were before you. (NAB Mt 5:10—12)

These people are not victims, and do not see themselves as victims, because they said *yes* to a call from God. They freely chose to accept suffering for the sake of love; for the sake of the kingdom of God. The Beatitudes were intended for the disciples, not non-believers.

There are many people, however, who constantly claim to be *victims* of abuse and persecution from others. They are not innocent, like little children. They bring on persecution and provoke abuse through their own behavior. Even some, who are persecuted for doing what appears to be good works, may have selfish reasons and not be doing it out of selfless love, or in obedience to the will of God. They are victims of their own selves, constantly complaining that others abuse them and take advantage of them; and constantly boasting of all the good they do. St. Paul says:

If I speak in the tongues of men and of angels, but
have not love, I am a noisy gong or clanging cymbal.
And, if I have prophetic powers, and understand all
mysteries and all knowledge, and if I have all faith,
so as to remove mountains, but have not love, I am
nothing. If I give away all I have, and if I deliver my
body to be burned, but have not love, I gain nothing.

Love is patient and kind; love is not jealous or
boastful; it is not arrogant or rude. Love does not
insist on its own way; it is not irritable or resentful;
it does not rejoice at wrong, but rejoices in the right.
Love bears all things, believes all things, hopes all
things, endures all things. (ICSB 1 Cor 13:1—7)

God loves us beyond understanding. He takes no pleasure in
seeing his people suffer. He takes no pleasure in seeing evil abound
in the world; but he cannot remove evil without violating our *free
will*. Instead, he brings good out of evil. Instead of removing *death*,
he gives us resurrection and eternal life. Instead of removing suffering, he comforts the afflicted and brings good from it. He gives
us joy in the midst of suffering, and our suffering is never in vain.

God does not call anyone to be a victim. He calls us to set the
victims free. Jesus was not a victim, because he came from heaven
and freely chose to suffer and die for our sake. He came to set victims free. A victim is one who suffers against their will. Those who
accept suffering and unite it to the suffering of Jesus are victims,
no longer. They are free, and freely love God and others.

Therefore, we can rejoice and embrace whatever trials, tribulations, suffering, loss, and even death that await us, for they carry the hope of glory. They will not be in vain. Even now, we can see on the horizon, great suffering for humanity, but we do not despair because we love God and know that out of it will come, new life. This is why St. Paul, and all the Saints with him, could exclaim: "Now I rejoice in my sufferings for your sake, and in my flesh I complete what is lacking in Christ's afflictions for the sake of his body, that is, the Church," (ICSB Col 1:24)

22

The Fruit of Suffering

I was just thinking about how few people really believe that good can come from suffering. Most people, today, wonder if there is any real purpose of suffering. If we are reflective we can see from our own experiences that suffering produces virtue, when accepted. We grow in patience, perseverance, fortitude, courage, strength, discernment, wisdom, knowledge, understanding, etc. But, what good could come from the passion and death of Jesus? How is suffering redemptive? How is death redemptive?

Jesus said, "Greater love has no man than this, that a man lay down his life for his friends" (ICSB Jn 15:13). To many people, this is foolish, and a waste. They value their own life more than the life of their friends, even if they think their friends will make better use of their life than they would. If they think they are better than their friends, this kind of sacrifice is even more foolish. There are, however, many people who are very humble and selfless. They would willingly risk their life to save others, like the helpless and innocent. Very few, however, would risk their life to save a criminal or great sinner; perhaps, none, except for mothers for their children. Many people are also willing to risk their life for a good cause, like protecting their country. But, how many people could risk their life, or lay it down, if there was no honor in it; if they had to lay down their reputation and good name as well as their life? Jesus laid down his life, freely, in order to save sinners. He did it for the honor and glory of his Father, as well as to give eternal life to sinners. He also allowed himself to be taken for a criminal and a heretic, rather than a hero or martyr. Is there any greater act of love than this?

So, how did this love, this sacrifice of the life of Jesus help humanity? How has it saved anyone, let alone sinners? Jesus rose from the dead, proving that he can restore life and give eternal life; proving that he conquered sin and death; proving that he can deliver people from the slavery of sin and transform them into the image of God, by sending them the Holy Spirit. The evidence lies in the thousands of saints and holy souls that followed after him. It has affected even non-believers. It has even brought about a new evolution of humanity, in spite of all the evil that still exists in the world. The kingdom of God is growing in the hearts of human-kind and the world. I believe that our understanding of what the love of God is, has also grown, and continues to grow and deepen. Although they prophesied about the mystery of God's love, could the prophets have ever been able to conceive of the scope and mag-nitude of this love? Could they have understood a God who loved his enemies and the enemies of his people, who loved everyone; a God who loved unconditionally; a God who is so merciful, and so powerful that he can change the hearts of his enemies, of the most hardened sinner; a God who was willing to come among them and be with them, be one of them; a God who would lay down his life for them, in flesh and blood? Scripture says:

> Have this mind among yourselves, which was in Christ Jesus, who, though he was in the form of God, did not count equality with God a thing to be grasped, but emptied himself, taking the form of a servant, being born in the likeness of men. And being found in human form he humbled himself and became obedient unto death, even death on a cross. Therefore God has highly exalted him and bestowed on him the name which is above every name, that at the name of Jesus every knee should bow, in heaven and on earth and under the earth, and every tongue confess that Jesus Christ is Lord, to the glory of God the Father. (ICSB Phil 2:6—11)

God is love, and the greatest suffering in life comes from the rejection of love; for both, the one who is loved and the one who loves. God has revealed to us, long ago, that even if we are unfaithful, if we abandon him and reject his love, he will always be faithful to us; he will never abandon us, reject us, or stop loving us. He accepts the pain and suffering of our rejection without retaliation, even if we refuse to repent, and continues to love us. An example of his love is *unrequited love*. It is somewhat flattering to the one who is loved, at first. But, because they do not return the love, or cannot return it, they reject it. When the one who loves, continues to love, it becomes bitter to the one who is loved. They become angry, and then want to destroy the one who loves them.

The suffering that results is terrible for both, the one who loves and the one who is loved. Jesus wept over Jerusalem because they did not realize what was being offered to them, and the consequences of their rejection. (Mt 23:37)

I do not mean to imply that the pain we cause God by our rejection of his love is the same as that experienced by a person who experiences *unrequited romantic love*. Unrequited romantic love is painful to the ego and is not selfless love. One is in love with an illusion, or the idea of being in love, rather than in love with a real person. Nevertheless, it can be very painful. In a mysterious way, Jesus is with us, as well as in heaven. Therefore, the *unrequited love* of God causes him pain; not because our rejection of him hurts him, but because it hurts us. God pursues us with his love like "the hound of heaven," but he never forces his love upon us. He weeps over us because our rejection leads us toward death. An example of God's pain of *unrequited love* is the pain of the Father in the parable of *The Prodigal Son* (Lk 15:11—32), and Jesus, *weeping over Jerusalem*. (Lk.13:34—35).

Personally, I can recall several times in my own life, when I experienced *unrequited love*. It seems that I was always attracted to someone who was not attracted to me; attracted to someone who was not available; or attracted to someone who was not a good match for me. I think this is true of God's love for us, as well. The difference is that we are all made for union with God; and even though we are not a good match for him right now, he has promised to transform us into the image of his Son. Nevertheless, the suffering that I experienced from *unrequited love* was intense and I think that this suffering helped me to understand a little of what God experiences from our rejection of his love.

God loves us unconditionally, with *unrequited love*. Our rejection of his love brought about his crucifixion. When the first man and woman sinned, it was a rejection of God's love, and if God had been flesh and blood, their rejection would have resulted in the passion and death of God upon the tree of life. The crucifixion of Jesus is a reenactment of the effect of sin upon God and humanity. Jesus accepted our rejection knowing what it would lead to—even before his incarnation. It was the Father's will that his son love unconditionally, with the same unrequited love. Love does not, however, end with the cross; with crucifixion. Jesus rose from the dead, revealing the power of enduring love. The cross is not the last word. The cross is God's act of mercy. The *unrequited love* of God will eventually conquer death and separation and transform our relationship with him into the union of love; not because of us, but because of God's unending mercy, his ultimate act of love.

I doubt if the power of unconditional love was immediately evident at the time of Jesus' death. I think this was revealed to his disciples after his resurrection. I also think that it continues to be revealed throughout the ages, through subsequent disciples who love unconditionally, until the kingdom of God is fully established on earth. Jesus said: "A servant is not greater than his master" (ICSB Jn 15:20). If they persecuted Jesus, they will also persecute his disciples. All suffering in life, even that of the totally innocent can be traced back to sin—to *original sin*—the rejection of God's love.

It seems to me that when the love of God enables us to accept suffering, and unite it to the suffering of Jesus, we continue to proclaim the Gospel, the Good News, and to manifest the unconditional love of God for humanity. When humans accept the *mercy* of God, his unconditional love for them, even though they do not deserve it, they enable the power of his resurrection, the power of unconditional love, to be made manifest in the world.

Was not this the message of the prophet, Hosea? His own relationship with his unfaithful wife became a metaphor for the relationship that God has with his people, as well as the whole human race. It has also served to deepen our understanding of the indissolubility of marriage, and the kind of love a married couple should have for one another (Hos 2). There have been many marriages in which one spouse, at some point, stops loving the other spouse or rejects their love. If the other spouse continues to love, unconditionally, there will probably be much suffering and conflict, for a while. If they persevere, however, it may eventually win the other over. There may need to be a period of separation (a time-out) to allow for a change of heart, like the wife of Hosea (before one of them destroys the other). I think, however, that if they do not get a divorce, there is always hope for a reconciliation and union of love. I think that this is why it is necessary for those who enter into marriage, to make a commitment for life and to stay in the marriage.

Marriage is a covenant of love and there is no love without sacrifice or suffering. Marriage is in sickness and health, for richer or poorer, in good times and bad. The same is true with our covenant with God. We have to trust in him and in his love for us. God never gives up on us and continually pours out his love and mercy on us.

Scripture tells us that in a true marriage, there can only be one husband and one wife. Jesus said:

> Have you not read that the creator from the beginning *made them male and female* and that he said: *This is why a man must leave father and mother,*

and cling to his wife, and the two become one body?
They are no longer two, therefore, but one body. So
then, what God has united, man must not divide."
(JB Mt 19:4—6)

God took woman from out of man and formed her (Gen 2:21—
24). He created man and woman for union; to be one, through
marriage. This is not so, of two women or two men, or of a human
with an animal, or of a man and woman outside of marriage, or of
an adult and a child. A husband and wife should be a matched pair,
like two shoes, the same size and style, but, a left shoe and a right
shoe. A marriage should be a perfect fit, a good match. If it is not,
the two cannot become one, and there is no true marriage. The relationship will be disordered and out of balance.

Once, long ago, I was praying for the marriage of some friends.
Then, I had a dream. In the dream, I saw a pair of shoes. The soles
from both of the shoes were separated from the shoes. On one
of the shoes, the nails that connected the sole to the shoe were
fairly straight and the sole was easily reconnected to the shoe with
the use of a hammer. The nails on the other shoe, however, were
very crooked and damaged. The sole could not be reconnected
to the shoe. The shoes were no longer a pair, and the two could
not walk together. Some good marriages become so damaged and
broken that only the *Master Shoemaker* can fix them; only a miracle can fix them.

The relationship between a husband and wife is an exclusive
relationship. They each jealously guard this relationship against
false lovers who attempt to break their covenant with each other.
Righteous jealousy should not to be confused with the jealousy

that comes from our ego, or lower nature. Righteous jealousy is comparable to the zeal of the shepherd who guards and protects his sheep from the thief and the wolf, who comes to steal and to destroy the sheep (Jn 10:11 — 16); *God is a jealous God!* There can only be one God, who is God over all peoples. The *bride* is a metaphor for the human race, the people of God. The bride is inclusive of all humans. There is only one God who can make a covenant with all humans; beginning with the first man and woman, who represent all humans. There is no place for false gods in this covenant relationship. There is only one *Shepherd*. God jealously guards his people against thieves and hirelings who try to take his place, but he will not stoop to compete with them. He jealously guards his people because of what will become of them if they become slaves of false gods, and so he will never abandon them. He goes in search of them when they become lost, and never gives up until he rescues them. Jesus came to save the whole world. Not all of the sheep know the voice of the Shepherd, or follow him. They are not yet part of the flock. God will not rest until he has all his sheep back: "And there are other sheep I have that are not of this fold, and these I have to lead as well. They too will listen to my voice, and there will be only one flock, and one shepherd." (JB Jn 10:16)

As I reflect on how God gradually revealed his love throughout the Old Testament, I am reminded that in the book of Jonah, the message was that God is the Creator of everyone, and loves everyone. God has no favorites. The "chosen people" were called for the sake of all nations, to be a light to the nations and direct them to God; to be a spokesman for God to reveal his love to all peoples. In the book of Job, the message was that suffering is not punishment from God for sin. Suffering comes to good people as well as bad. All behavior has its own consequences, we reap what we sow. Nevertheless, the innocent suffer as well as the guilty, and the evil man prospers as well as the righteous man. When we have turned away from God, suffering can be a gift to turn us back to God. When we are righteous, as Job was, and suffering comes to us, we need to trust in God; accept the suffering and continue to trust that God is with us in the suffering and will bring good from it.

God takes no pleasure in seeing his people suffer. Through one person's sin, all of creation was wounded. This causes me to reflect that, in some mysterious way, all of creation is connected. When one person suffers, the whole of creation suffers. Through one person's perfect act of love the whole of creation is healed and renewed—transformed. God did not come to destroy the world, but to save it. To me, sin is like the radio-active fall-out from a hydrogen bomb. It affects everything; all life on earth; people, animals, plants, water, air, and earth. I do not believe that God sends natural disasters to punish us. I think that they come from the impurities and imbalance in nature caused by sin. If a whole city repents (Nineveh) and turns to God, the elements of nature are affected, as well. To repent is to be with God; to receive his love and protection. To be separated from God is to be subject to destruction. God is not a destroyer. I do not think that the plagues of Egypt came directly from the hand of God. When we refuse a blessing from God, it seems to me that we choose to be cursed. Perhaps, the plagues were the result of nature rebelling against sin—cause and effect. Suffering is the result of our rebellion against God, because we were created for union with God. God could have intervened and stopped the plagues if Egypt would have allowed him to (as Jesus calmed the storms at sea). It seems to me that the Hebrew people were saved, or spared by God, because God was with them and they were with God, through obedience. The human body is always trying to heal itself of its impurities and disease. I think that nature does the same, through what appears to be natural disasters or interventions of God. God did not destroy Egypt, he saved the Hebrews.

I have heard that some holy souls absorb the impurities of others into their own body like one who sucks out the venom of a snake bite in another person. I think that some nations do the same. They are a sign of the Cross for the world. These are the poor and the innocent ones. They become a sacrifice of love, uniting their suffering with Jesus—the sacrificial Lamb of God who takes away the sin of the world. Jesus taught: "Blessed are the poor in spirit, for theirs is the kingdom of heaven" (ICSB Mt 5:3). I would say that the kingdom of heaven is the *fruit of suffering*.

23

There is Only One God, Only One!

*I*n every generation since the beginning of time, it seems that God has to remind us: *"There is only one God, only one; and it is not you!"* I remember, as an adolescent, my father saying to me, "I am the king of this castle, not you." I wondered why it was so important for him to be *king of the castle*. When I grew up and had children of my own, I understood why. It was not important to my father to be king, it was important for me to know he was king; and that I was not.

There is so much division in the Church right now. Humans cling to the need for infallible truth and doctrine as though, without it, we would lose God, and the Church would be destroyed. We pride ourselves that we have a full-proof method to determine what is fallible, or heretical teaching, and what is the infallible, teaching of God. How did the apostles ever manage, without the cannons of Scripture and Cannon Law? Does faith only come from hearing and seeing the Word of God in black on white paper?

Why are we so afraid of heresy? Of what is imperfect, what is subject to error, what is fallible? Are we fearful of being merely creatures, of being human, of being less than the angels, or of not being God? Do we not believe that we can serve God, or that he can use us in spite of our limitations, errors, and fallibility? Are we afraid of being separated from him if we are not Gods, not equal to him? Are we afraid of powerlessness, fallibility, and servanthood? Have we forgotten that these are the things necessary for salvation and mercy? Why do we always tend to *throw out the baby with the bath water*? We are so afraid of change or anything new, of anything we cannot prove, of anything that requires faith and trust.

The worst kind of heresy is not philosophies or teaching that is contrary to our beliefs, but calumny, detraction, lies, ridicule, and gossip that can destroy people's reputations and lives. We have learned from experience that it is futile to try to fight heresy through protest mobs that end in violence, public condemnation, exclusion or excommunication, or by burning heretics at the stake. This is not the example that Jesus gave us. At times, Jesus had to rebuke or correct the Pharisees, as well as his disciples, when they were in error or given to heresy. He knew that he was the *Truth,* and that he had more authority than them; he had all authority in heaven and on earth. Jesus responded to heresy and error by teaching the truth. To those who were not open to the truth, he was silent. Instead, he let his actions speak for him.

Jesus proved that he was who he said he was; that he was not just a good man with a messiah complex. He proved he was the Son of God, and did so as a human person. He proved it, not with mere words; not with a new code of ethics or morals; not with new rules, regulations, laws, and doctrines. He proved it by his deeds, by doing the impossible works of God: he forgave men their sins, removing guilt and shame; he healed the deaf and the blind; he cast out demons and raised the dead; he calmed the seas and walked on water; he multiplied bread and fish to feed the hungry. He proved it by his humility, wisdom, and love for even his enemies; by accepting suffering, persecution, and crucifixion, although he was innocent of all wrong-doing; by rising from the dead on the third day in his body, and ascending into heaven; and by sending the Holy Spirit to empower, teach, guide, and transform all believers. He came pre-announced and fulfilled all the prophecies that referred to him. Jesus is the *Truth* and the *light*. He is within us, and speaks to us from within, as well as through the Church. We receive his enlightenment from within our minds, through the Holy Spirit. We recognize the *Truth* when *our hearts burn within us* and cause us to exclaim, *yes!!!*

What would happen to Church leaders if they suddenly discovered that human error has always existed within the Scriptures, teaching, and doctrines of the Church? Would they lose their faith? Would they reject and abandon the Church? Would they deny and abandon Jesus?

Faith comes from hearing the Word of God. The Word of God is Jesus, and he speaks to us in many ways; from within our hearts and minds; through the Scriptures, the Church, and the sacraments; through one another; and through our life experiences. If only we have ears to hear! But, how do we know who Jesus is? How do we know it is him speaking to us, amidst the thousands of voices ringing in our hearts and minds? How do we *test the spirit*?

My knowledge of Jesus comes from the eye witness accounts of men who lived with Jesus; men who knew him as a brother; men who saw and heard what Jesus said and did, even when they did not fully understand what he said and did. Understanding came in time; from the Holy Spirit and from what they experienced. I believe in their testimony because of the fruit they manifested in their own lives, and from the witness of the Holy Spirit within me. The apostles proved they were men of faith and holiness by their deeds and words, and by laying down their lives for the kingdom of God. Even though they were fallible, they were not liars or deceitful. They loved the people and each other as Jesus loved them. They were not charlatans, false prophets, or false teachers. They did not live for themselves. If not for their testimony, I could not know who Jesus is; who it is that speaks to me from within me. I could not know his *name*. I recognize him because of their testimony. And, even though not all of their successors had their integrity or were men of faith, hope, and love, it could not detract from their testimony.

Is there anyone other than God who can claim to be truly infallible? Even if every pope, bishop, priest, deacon, and saint throughout the past two thousand years agreed upon something, could it be said to be the infallible *Word of God*? Does the sum of humanity equal God? Could there ever be enough words to fully explain what is in the mind and heart of God? If God came to us and spoke his Word to us in person, (which he did) could anyone claim to infallibly interpret or understand what he says? Would it not be like a foreign language to us even if it was in our own tongue? Could we interpret or understand what he says? Would it not be even harder, than for animals to understand humans? Gradually, we might catch on to a few commands, praises, or signs, but could we ever communicate or converse with God, the creator of heaven and earth, on an equal level? If God became man, (which he did) would he not have to submit to the limitations of humans in order to communicate with us? Would he not be subject to human error and the need for growth in human wisdom and knowledge, within a human body? Would we accept him, or crucify him? Could we follow him or accept his divinity, based on supposed infallibility? Would it not, instead, require us to have faith, hope, love, and trust? Would it not take actions instead of just words for him to prove that he was God? Every word from God brings a thousand questions. No wonder God is silent most of the time. His most frequent words must be "that is not what I am saying." It is only by and through the Holy Spirit that we can hear and understand what God is trying to convey to us. Even so, we think and reason like little children; and this side of heaven, we see "in a mirror, dimly" and "know in part"; not fully. (ICSB 1Cor 13:12)

Did Jesus ever claim that every word of Scripture is literally the infallible word of God? Did he ever claim that his Church would be infallible? Or, instead, did he say that in spite of human errors and limitations, his message would live on because of their love for one another, and because of the Holy Spirit? Did Jesus not teach us to look for the fruit: *he who hears the word and understands it;* bears good fruit? (ICSB Mt 13:23). Did he not say, *I am the way, and the truth,* (ICSB Jn 14:6) and *the truth will make you free* (ICSB Jn 8:32)? Did he not promise that there would always be a remnant of his Church to pass on his message until he comes again?

Why did Jesus really come to us? What message did he want to convey to us? What did he say and do that could save us; change and transform us into his likeness? What did he mean when he said, *on this rock, I will build my Church, and the gates of Hades shall not prevail against it* (ICSB Mt 16:18)? Who and what is his Church? Why did he give the keys of the kingdom to Peter?

We know that those keys represent power, truth (infallibility), and authority, but do they not also represent faith, hope, and love? Why did Jesus trust Peter? Why did he tell him *whatever you bind on earth shall be bound in heaven, and whatever you loose on earth shall be loosed in heaven* (ICSB Mt 16:19)? Why did he not say *whatever is bound in heaven will be bound on earth, and whatever is loosed in heaven will be loosed on earth*? Was he saying that Peter is greater than, or equal to God? Or was he just saying: *Because you love me and have faith in me, I trust you to use your best judgment, and to yield to the Holy Spirit. I have your back. I will defend you and not hold your limitations against you. I know that I can work all things for good, even your human errors, failures and sins; because the Holy Spirit will never leave the Church.*

God gave Moses authority over the Law and the people; and yet, Moses allowed the men to divorce their wives. Even though it was not part of God's plan in the beginning, God allowed Moses to do this, and honored the authority he gave him. It did not mean that Moses *got it right!* Will God not do the same for the Church? Is not this the same kind of authority that God gives to parents over their children? As long as parents love their children, putting them first before their own selves, and do the best they can within their knowledge and means, God honors the authority he gives them, and blesses them.

What would be our response if Jesus asked us: "If everything in Scripture was only 90%, or 80%, or 70% infallible or true, would it be in vain? Why do you turn Scripture into an idol? If the teaching tradition of the apostles and the Church was only 90%, 80%, or 70% infallible or true, is it still not valuable? Why do you turn it into an idol? Can you not learn from error, or grow from it? Why do you expect man to be God, when even the Son of God did not demand equality with God?" As Scripture says:

> Have this mind among yourselves, which was in Christ Jesus, who, though he was in the form of God, did not count equality with God a thing to be grasped, but emptied himself, taking the form of a servant, being born in the likeness of men. And being found in human form he humbled himself and became obedient unto death, even death on a cross. (ICSB Phil 2:5—8)

Jesus always said what the Father wanted him to say, not because the words were the literal and infallible words of the Father, but because the Father's words were life-giving spirit for humans. It was the Father's love that Jesus spoke. Jesus came to reveal the nature and heart of the Father, not just words. Jesus is the Word of God, not written or spoken words. Jesus came to reveal the love of the Father for the world; to teach us to love as God loves us. He came to forgive and to reconcile man with God. He came to give us his Spirit so we can become like him; and love, think, and act like he would if he were in our skin. He came to give us *eternal life* and to destroy the fear of death.

The mission of Jesus was two-fold. He came first, to make disciples; to form a community of disciples, his Church. He came to gather the faithful believers, and those prepared by John the Baptist. He went among his own people. He went to the temple and the synagogues, towns and villages. He went to those seeking the Lord. He told them, *Come, follow me; live with me; do as I do.* He formed them by the words of Scripture, the Sermon on the Mount, the Beatitudes, and taught them how to pray. He revealed himself to them. Jesus is the *Revelation of God*. Jesus said, "He who has my commandments and keeps them, he it is who loves me; and he who loves me will be loved by my Father, and I will love him and manifest myself to him" (ICSB Jn 14:21). Most of the Jews were people who kept the commandments, who loved God and their neighbor. Some were great sinners but had hearts made for God, hearts of mercy and compassion. He prepared them all to receive the Holy Spirit. Jesus came to form disciples who would become holy, filled with the Holy Spirit, and die to their own selves, so that he could be made manifest through them in order to show the world the *way, the truth, and the life;* (ICSB Jn 14:6)

The second part of his mission was to *set captives free* (Lk 4:18). Jesus went to those in need of a Savior, of deliverance. He forgave sins; he healed the sick. He went to prisoners, those held captive by demons and sin; he gave sight to the blind and opened the ears of the deaf. He went to the poor, the hungry, the homeless, the outcasts, the dying, the lepers, and those who did not know good from evil. He went to prostitutes and thieves. He did not judge or condemn them; he gave them hope, good news of salvation. He fed, healed, forgave, delivered, and taught them. He taught them to love God because God loves them, and to love others the way God loves them; to do unto others, even their enemies, what they would want done unto them; that everything they do to others, good or evil, will come back upon them. He gave them the anecdote for *bad karma:* penance, forgiveness, prayer, almsgiving, fasting, sacrifice, and to carry their cross. He taught them that they would need the Holy Spirit in order to be good and to do good to others.

He also taught them not to live for this life, alone, because there is life after death in the kingdom of God. He embraced them, touched them, and loved them. Jesus commanded his disciples to follow his example and continue his mission. Jesus wanted to send his disciples out into the world to do as he did, so he sent them the Holy Spirit to clothe them with power.

All people are searching for love; to love and be loved. All people are searching for acceptance, and for purpose and meaning for their life. All people are longing to be set free from fear, shame, and guilt. All people fear suffering, rejection, loss, and death. Who are the faithful followers of Jesus, today? Who are the Pharisees of our day? Who are the Romans of our day? Who are the Zealots of our day? Who are the outcasts of our day? Who are the captives of our day? Who are the blind and the deaf, the hungry and the poor today? Who are the hopeless, the faithless, and the unloved today? Who are the sick in need of a physician today?

I believe that God has spoken to men and women throughout time and history, to anyone who was searching for him and open to listen. I believe in the covenants that God made with all the servants of God mentioned in Scripture. I believe in the authority God gave them, and his trust in them. I have doubts, however, that every word they heard was the divine word of God; or that they always fully understood what they heard. Nevertheless, I believe they heard enough of the truth to satisfy God; and that their wisdom, insights and teachings far exceeded those of secular scholars and philosophers, and other religious leaders. This was accomplished in spite of human fallibility and error, not because of inerrancy. It was accomplished by the Holy Spirit, and continues to be accomplished by the Holy Spirit.

256

I believe in Moses, Abraham, the Prophets, David, and all the great figures of the Old Testament. I also believe in Buddha, Gandhi, Lao Tzu, and other great religious reformers. Jesus said: "He who receives a prophet because he is a prophet shall receive a prophet's reward, and he who receives a righteous man because he is a righteous man shall receive a righteous man's reward" (ICSB Mt 10:41). Most of all, I believe in Jesus, that he was the only begotten Son of God, and that everything he taught was the divine word of God. I believe in the virgin, Mary, and the apostles and their teachings. Whether everything they wrote was exactly as Jesus taught it, I do not know; but I accept it because God accepted it. The same is true for the teachings of the Church. It would not surprise me, however, or shake my faith to discover that there always has been a margin of error throughout the teachings of the Church. If it does not bother God, why should it bother me? If God can accept their limitations, so can I. I believe that the Church was divinely instituted by Jesus, but I do not believe the Church is divine. I believe the Church is a human sacrament through which God works, but the Church is not God. The Church is a window, or image of Jesus; like a photograph that helps us to identify Jesus when we see him. She is only the *bride of Christ*, his representative in the world. When Jesus returns, he will transform the Church and she will put on immortality, and be divinized. She will become one with Jesus. Until then, she is not yet finished.

I believe everything I profess in the creed. I believe in the Trinity, three persons in one God; but I do not fully understand it. I believe that there is only one God; but I also believe that God, the Father, has always been in relationship with *another,* like him; who is one with him. God is love, and love is always relational.

That *other* is divine. That *other* is Jesus, who is one with God the Father, but also became one with humanity, born of the virgin, Mary. I believe that Jesus was conceived by the Holy Spirit, who is one with the Father and the Son.

Who is Mary? Is she the fourth person of the Trinity that we did not know about? Did she come from God as Jesus did? I do not think so! But, the creation story seems to suggest some form of hierarchical progression. God created Adam out of earth and his spirit. Eve came forth from Adam, and humanity came forth from Eve and Adam. I believe that Jesus ascended into heaven, body and soul. I also believe that Mary was assumed into heaven, body and soul, and represents what lies ahead for the rest of the Church. I believe Mary is the new Eve, the mother of a new humanity, and my mother. If Jesus is the new Adam, then there must also be a new Eve. If there is male, there is also female. But, I am only a fallible human, so I could be wrong.

Even St. Paul seems to believe in a margin of error, until Jesus comes again. In his first letter to the Corinthians, he has this to say:

> Love never ends; as for prophecies, they will pass away; as for tongues, they will cease; as for knowledge, it will pass away. For our knowledge is imperfect and our prophecy is imperfect; but when the perfect comes, the imperfect will pass away. When I was a child, I spoke like a child, I thought like a child, I reasoned like a child; when I became a man, I gave up childish ways. For now we see in a mirror dimly, but then face to face. Now I know in part; then I shall understand fully, even as I have been fully understood.

So faith, hope, love abide, these three; but the greatest
of these is love. (ICSB 1 Cor 13:8—13)

In this life, it really comes down to faith! I do not think it will
matter to God if everything the Church teaches is not infallible.
The real test will be the fruit that it produces. I think the important
concern will be faith; why we have faith or why we do not have
faith. Perhaps we will not know until perfection comes; until Jesus
returns and gives the final judgment; until he comes to *separate
the chaff from the wheat*, and to *remove all the darnel sown by the
enemy*. In the meantime, St. Paul urges us not to resist the movement of the Holy Spirit by concealing our gifts and not using them
for the benefit of others; or by rejecting the gifts of others, manifested through prophesy, teaching, and revelations. He merely tells
us to test everything to be sure they do not contradict the word and
spirit of Scripture, and all that was handed down by the apostles
and the Church. He tells us to keep the good and discard what is
not good: "Do not quench the Spirit, do not despise prophesying,
but test everything, hold fast what is good, abstain from every form
of evil" (ICSB 1 Thes 5:19—22). All heresy contains both, truth
and error. Perhaps we need to focus on separating the good from
the bad and truth from error, instead of condemning all heresy and
heretics. Otherwise, we may end up condemning all Christians.
Heresy and fallibility are not the causes of division and schism;
sin—the lack of faith, hope, and love—is the cause.

I no longer care if I do not get it right. I believe in Jesus' love
and mercy, because I need it. I cannot help thinking that Jesus has
always been trying to tell the Church, *You will never get it right!
That is ok! I do not expect it. You are only human, and only I am*

God. But one day, I will make you like God, each in accordance to his nature. To err is human. Error is not simply a miss-print, a misunderstanding, or something that is blatantly false. Error can be saying the right thing, or truth, at the wrong time. It can be speaking the truth in the wrong way or with the wrong intention. It can be saying a half-truth or incomplete truth. It can be speaking the truth out of context. It can also be clinging to a truth when we are called to step out and go forth in trust. For Christians, the *Truth* is Jesus, not facts or doctrines (Jn 18:37). The *Truth* is a Spirit, the Holy Spirit. We are called to listen to the Spirit; to follow and yield to the Holy Spirit. Sometimes, it can seem like the Holy Spirit is taking a detour—backwards before we can go forward.

I am no longer afraid of speculation, even though I know I may be wrong; I do not cling to my speculations or private revelations. I know life will turn out better than my speculations and beliefs. But, to speculate is to have a dream, a vision for the future; to wonder; to risk; to step out in faith. To know that I am fallible and do not have the whole truth is to always be open to God; to always be in need of God. I love the Church, and respect all that she teaches. But, in this life, she is still only human. She is in process of becoming the *bride of Christ*. She may be instituted by Jesus, but she is not divine. Of course, I am only a fallible human, not God, so I could be wrong!

Would it not be something, if our Catholic saints, after getting into heaven, discovered that Martin Luther was the greatest saint in his time? I think they would be very happy, even if it meant that they were wrong about their judgment of him. We have labeled him as a heretic and schismatic, but divine providence has a way of righting all the wrongs in life. Even though the *Reformation* caused much division and suffering among Christians, the real cause of the Reformation was sin among Christians. Looking back, the Reformation may have protected the Church and prevented her from being over-come by the *gates of Hades*.

I think that the Church is infallible, not because she always manifests the incarnate truth, but because the incarnate truth resides within her. She is infallible because she cannot be conquered or destroyed by Satan, sin, or evil; because the Holy Spirit will not allow it. The wounds of the Church are not mortal because she has eternal life. If she appears to die, she will rise again through the providence and power of God. The Holy Spirit is always with her. The mission and message of Jesus will always continue until he returns.

Life is wonderful today, in spite of all the division, chaos, suffering, and death. Theology, Scripture, spirituality, and the teaching of the Church are so exciting and full of wonder, in spite of the errors and heresy, and even the lies and fake news. There are so many beautiful minds working together; searching, challenging, provoking, correcting, and inspiring us to reach beyond the stars, and to *seek the Lord while he may be found*.

One thing, however, rings true over everything else! If we want peace and joy in our hearts, if we want to love and be loved, if we want the fulfillment of becoming the person we were created to be, if we want eternal life—life beyond the grave; then we must *love God with all our heart, mind, soul, and strength, and love our neighbor as ourselves*. Of course, to do this we need to know what *love* is, who God is, and who our neighbor is. We can know the answer to these questions by looking at Jesus; by following him; and by living with him. Mary, our mother, and the Church can lead us to him.

24

Daughters of the New Eve

$\mathcal{M}$ ary, the mother of Jesus, is the "woman" of Genesis, and the new Eve of the kingdom of God. She reigns upon the earth alongside of Jesus, the New Adam. All the popes that have reigned in my life time, from Pope Pius XII to Pope Francis, seem to have the heart of a mother. They all have had a great devotion to Mary, as the mother of Jesus and the mother of the Church; they all have manifested a great devotion to mothers everywhere and to all women in general; they all have, in some way, acknowledged the feminine genius in women, and the need for women and their unique gifts, for the salvation of the world. All women, today, are called to be *daughters of the new Eve*. What does this really mean for women, today?

Whenever I think of Pope Paul VI, I am reminded of the pilgrimage I made to Rome, many years ago. When I was there, I had an opportunity to have an audience with Pope Paul VI. This was the same pilgrimage in which I saw the Eucharist multiplied. I really had no desire to meet the pope, so I was greatly surprised when my chaplain chose me to accompany him for an audience with him. I was even a little indignant, as I thought of the thousands of people who came to Rome to see the pope, and who would give anything for an audience with him; people much more deserving than me.

As we were preparing to go for the audience, the people in my group said to me, "You must be so nervous and excited." I thought to myself, "Why should I be nervous, he is only a man." Then, I heard the Lord say to me, "This man is my servant!" I began to weep, openly, and could not stop weeping until after the audience. My knees were shaking as I bent to kiss the pope's ring, and I fell to the floor. Pope Paul helped me up. Not knowing what to say, I addressed him as "Your Majesty." As he raised his hands to bless me, I had what I think was an intellectual vision, I saw Mary and the pope united in the same person. It was as though I was seeing right into his soul. He was one with the Blessed Mother, as Mother of the Church, and I saw them both as one person. It was as though his heart was pierced; he was kneeling in prayer, weeping, and crying out to God, with his hands raised up. He said, "Oh, Lord, why did you choose me? Your people are so vast, and everyone is in a different stage of growth. Whatever I say or do that will help one will hurt another. Come Holy Spirit, give me wisdom, knowledge, and understanding to know how to guide and teach your children." He appeared to me, like a mother, weeping and interceding for her children. While he was blessing me, I felt this great love and indescribable light emanating from him. It was awesome! There really are no words to describe it.

When I returned home and shared this experience with my protestant friends—simply witnessing, not preaching—one of them responded by saying, "I think the Lord wants us to pray for the pope"; and so we did. Then, in 1972, not long after this pilgrimage, maybe a year, more or less, I returned to the States. I was invited to give a "witness" at a charismatic Episcopalian Church. I prayed and prayed, not knowing what I would say, and somewhat fearful of speaking before such a group. My husband said to me, "Trust in the Lord, he will give you the words to say." This was strange for him to say, and out of character, because he would never do what he told me to do.

The Lord did give me the words. I shared about my pilgrimage to Rome—about the Eucharist and Pope Paul VI. The response was overwhelming. Even the priest, not Catholic, was edified. There were many former Catholics in the group, who believed they were excommunicated because they were divorced. Many women came up to me, crying, saying, "I want to come home, is there any hope for me?"

Later, as I reflected on this, I thought to myself, it is a shame that Pope Paul VI does not know the impact that he has had on these people. Then, I felt the Holy Spirit prompting me to write him and tell him. I struggled against this, thinking, "How can I write a letter to a pope?" I wrote the letter, however. One minute, I was a docile child speaking to her father, and the next minute, I was a mother, speaking to her son—telling him not to retire but to remain where he was until the Lord came for him. I prayed for discernment, again doubting that this was from the Lord. Then, I thought, "It would be a miracle if he even received it, because he must receive thousands of letters every day, and I do not even know where to send it." So, I felt that I had nothing to lose. If God wanted him to have this letter, he would receive it, and if it was not God's will, he would not receive it.

While I was in Europe, I met a priest who was the secretary for a prominent cardinal in Rome, and he gave me his card and told me that if I ever came to Rome, to let him know. So, I sent the letter I wrote to Pope Paul VI to this priest and asked him to deliver it. To my surprise, within a couple weeks I heard from the priest, that the letter was on the pope's desk. Shortly after, on November 29, 1972, I received a letter from the pope's secretary, thanking me on behalf of Pope Paul, with an Apostolic Blessing, and a gold medal—a dove with an olive branch in its beak. Shortly after this, I read that Pope Paul decided not to retire; not that my letter persuaded him, but it may have been a confirmation for him.

I was so proud of that medal that I even thought of having it made into a necklace that I could wear; but the Holy Spirit convicted me of my pride and attachment. There was a woman who came to daily Mass, who was tormented by evil spirits. These spirits would constantly taunt her and blaspheme Jesus and the Church. She could not get anyone to help her or deliver her. I had befriended her. When she saw the medal I received, she was filled with awe and tears. Prompted by the Holy Spirit, I was moved to give her the medal from Pope Paul VI. The woman was overwhelmed with joy and gratitude, and was delivered from the evil spirits that tormented her. As far as I know, she never heard those voices again. Praise God!

Many people have proclaimed Pope Paul VI to be a prophet for our times. His following words are indeed very prophetic. On December 8, 1965, at the closing of the Second Vatican Council, Pope Paul VI addressed these words to all women:

> And now it is to you that we address ourselves, women of all states—girls, wives, mothers and widows, to you also, consecrated virgins and

women living alone—you constitute half of the immense human family. As you know, the Church is proud to have glorified and liberated woman, and in the course of the centuries, in diversity of characters, to have brought into relief her basic equality with man. But the hour is coming, in fact has come, when the vocation of woman is being achieved in its fullness, the hour in which woman acquires in the world an influence, an effect and a power never hitherto achieved. That is why, at this moment when the human race is under-going so deep a transformation, women impregnated with the spirit of the Gospel can do so much to aid mankind in not falling.

You women have always had as your lot the protection of the home, the love of beginnings and an understanding of cradles. You are present in the mystery of a life beginning. You offer consolation in the departure of death. Our technology runs the risk of becoming inhuman. Reconcile men with life and above all, we beseech you, watch carefully over the future of our race. Hold back the hand of man who, in a moment of folly, might attempt to destroy human civilization.

Wives, mothers of families, the first educators of the human race in the intimacy of the family circle, pass on to your sons and your daughters the traditions of your fathers at the same time that you prepare them for an unsearchable future. Always remember that by her children a mother belongs to that future which perhaps she will not see.

And you, women living alone, realize what you can accomplish through your dedicated vocation. Society is appealing to you on all sides. Not even families can live without the help of those who have no families. Especially you, consecrated virgins, in a world where egoism and the search for pleasure would become law, be the guardians of purity, unselfishness and piety. Jesus who has given to conjugal love all its plenitudes, has also exalted the renouncement of human love when this is for the sake of divine love and for the service of all.

Lastly, women in trial, who stand upright at the foot the cross like Mary, you who so often in history have given to men the strength to battle unto the very end and to give witness to the point of martyrdom, aid them now still once more to retain courage in their great undertakings, while at the same time maintaining patience and an esteem for humble beginnings.

Women, you do know how to make truth sweet, tender and accessible; make it your task to bring the spirit of this council into institutions, schools, homes and daily life. Women of the entire universe,

whether Christian or non-believing, you to whom
life is entrusted at this grave moment in history, it
is for you to save the peace of the world. (Pope
Paul VI 1965)

In response to the prophetic word from Pope Paul VI, many
holy women have given birth to ministries and apostolates for
women. Some examples of these apostolates are: *Women of
Grace®*, a Catholic apostolate for women, with many media out-
reaches, founded by Johnnette Benkovic in 1988; *Foundation of
Prayer for Priests,* with *Spiritual Motherhood* as an outreach ministry, co-founded by Kathleen Beckman in 2013; and *Magnificat, A
Ministry to Catholic Women,* founded by Marilyn Quirk and com-
panions in 1981.

᭝ The mission of Magnificat, inspired by the visitation of Mary to
her cousin, Elizabeth, is "to evangelize and to encourage Catholic
women to grow in holiness through opening more fully to the
power and the gifts of the Holy Spirit" (Magnificat HB). Since its
inception, Magnificat has grown from a hand full of spirit-filled
women to a ministry that has many chapters of women all over
the world. Their primary goal is for each chapter to present four
meals a year. The *Magnificat Meals* are an opportunity for women
to come together to share a meal; to support and encourage each
other by witnessing their faith; to praise and worship God; and to
listen to a speaker share their testimony of how God has worked
in their life. This is the main focus of the meal because it is what
evangelization is all about—to witness, inspire, encourage, and
proclaim the Gospel of Jesus Christ.

Almost thirty years ago, my spiritual director at the time, told me that he thought I was "the religious woman of the future." I really did not understand what he meant, and believed that God was calling me to become a nun in a traditional religious order. So, I proceeded to pursue a religious vocation. After ten years as a nun, I discovered that wasn't where God was calling me to live out my life. Life as a nun was an important part of my formation, and I am very grateful for the experience; however, for me, it was only a temporary preparation for the future. The Lord led me from the convent to the desert. Almost immediately, I became involved in Magnificat, as a member of the service team of the Palm Desert Chapter; founded by Donna Ross. Presently, Donna is the international coordinator of Magnificat's Central Service Team (CST). In the desert, I discovered that I can be a religious woman, today, right where I am; regardless of whether I am single, married, or a nun; or even if I am a mother, grandmother, and great-grandmother. All I have to do to be a religious woman — of the past, present, and future — is to say "yes" to whatever God asks of me; for me, this is a four-fold call:

- A call to conversion and holiness.
- A call to be a witness of Jesus, and to what he has done for me; to evangelize.
- A call to be a handmaid of the Lord; to serve and to do the will of God.
- A call to be a spiritual mother for the Church and the world.

I get the sense that Mary, our holy mother, is forming her own religious order today, in our particular time in history. One of the titles that Jesus gave Mary was *woman*. It seems to me that she is forming an order of *little women* to follow in her footsteps, in order to become spiritual mothers for the Church and the world, and especially for the priesthood. She wants to re-form women; with their natural attributes of receptivity, trust, humility, and surrender. These attributes are natural to the feminine nature of a woman's body and soul.

It seems to me our Lady wants to give women her charisms of contemplation, chastity, obedience, poverty, service, prophecy, intercession, advocacy, faith, redemptive suffering, and spiritual motherhood; in accordance with the measure of grace we receive, and for the common good of the whole Church and world. This is a vocation for women in every state of life—single, married, religious sister, divorced, separated, and widowed—all women, regardless of their past or present circumstances.

For the Catholic woman, *spiritual motherhood* is more than being a spiritual mother for the Church and priests; it is also being a handmaid of the Lord and a bride of Christ. Our holy mother Mary is, and always will be, a *handmaid of the Lord* and a *bride of Christ*. She is the spouse and handmaid of the Holy Spirit; the Mother of Jesus, the Son of God; and she is the *spiritual mother* of the Church and all priests. Mary is the perfect model of the whole woman. Her body and soul are fully integrated, one in being, and feminine to the core. She fulfills the whole call and purpose of *woman*—as handmaid, mother, and bride of Christ. She is the Christ-bearer, and an eternal life-bearer for the world.

I believe that all women are called to be *spiritual mothers*, whether we are barren or fertile; married, single, divorced, or a nun; Catholic or Protestant, Christian or non-Christian. Women were created for motherhood, including those who can never be a biological mother. As biological mothers, we are called to surrender our will, our body, and all that we have, for the sake of our children. We put them before ourselves. We are committed to give life, to nurture and protect them, to intercede for them, to be an advocate and mediator for them, and to defend their human dignity. No sacrifice is too much. We are there for them at every stage of development—at their first hour and at their last hour, as Mary was. Whatever belongs to us also belongs to them. We give to them all that God has given to us. All that we do for them, all that we give to them, is no more than what is expected of us by God, because he loves them even more than we do. We are filled with gratitude for them and delight in them. We encourage and exhort them to be all that God created them to be. All that we receive is for their sake, and given to them. When we must admonish or correct, we do so with gentleness and love in order to teach them. All that we do and say is for their good; not out of anger, revenge, or to exact payment. As *spiritual mothers*, we are a mother for the Church and the world in the same way that we are a mother for our own birth children; especially our priests and pastors.

Mary, the Mother of Jesus, is the new Eve; the new woman. This is her time to reign. She is calling all women to reign with her; to become the new Eve, the new woman, walking in her footsteps. It is time for women to discover their true genius as women; their unique gifts for the family, Church, and all humanity. It is time for women to discover their true vocation and mission in the world.

Are we, as women, ready to say "yes" to the will of the Father, as Mary was? Are we able to believe the promises given to us by God? Are we able to believe that we can be *full of grace*, as Mary is? Do we believe that we can find favor with God, as Mary did? Nothing is impossible for God! Is not this what God wants for all women? We are not Mary, and we do not have all the gifts that she has, but if we become the woman God created us to be, with the help of his grace, we can sing with Mary, "My soul magnifies the Lord, and my spirit rejoices in God my Savior, for he has regarded the low estate of his handmaiden." (ICSB Lk 1:47—48)

25

The Bride of Christ

*G*od became flesh in the person of Jesus Christ, so that the Bridegroom could be joined to his Bride, and the two would become one flesh. In this way, God could become flesh with his people, and he would always be with them. Together, they would renew the face of the earth. This was God's plan from the beginning when he joined Adam and Eve in marriage, in order to prefigure the heavenly Marriage between the Lamb and his Bride.

> "Hallelujah! For the Lord our God the Almighty reigns. Let us rejoice and exult and give him the glory, for the marriage of the Lamb has come, and his Bride has made herself ready; it was granted her to be clothed with fine linen, bright and pure" — for the fine linen is the righteous deeds of the saints. (Rev 19:6—8)

The Church, all those born from the side of Jesus upon the Cross, as Eve was taken from the side of Adam, are the Bride of Christ, being prepared for the final marriage feast.

> So the Lord God caused a deep sleep to fall upon the man, and while he slept took one of his ribs and closed up its place with flesh; and the rib which the Lord God had taken from the man he made into a woman and brought her to the man. Then the man said, "This at last is bone of my bones and flesh of my flesh; she shall be called Woman, because she was taken out of Man." (Gen 2:21—23)

In this world, the bride is the betrothed, awaiting the final consummation of her marriage, while the Groom goes ahead to prepare a home for her. Upon his return, she will be clothed in fine linen and adorned with precious jewels, forever joined to her Bridegroom. Her body will belong to him and his body will belong to her. "For the wife does not rule over her own body, but the husband does; likewise the husband does not rule over his own body, but the wife does." (1 Cor 7:4)

Before this great marriage feast takes place, the bride is carried off to a place in the desert where she will be protected against the *gates of hell,* washed, and dressed for the marriage feast. "And the woman fled into the wilderness, where she has a place prepared by God, in which to be nourished for one thousand two hundred and sixty days" (Rev 12:6). This place of refuge is not an escape from the world, but a state of being; to be tested, cleansed and purged through a *baptism of fire*, and clothed with the gifts of the Holy Spirit and deeds of virtue.

Before we can really recognize the Church as the bride of Christ, we need to go back to see the original bride of Christ. A man always looks for a bride like his mother. Mary, the mother of Jesus, prefigures the image, character, beauty, and gifts of the Church. The bride, like Mary, would be "a woman clothed with the sun, with the moon under her feet and on her head a crown of twelve stars." (ICSB Rev 12:1)

Who is Mary? Who is this bride of Christ and icon of the Church? Mary has many titles and many faces. To name a few:

New Eve
Woman of Genesis
Immaculate Conception
Spouse of the Holy Spirit
Handmaid of the Lord
Mother of God
Mother of the Church
Queen of Angels
Queen of Apostles
Queen Mother
Ark of the Covenant
Tabernacle of the Covenant/Eucharist
Co-Redemptrix
Mediatrix of all Grace

According to tradition, at a very young age, Mary consecrated her life as a *handmaid of the Lord,* including her virginity, forsaking all others. She was obedient to the covenant in every way; to the Law and the Prophets. She was a true daughter of Israel. The angel, Gabriel, tells us that she was *full of grace*, full of love, and especially favored by God; chosen to be the Mother of God's only Son. One cannot be *full of grace* unless they are free of all sin; including *original sin*. When Gabriel greeted Mary with the words, *Hail, full of grace*, she was *greatly troubled*. This was a sign of her great humility and reverence for God; she did not feel worthy of such a salutation. The angel assured her that it is due to God's favor of her; because God chose her. When Gabriel told her what God was asking of her, Mary did not presume to understand all that was said, but responded in humility, asking: *How can this be, since I have no husband?* She knew that God would not ask her to break her vow of virginity, so she would not assume that this would happen through natural means. Mary had the humility and child-like trust to be able to ask God for what she needed to know. Gabriel answers her, telling her that "The Holy Spirit will come upon you, and the power of the Most High will overshadow you; therefore the child to be born will be called holy, the Son of God" (ICSB Lk 1:35). This was Mary's Pentecost! Mary was the first to receive the gift of the Holy Spirit, which resulted in the incarnation of the Son of God. This was the greatest gift, and most powerful gift of the Holy Spirit that anyone has ever received. Gabriel also tells Mary about her cousin, Elizabeth. Mary responds to this invitation from God, saying, *Behold, I am the handmaid of the Lord; let it be done to me according to your word* (ICSB Lk 1:38). She surrenders all to God, and to the will of God. We could assume that Mary also received many other gifts of the Holy Spirit; mentioned in Isaiah. (Is 11:1—5)

Scripture tells us that "In those days Mary arose and went with haste into the hill country, to a city of Judah, and she entered the house of Zechari'ah and greeted Elizabeth" (ICSB Lk 1:39—40). Mary is a true servant; whenever she recognizes someone with a need, she responds immediately, and goes to their aid. This was no easy journey for her to make, but Mary was always ready to accept any hardship that life had to offer her. Mary is also anxious to share Elizabeth's great joy in having conceived a son, after being barren for so many years. She wants to honor Elizabeth. An extraordinary thing happens with this visitation. The very sound of Mary's voice imparts the Holy Spirit to Elizabeth, and to John the Baptist, while in her womb. Elizabeth receives the gift of prophecy. She realizes that Mary is not just her little cousin, but the mother of her Lord. She honors Mary, recognizing the importance of Mary's faith and trust in God.

> And when Elizabeth heard the greeting of Mary, the child leaped in her womb; and Elizabeth was filled with the Holy Spirit and she exclaimed with a loud cry, "Blessed are you among women, and blessed is the fruit of your womb! And why is this granted me, that the mother of my Lord should come to me? For behold, when the voice of your greeting came to my ears, the child in my womb leaped for joy. And blessed is she who believed that there would be a fulfillment of what was spoken to her from the Lord." (ICSB Lk 1:41—45)

Mary begins to rejoice in God, to praise God and thank him for her vocation, while acknowledging her lowliness; and to prophecy the *Magnificat*. She remained with Elizabeth for three months, to care for her. (Lk 1:46—56)

Mary's *fiat* placed her at risk of being stoned to death, but Mary had complete trust in God. She was not naïve, however. Mary is a true contemplative, always praying, reflecting, and pondering everything in her heart. (Lk 2:19, 51). She was a faithful and devout wife, always at Joseph's side, and ready to follow him wherever he went, no matter what hardships it would bring her. They make the hard journey to Bethlehem, even though she was ready to give birth. She gives birth in a stable, without any of the comforts of home, depending totally on the providence of God. She graciously receives the shepherds and the *Wise Men from the East*, pagan astrologers. She graciously receives the gifts the wise men offer her. She does not differentiate between the rich and the poor, Jews or Gentiles. She is without prejudice or bias. She is obedient to the ordinances of her faith, in spite of danger and hardships. In obedience, she has Jesus circumcised and makes the prescribed offering in the temple. When the prophet, Simeon, prophesied, regarding Jesus, Mary listened intently, and marveled at what he had to say. She was always full of joy and gratitude to God. Simeon also prophesied concerning Mary, saying, "(and a sword will pierce through your own soul also), that thoughts out of many hearts may be revealed" (ICSB Lk 2:35). We know that this prophecy was fulfilled, as well. Mary was so bonded and united with Jesus that she experienced all his hopes, dreams, and joys, as well as all his pain and sorrow. When his heart was pierced upon the Cross, her heart was also pierced.

After the presentation in the temple, Mary and Joseph flee from their country, to Egypt, in order to protect the life of Jesus. Being the mother of Jesus was no easy life. Mary nurtured the Son of God, taught him all that she knew, and protected him from all harm. After their return to Nazareth, Jesus is separated from his parents when he is twelve years old, while on pilgrimage to Jerusalem. They search for him, anxiously, for three days. After they finally find him in the temple, Mary asks Jesus, with the same desire to understand that she questioned Gabriel, why he stayed behind and did not join the others. Jesus responded, "Did you not know that I must be in my Father's house?" Jesus must have assumed that Mary would know where to find him. Again, Mary *pondered these things in her heart*. She had to accept her own humanness, limitations, and helplessness. Nevertheless, she taught Jesus obedience and raised the God-boy to manhood. (Lk 2:1—52; Mt 1:18—25; 2:1—12)

Mary was always a part of Jesus' mission. She was with him to initiate his *first hour*, at the marriage at Cana, and to finish his *last hour*, on the Cross. At Cana, she is quick to notice the needs of the wedding party, and does not hesitate to ask Jesus for help. She seems to know, however, that there is another reason to ask Jesus for help. She is a prophet, after-all. She seems to sense that the hour has come for Jesus to reveal who he is. It almost seems like Jesus is testing her, or looking for a confirmation. He addresses her as *woman*, (the new Eve). With certitude in her heart, and great trust in her son, Mary simply turns to the servants and says, "Do whatever he tells you." She is a servant, herself, and knows how to teach others how to serve. This is an important part of Mary's vocation. She is a *help-mate* to Jesus, always leading others to listen to him and *do whatever he tells them*. From the Cross, Jesus,

279

again addresses his mother as *woman*, and commissions his mother to be the mother of the Church, to embrace all his disciples as her children; and he commissions his disciples to accept her as their mother. (Jn 2:1—11; 19:26—30)

The disciples loved Mary, as their own Mother, and called her *blessed*, just as Jesus did. Mary loved all the disciples, as her own children, especially the apostles. We know from tradition, that Mary was assumed into heaven, body and soul, when she died; and also crowned by the Holy Trinity, as Queen of heaven and earth. (CCC 966)

Mary continues to be our spiritual mother, today, and is always interceding for us, and comforting us. She suffers with us, just as she did with Jesus. Her love for priests, however, is magnanimous. She has a very special love and concern for her sons, all priests, because they represent Jesus: *Blessed is he who comes in the name of the Lord*. (Lk 13:35)

Mary is the Mother of God because she is the mother of Jesus, and Jesus is God; one person with two natures; Son of God and Son of Man. His divinity cannot be separated from his humanity; he ascended into heaven with his resurrected body. (CCC 466, 495, 509)

Mary is the mother of the Church because the Church is the *body of Christ*, and cannot be separated from Jesus; and because she is the new Eve and Jesus is the New Adam. As mother of Jesus, she is also mother of the Church. Mary was assumed into heaven in her resurrected body, by Jesus. (CCC 968—970)

Mary is the new Eve because she is the *woman* of Genesis; the mother of Jesus and the *body of Christ*, the Church; because she is one flesh with the New Adam. From the beginning, God said: *I will put enmity between you and the woman, and between your seed and her seed; he shall bruise your head, and you shall bruise his heel.* (RSV Gen 3:15) (CCC 411)

In the first place, God is speaking to Adam and Eve, and to their *seed*, their descendants; and to the *serpent*. In the second place, God is speaking to Jesus and Mary, the New Adam and new Eve, and to their *seed*, the Church. (CCC 411)

When God addressed Adam and Eve and asked "What is this that you have done?" He was speaking to both of them as one person, one flesh. Adam and Eve were created one flesh (Eve was taken out of Adam). They were forever married, one flesh in relationship. Whatever God says to Adam, he also says to Eve, and whatever God says to Eve includes Adam. Because of their sin, their relationship is fractured. The consequences are the same for both of them, yet, in accordance with their gender and nature. (Gen 3)

What is the seed of the serpent? The serpent represents Satan, the devil, or Lucifer. His *seed* represents evil; Satan and the fruit of Satan. Evil includes Satan, or Lucifer; all the demonic powers that he manifests; all the fallen angels that fell with Lucifer; and all those who follow Satan. The seed of the woman is Jesus, and all the descendants of the new Adam and Eve. The seed is taken out of the *woman*, Mary, as Eve was taken out of Adam. The process is reversed. The promise is made to Adam and Eve, together, as well as Jesus, the New Adam, and Mary, the new Eve; as well as all those who enter into Jesus Christ. (1 Cor 15:21—23). The new Adam and Eve will crush the serpent's head. (Gen 3:9, 15; CCC 410)

Jesus is the Son of God and the Son of Man, together; inseparable, as one person. From the moment Jesus is conceived, Mary is made one with Jesus. Her DNA is in him, and his DNA is in her. They are inseparable in God's plan of salvation and redemption.

Jesus would not exist without Mary, his mother, and Mary, the new Eve, could not exist without Jesus, the New Adam. Jesus was birthed by Mary and Mary was birthed by Jesus.

When Jesus' side was pierced on the Cross, and blood and water flowed forth, Mary's soul was also pierced as well (Jn 19:31 – 34). Mary and Jesus, together, gave birth to the Church. Simeon, the prophet, prophesied: "and a sword will pierce through your own soul also), that thoughts out of many hearts may be revealed" (ICSB Lk 2:35). Mary shared in her son's redemptive suffering. Together, they crushed the head of the serpent. The Sacred Heart of Jesus and the Immaculate Heart of Mary triumphed, and together they reign as the New Adam and the new Eve; a new creation of sons and daughters of God. The blood and water flowing from their hearts, prefigures the birth of the Church; through water, by baptism of water and the Holy Spirit; through blood, by *baptism of fire* and the Eucharist. (See Luke 3:16)

At the wedding of Cana, Jesus mission begins with the miracle of changing water into wine. Mary is included in this miracle, with Jesus. Mary says to Jesus, *They have no wine*. Jesus responds by addressing her as *woman* (Gen 2:23), and asks her, *O woman, what have you to do with me? My hour has not yet come* (ICSB Jn 2:4). In other words, *what does this have to do with our mission?* Jesus seems to be *testing the spirit*, to know if this is just Mary's human concern, or from the Holy Spirit moving her to announce the time to begin his mission. Mary, motivated by the Holy Spirit, simply turns and tells the servants to *do whatever he tells you*. This wedding seems to represent a mystical marriage between Jesus and Mary, in regards to their mission and *final hour*, and prefigures the wedding between Jesus and the Church. One of the graces given to Mary when the Holy Spirit over-shadowed her was the gift of prophecy. The Incarnation of Jesus was her Pentecost. (Jn 2:1 — 11)

Throughout the life of Jesus and Mary, there is *enmity* between them and Satan; spiritual warfare. When Jesus dies on the Cross, the head of Satan is crushed; "It is finished" (Jn 19:30). This completion is also a new beginning. Satan goes in pursuit of the Church: "Then the dragon became angry with the woman and went off to wage war against the rest of her offspring, those who keep God's commandments and bear witness to Jesus" (NAB Rev 12:17). This warfare will continue until Jesus returns again and fully establishes his kingdom upon the earth. His Second Coming will be preceded by Mary, in her prophetic role, to *prepare the way of the Lord*. Many apparitions of Mary have been reported during our time, as well as throughout the history of the Church, such as Fatima and Lourdes.

All of this is a mystery, and we cannot yet see or understand how it will all be played out, and how all that God has revealed to us fits together without contradiction or error. Mary was one flesh with Jesus, and her *soul would be pierced* along with Jesus. As I ponder that, I have the sense that Mary shared in the passion and death of Jesus because of her close union with him. Mary was not with the other women who went to the tomb to anoint Jesus. None of the apostles mention Mary in Scripture, from the moment of Jesus' death until Pentecost. Why is this? Where was Mary? She mysteriously seems absent from the time of Jesus' death until Pentecost, the birth of the Church. Was she with Jesus in spirit? Was she in some sort of deep sleep? Was she preparing to give birth to the Church along with Jesus? Nothing is impossible for God! For instance, many saints experienced the gift of bilocation, being able to be in more than one place at the same time. The Son of God was always part of the Holy Trinity, even before the Incarnation of Jesus. Jesus is the one Mediator between God and humankind. He took on flesh in the womb of Mary. The Son of God is part of the Blessed Trinity, three persons in one God. He always existed from eternity. The Incarnation of the God-man, Jesus Christ, was not from all eternity. It took place in the fullness of time, in the womb of Mary. Redemption comes from God, from the Second Person of the Holy Trinity, who took on human flesh in the womb of Mary at the moment of his conception, through the Holy Spirit. This event not only affected the God-man, Jesus Christ, but his mother, Mary, as well. It was the beginning of the Son of God in the person of Jesus Christ. His DNA was in his mother and her DNA was also in him; this is not true of any other human being, and perhaps why both Jesus and Mary needed to remain virgins. The Son of God could not enter humanity except through the body of Mary, through her seed; and through her permission, her "yes" (Lk 1:38). Therefore, Jesus is our Redeemer because he is both God and man, and Mary is our co-redemptrix because she is the mother of Jesus, and brought him into the world, by the power of God working in her and through her. She shares in the life and mission of Jesus from the moment of his conception.

In the first covenant, Adam came first, and Eve was taken from him (Gen 2:21—22). Under the new covenant, Mary comes first, and Jesus is taken from her; the *first-born of a new creation*. Then, after Jesus' death, after his side was pierced, Mary is taken from Jesus and becomes the new Eve. She is separated from him by death. (Jn 19:33—34)

As co-redemptrix, Mary is not equal to Jesus. The prefix, *co* means *with*. Jesus with Mary is the Redeemer of the world. Mary had a human mother and father. Jesus had a human mother and a divine Father. Mary had only a human nature. Jesus had two natures, human and divine. Mary is the new Eve and Jesus is the New Adam, but only Jesus is Lord of heaven and earth; Mary is subject to him in all ways. Jesus suffered the consequences of *sin* through his flesh, his body and blood, on the Cross. His body came from Mary. His body is what saves us. His divine nature could not die. Mary suffered the consequences of sin only in her soul, not her flesh. Her soul was pierced. Jesus is the only begotten Son of God and Son of Man. Mary is not the begotten daughter of God; she is the daughter of a man and a woman, and along with Jesus, a descendant of Adam and Eve. Mary cooperated with God, but Jesus was God.

God became *like us in all things*, except for sin, taking on human flesh (Phil 2:6—8). For God to become like us he has to, in some way, become like man and woman; become Jesus with Mary; the New Adam *with* the new Eve. Mary is not God, but God adopted her from the beginning of her Immaculate Conception. God became *like* woman, as well as man, by virtue of Mary's relationship with Jesus. (CCC 490—493)

The first Adam and Eve became living souls, able to pass on the earthly body/soul to procreate life. The last Adam and Eve became life-giving spirits, able to pass on the Holy Spirit, giving new life to others (1 Cor 15:45). It was through the voice of Mary as well as the presence of Jesus in her womb, that Elizabeth and John the Baptist received the Spirit (Lk 1:43—45). As co-redemptrix, Mary is also able to give graces to humans; to be a mediatrix of all grace. (CCC 969—970)

Mary is the model, icon, of the Church. The Church is the *body of Christ*, as well as *spiritual mother* of the faithful. The role of the Church as *Mother* has always been understood since the time of the apostles. (Rev 12)

It is only when we enter into Christ, becoming part of his body, that we become adopted sons of God; that we can share in his divine life and enter into his relationship with the Father; that we become partakers of his divine nature; that we become participants in his priesthood; that we share in his redemptive suffering for the salvation of the world (Rom 8:22—23; Gal 4:4—7). By virtue of being the New Adam, Jesus is in all humans; but not all humans are in Christ, part of the body of Christ. The fullness of the revelation of God for our salvation came to humans through Jesus, *with* Mary, in the form of many pieces of a puzzle. It is only over time, that the Holy Spirit helps us to fit those pieces together. God chose to come to us, man and woman, to become like us, man and woman, in all things except for sin (Phil 2). God did not become a man and a woman, but a man *with* his mother (woman), making Mary subject to Jesus. Without Jesus we can do nothing; with Jesus we can do all things. Mary is mediatrix of all graces because she is forever *with* Jesus. Apart from him, she can do nothing. Apart from Mary, Jesus could not exist. They are never separated.

God made a covenant with Adam and Eve, not just with Adam; with Abraham and Sara, not just Abraham; with Isaac and Rebekah, not just with Isaac; with Jacob and Rachel, not just Jacob; with David and Bathsheba, not just David. The *seed* of the covenant always came from the man through the woman, to the world. Jesus and the Church are made one in a spiritual marriage; bride and Groom. This begins with the Incarnation of God in the person of Jesus Christ, in the womb of Mary, his mother.

Mary is the *new Eve*, the *woman*, the first member of the Church; taken from the side of the *New Adam*, Jesus Christ, her Son. She was the first to be redeemed, even before she came to be born. She was filled with the Holy Spirit, *full of grace*. We need faith to believe in Jesus, our Lord and Savior, fully God and fully man. We need faith to believe that Mary is also our mother, as well as the mother of Jesus. We need faith to believe that the Church is also our mother, and to love her, as her sons and daughters. We cannot love Jesus without also loving the Church. Jesus said to his apostles: "Truly, truly, I say to you, he who receives any one whom I send receives me; and he who receives me receives him who sent me" (ICSB Jn 13:20; Lk 10:16). We are in the Church and the Church is in us. We are in Jesus and Jesus is in us. Jesus is in the Father and the Father is in him. Mary is in the Church and the Church is in Mary. The Holy Spirit is in the Church and the Church is in the Holy Spirit. These are all mysteries. In Jesus, humanity and God became one person. The Church is also a type of the *new Eve*, born from the side of Jesus, through blood and water, from the Cross; and like Mary at the Annunciation, was over-shadowed by the Holy Spirit at Pentecost.

> The Church is born primarily of Christ's total self-giving for our salvation, anticipated in the institution of the Eucharist and fulfilled on the cross. "The origin and growth of the Church are symbolized by the blood and water which flowed from the open

side of the crucified Jesus." "For it was from the side of Christ as he slept the sleep of death upon the cross that there came forth the 'wondrous sacrament of the whole Church.'" As Eve was formed from the sleeping Adam's side, so the Church was born from the pierced heart of Christ hanging dead on the cross. (CCC 766)

Just as Eve was taken from the side of Adam, Mary was taken from the side of Jesus, on the Cross, when his side was pierced and blood and water poured out. Mary was united with Jesus on the Cross. At the same time, when Jesus' side was pierced, Mary's soul was pierced, as well. The prophet, Simeon, prophesied about Mary, saying: "And (a sword will pierce through your own soul, also)," (Lk 2:35). Therefore, the Church, a type of the *new Eve*, is born from Jesus and Mary, together. Jesus and Mary are the New Adam and the new Eve of the new creation, the new humanity, the kingdom of God on Earth. (Jn 19:26—27)

The Church, and Mary, the *new Eve* and icon of the Church, are referred to as the mother of all believers; all those destined for the kingdom of God. Like Mary, the Church also has many faces and titles. As our mother, the Church is also a type of *new Eve*. Some refer to the Church as a "sacrament for the world." (CCC 774—776)

The Church, modeled after Mary, is the *bride of Christ*; and made up of all believers, being prepared for the heavenly banquet and union with the eternal *Bridegroom*, Jesus Christ. The Church, like Mary, is the spiritual mother of Jesus, giving birth to Jesus within every one of her children; nurturing them to the fullness of life through the sacraments, her teaching, and the Word of God.

The Church is like the *Good Shepherd*, feeding and tending her sheep and lambs, through the chair of Peter and the magisterium (pope and bishops).

> At once virgin and mother, Mary is the symbol and the most perfect realization of the Church: "the Church indeed...by receiving the word of God in faith becomes herself a mother. By preaching and Baptism, she brings forth sons, who are conceived by the Holy Spirit and born of God, to a new and immortal life. She herself is a virgin, who keeps in its entirety and purity the faith she pledged to her spouse." (CCC 507)

The Church and the Holy Spirit, like Mary and the Holy Spirit, have a unique bond that is a mystery, not fully seen or understood. Mary is the spouse of the Holy Spirit, and Jesus established the Church to be his spouse through the Holy Spirit. Since Mary is an icon of the Church, she is a visible representative of what Jesus intended the Church to be.

> By her complete adherence to the Father's will, to his Son's redemptive work, and to every prompting of the Holy Spirit, the Virgin Mary is the Church's model of faith and charity. Thus she is a "preeminent and ...wholly unique member of the Church"; indeed, she is the "exemplary realization" (typus) of the Church. (CCC 967)

The Church, like Mary and the Holy Spirit, is an *advocate* and a *witness*. The Church also represents the Divine Offices of Priest, Prophet, and King. The Church was instituted to fulfill the mission began by Jesus Christ. There are many and diverse images and roles of the Church. (Mt 17:1—8; CCC 554—555)

Is it not strange, or is it, that those who reject the authority and role of the Church, seem to also reject Mary, and those who reject Mary also reject the Church? Those who love Mary love the Church, and those who love the Church, also love Mary. Do we really think that Jesus, who was not only God, but also a righteous Jewish man, would not honor his mother and make a special place for her in the Church and in his kingdom? Jesus said: "In my Father's house are many rooms; if it were not so, would I have told you that I go to prepare a place for you? And when I go and prepare a place for you, I will come again and will take you to myself, that where I am you may be also" (ICSB Jn 14:2—3).

☙ Perhaps one of the reasons so many Catholics have left the Church is because they have a distorted or limited perception of what the Church is, and what she represents. They do not see the feminine side of the Church, as the new Eve, the *beloved* daughter of the Father, the bride of Christ, or the mother of Jesus in the world. They see the Church as only masculine, and our culture has a warped image of the masculine, of man, today. When people look at the Church, today, they see a human institution, a manmade organization, a bureaucracy, hierarchy of men, or as a *Good Ole Boys Club*. Our culture has little respect or esteem for men and fathers today. They are portrayed in comedy and satire, as ignorant, adolescent, crude, bigoted, narcissistic, and boorish. More and more, this is the image that is projected onto the Church. Our culture has

CHAPLET OF THE PRECIOUS BLOOD

This devotion consists of seven mysteries in which we meditate on the seven principal sheddings of the Most Precious Blood of Jesus. The Our Father without the Hail Mary is said five times after each mystery except the last, then it is said three times—in all, thirty-three times in honor of the thirty-three years of Our Lord's life on earth.

V. O God, come to my assistance!

R. Lord, make haste to help me!

V. Glory be to the Father, etc.

R. As it was in the beginning, etc.

FIRST MYSTERY

Jesus shed His Blood in the Circumcision. Let us ask for chastity of soul and body.

Our Father five times, Glory be to the Father once

V. We pray you, Lord help your servants!

R. Whom you have redeemed with Your Precious Blood!

(This invocation to the Precious Blood is said after the Our Father and Glory be of each mystery.)

SECOND MYSTERY

Jesus shed His Blood in the Agony while praying in the Garden of Olives. Let us ask for the spirit of prayer.

THIRD MYSTERY

Jesus shed His Blood in the Scourging at the Pillar. Let us ask for patience and self control.

FOURTH MYSTERY

Jesus shed His Blood in the Crowning with Thorns. Let us ask for humility to atone for pride.

FIFTH MYSTERY

Jesus shed His Blood while carrying His Cross to Calvary. Let us ask for acceptance of our daily crosses.

SIXTH MYSTERY

Jesus shed His Blood in the terrible Crucifixion. Let us ask for contrition.

SEVENTH MYSTERY

Jesus shed Blood and water from His side pierced by the lance. Let us ask for perseverance.

Wm.J. Hirten Co. Inc.   4022H

rejected the positive qualities of patriarchy, hierarchy, authority, and masculinity. We have blurred the distinction between male and female, and can no longer recognize what is truly feminine and what is masculine. The human person has become a false persona, a mixture of the negative elements of femininity and masculinity, of male and female. We cannot distinguish Eve from Adam, woman from man, or humans from God.

The Church was instituted by Christ, with an order and structure that enables her to live in the world of space and time, just as the soul needs to dwell within a physical body in order to be relevant in a physical and material world. For the same reason, the Church has a hierarchy of values, principles, gifts, ministries, beliefs, and persons. Some are more necessary for the common good than others; some are more beneficial for the common good than others; some are more indispensable for the common good than others. (1 Cor 12:4—11; Eph 4:7—14)

The outer persona of the Church is male, because Jesus was a male, the Son of Man, and because he chose twelve male apostles to carry on his mission in the world as the foundation stones of his Church, just as the twelve tribes were the foundation stones under the old covenant. Part of the mission of Jesus was to reveal to the world, the person of the Father. He did this by revealing the relationship between the Father and the Son. This is the role of the *New Adam*. Jesus, who is equal to the Father and the Holy Spirit, revealed to us our role in relationship to the Father, by submitting in humble obedience to the Father; not demanding his equality with God (Phil 2:6—8). This is the role of the apostles in relationship with Jesus; the role of the Church in relationship with Jesus; and the role of woman in relationship to man. For our sake, the Holy

Trinity reveals to us a hierarchy of authority and relationship roles. The Son is subservient to the Father, and the Holy Spirit is subservient to the Son.

In my opinion, the most exemplary quality of woman is humility. This is a feminine quality. Woman is not as visible as man in the outer form, or persona of the Church, because, like humility, she is hidden in the heart. Woman takes her place hidden behind man, so as to make man more visible. Like the Holy Spirit, *woman* is the driving force, or principle, within, behind, and to the side of *man*, as his helpmate, pushing him towards excellence and bringing out the best in him. In my opinion, *woman* is excellence, representing the best part, the soul of *man*. She does not lead, as *man* leads. Instead, she moves *man* from behind; she motivates him. This is her primary role as helpmate. I believe that Jesus sees the Church as his beloved, his first born son in the order of a new humanity. He also sees the Church, male and female, as his beloved bride; as his mother; and as woman, the new Eve.

Life began with a couple; with a marriage between one man and one woman, Adam and Eve. But, this couple was always intended to become a family, a people, a nation, and finally, the kingdom of God, or Church. The kingdom of God on earth began with a couple, with the mystical marriage between Jesus and Mary, the new Adam and Eve. It became a family when Jesus said: "And I tell you, you are Peter, and on this rock I will build my Church, and the gates of Hades shall not prevail against it" (ICSB Mt 16:18).

The Church began her mission after Pentecost and was sent out into the world. They were in the world but not of it. The visible Church, instituted by Jesus was very different than it is today. She was poor, but rich in the Holy Spirit. She was given many gifts of the Holy Spirit, and various ministries. She had apostles, chosen by Jesus, who were also later called bishops. She had the sacraments, although they were administered differently than today. All seven of the sacraments can be traced back to those early days. She had witnesses to tell the story of Jesus and what he did. She had no temples, no great cathedrals; only fields, catacombs, and houses to gather together in prayer and worship. The Church lived among the people, believers and unbelievers; friends and enemies. They did not hide away. But, they often had to worship in secret hidden places when the persecutions started. Nevertheless, they did not hide their light or retreat from the world. When they lost their temples, they found other places to gather together to worship. They had Eucharist in their homes. (Acts 2:41 — 47). They worshipped God in "spirit and truth." (Jn 4:23 — 24)

The Church, like Jesus had a very humble beginning. Jesus was born in a stable because there was no room in the Inn. The day is coming when the Church may have to return to the stable. Mary prefigures the Church. If we want to know what will happen to the Church, we only have to look at the life of Mary. Mary is making herself known upon the earth, today, to prepare the way for her Son, Jesus, to return, just as she was the way through which Jesus, fully God and fully man, came into the world at his first coming. She comes to us today, as a prophet, always leading us to Jesus. She is the immaculate, chaste, model of what the Church is to become. If we turn to her, we will see what it means for the Church to be mother and bride. Her assumption into heaven prefigures the assumption of the Church into heaven.

I wonder if we are *reading the signs of the times*. Does Pope Francis know something he is not telling the rest of the Church?

It seems that he has been working hard to reduce the power of the Vatican and the papacy and to divert that power to local bishops. Are our local bishops prepared to become apostles and martyrs, to be sent out into the world to make disciples, as the early Church was? Jesus never promised that the Church would always remain a powerful and great institution in the world, as it is today. What happened in Jerusalem to the Church and the temple, two thousand years ago, can happen again, today, to the Church in Rome, in America, and throughout the world. Are we prepared? Is the Gospel written on our hearts? Do we know the basics of the Gospel and of our faith? Are our bishops prepared to maintain the basics of our Liturgy and the Eucharist without all the frills and guidelines, pomp and ceremony? Are we prepared to carry on the mission of Jesus from the catacombs, in the desert, in our homes, or in a stable? Are our bishops prepared for martyrdom and to pass on the faith among the poor and disenfranchised? Are they able to walk in the footsteps of the apostles? Are the people of God ready to be washed *in the blood of the lamb* (Rev 7:14), to trust in God when all their visible supports and structures are removed? Are they ready to leave everything behind that they cling to? Do they have fuel for their lamps? Will they remain united in their faith, united in their love for God and one another? Are they able to replace the visible churches as they continue to witness, and to *worship the Father in spirit and truth*? (Jn 4:23)

Before the *marriage of the Lamb and his bride*, the Church must be *baptized in fire* and made ready for the Bridegroom. She must be washed in the *blood of the lamb*.

26

A Sign of Contradiction

*P*ope Francis is considered by many today, to be *a sign of contradiction*. He frequently seems to contradict himself in many things that he says. He embraces sinners, and even non-Catholics, while seemingly, rejecting the princes of the Church. He hates sin but loves sinners, and even feels comfortable around them. He hates war and violence but loves criminals. He is always on the side of the poor and those rejected by society. He avoids talking about morality but instead, preaches on the virtues and Beatitudes. He is common and unsophisticated. He is not impressed by dignitaries, or men of power, nobility, and wealth. He lives a simple life and identifies with refugees and the homeless. He has a distain for formality, and is not always politically correct. He loves Scripture but avoids discussing doctrines and Cannon Law. He is unpredictable and people do not know where he really stands on Church teaching. Hmm! He is starting to look a lot like Jesus and his apostles!

Why should Christians be surprised? After all, Pope Francis walks in the *shoes of the fisherman*. Jesus was always *a sign of contradiction;* a stumbling block for the leaders of the Jews, the elite, the successful, the proud, the rich, the famous, and the powerful. So was Mary, his mother, and all his apostles. They were all people of the *Beatitudes* (Lk 6:20—23). These *Blessings and Woes* were a major contradiction for the rich. The Jewish leaders, along with everyone else, except the poor and the humble, would not have understood them or accepted them.

When Mary and Joseph presented the infant, Jesus, in the temple, the prophet, Simeon, prophesied: "Lord, now let your servant depart in peace, according to your word; for my eyes have seen your salvation which you have prepared in the presence of all peoples, a light for revelation to the Gentiles, and for glory to your people Israel." Then, Simeon said to Mary, "Behold, this child is set for the fall and rising of many in Israel, and for a sign that is spoken against (and a sword will pierce through your own soul also), that thoughts out of many hearts may be revealed" (Lk 2:29—32, 34—35). We can also see a semblance of this prophecy, in the *Beatitudes*, and in Mary's song of praise, the *Magnificat.* (Lk 1:47—55)

That Jesus would be a *light unto the Gentiles* was a contradiction for the Jews; nevertheless, it was foretold long ago. St. Paul quotes Moses and Isaiah: "I will make you jealous of those who are not a nation; with a foolish nation I will make you angry"… "I have been found by those who did not seek me; I have shown myself to those who did not ask for me" (ICSB Rom 10:19—20). Paul is referring to the Gentiles, who Simeon prophesied about.

Of Jesus, it was said, "Behold, I am laying in Zion a stone that will make men stumble, a rock that will make them fall; and he who believes in him will not be put to shame" (ICSB Rom 9:33). It was *a sign of contradiction* that "the very stone which the builders rejected has become the cornerstone" (Lk 20:17). After healing a cripple, Peter preached to the people: "This is the stone which was rejected by you builders, but which has become the cornerstone. And there is salvation in no one else, for there is no other name under heaven given among men by which we must be saved" (ICSB Acts 4:11 — 12).

Another word for contradiction is "stumbling block," which brings rejection. Paul quotes Hosea, in speaking of the Jews and Gentiles called to be disciples of Jesus: "Those who were not my people I will call 'my people,' and her who was not beloved I will call 'my beloved.' And in the very place where it was said to them, 'You are my people,' they will be called 'sons of the living God'" (ICSB Rom 9:25 — 26). The Scriptures are full of contradictions, forever reminding us that God's ways are not our ways.

Jesus' whole life was a contradiction. He was the King of Kings, yet born in a stable in Bethlehem. He was the Son of God, yet he was poor. He chose apostles who were poor fishermen, not esteemed leaders. He was born of a virgin, thought to be an adulteress. He was crucified, dying the death of a criminal on a cross, though he was innocent. Jesus said things like, "Truly, truly, I say to you, unless you eat the flesh of the Son of man and drink his blood, you have no life in you; he who eats my flesh and drinks my blood has eternal life, and I will raise him up at the last day" (ICSB Jn 6:53 — 54). Another hard teaching was: "Love your enemies, do good to those who hate you, bless those who curse you, pray for those who abuse you." (ICSB Lk 6:27 — 28)

When it came to the subject of *sin*, Jesus focused on the motivations of the heart and mind; on unbelief and the lack of faith, hope, and love. Issues such as homosexuality, incest, cohabitation, and sexual promiscuity were all common in Jesus' day, but Jesus avoided those issues and focused on virtue and the Beatitudes; on repentance and forgiveness; on faith, hope, and love; and a personal relationship with the Father.

God works his power even through the messengers of Satan. St. Paul tells us: "And to keep me from being too elated by the abundance of revelations, a thorn was given me in the flesh, a messenger of Satan, to harass me, to keep me from being too elated. Three times I begged the Lord about this, that it should leave me; but he said to me, 'My grace is sufficient for you, for my power is made perfect in weakness" (ICSB 2 Cor 12:7—9). Of course, the greatest contradiction of all is the Cross. Again, St. Paul tells us:

> For the word of the cross is folly to those who are perishing, but to us who are being saved it is the power of God. For it is written, "I will destroy the wisdom of the wise, and the cleverness of the clever I will thwart." Where is the wise man? Where is the scribe? Where is the debater of this age? Has not God made foolish the wisdom of the world? For since, in the wisdom of God, the world did not know God through wisdom, it pleased God through the folly of what we preach to save those who believe. For Jews demand signs and Greeks seek wisdom, but we preach Christ crucified, a stumbling block to Jews and folly to Gentiles, Christ the power of God and the wisdom of God. For the foolishness of

God is wiser than men, and the weakness of God is
stronger than men. (ICSB 1 Cor 1:18—25)

The point is that the Scriptures, the pope, and the Church are
all *signs of contradiction* to the whole world, and we should not
be surprised! It is through these contradictions that the power of
God will save the world; through faith in Christ Jesus. Scripture
says: "For now we see in a mirror dimly, but then face to face. Now
I know in part; then I shall understand fully, even as I have been
fully understood. So faith, hope, love abide, these three; but the
greatest of these is love" (ICSB 1 Cor 13:12—13).

To the unbeliever or atheist of today, Jesus is a *sign of contradiction*, and so are the saints that followed him. The values of the
world are not the values of the kingdom of God. The prevailing
culture of our present time teaches us that life is a race, a contest; a
race that separates the winners from the losers, and everyone wants
to be a winner, to be better than everyone else. But, Jesus taught,
"Many who are first will be last, and the last, first" (Mt 19:30). How
can that be? It is a sign of contradiction!

The unbeliever wants to be first, to be the greatest, to be rich
and famous, and to have power over everyone else. The proud
person, when he compares himself with the rest of humanity, sees
himself as a winner; way out in front. But, when he compares himself to Jesus, or even to the least of the saints, he sees himself as
a loser. He cannot compete. If he admires them, there is a chance
for conversion. But, no, instead he becomes envious and angry. He
does not believe that Jesus is God. He believes that he is merely a
man like himself. He convinces himself that Jesus must be a fake,
an imposter; nothing more than a good magician; "Otherwise," he

thinks to himself, "I would be able to do the things he did, and even better." He then decides that it must be the Church who is to blame for this deception. He convinces himself that the Church has given Jesus and the saints a false persona, removing them from the reach of the rest of humanity, so that no one can compete with them; so that if anyone compares them with themselves, they will feel inferior, feel like losers. The crime of the century is to be a loser.

The saints love and serve the poor because they see Jesus in them; like Mother Teresa of Calcutta did. The proud serve the poor because it makes them feel superior and benevolent. Jesus loved the poor because he made himself one with them, and saw himself in them. He saw how much the Father loved them.

The unbeliever or atheist may want to be holy, holier than everyone else. He may want to be wise, wiser than everyone else. He may want to save the world, to be a messiah. But, he will end up last of all. He is still in denial of who is who; who he is and who God is.

Jesus is *a sign of contradiction* because he was not only human, he was also God. As a man, alone, he could never have done the things he did, or the things he continues to do in and through the saints. Our pagan culture refuses to believe this, to believe that Jesus is the only Son of God, fully human and fully divine. The unbeliever wants to strip Jesus of everything that smacks of divinity, everything that makes him different from other humans, so that he can compete with him on his own terms. He wants to do the same to all the saints because even if he could find a way to erase the historical Jesus from the history of mankind, how can he get rid of all the saints, as well?

The holy person does not compare himself with Jesus or the saints; he is not in a race to be first. He looks away from himself in order to see Jesus. But, when he sees Jesus, he also sees his own self, as in a mirror. When the humble person sees himself next to the saints, he sees their love. He rejoices in their goodness, and the goodness and power of God. He is given hope that he too, can become holy through God's grace. The proud person sees the saints as a threat, and despairs because he is a loser. His despair turns to anger and then to jealousy and envy. His only hope is to discredit them and bring them down so that he can appear greater.

When the saints look upon Jesus and the other saints, they are humbled. They realize that they are powerless to do any good thing on their own. They are powerless over God, others, and themselves. They are powerless over sin and evil. They saw themselves as last of all, as losers. They came to believe that God, through Jesus Christ, could redeem them and sanctify them. They made a decision to turn their will and lives over to Jesus. They said "yes" to the call to become saints. They put their faith and trust in God, in Jesus Christ, to change them and transform them into saints. This is why they could do the impossible, they died to themselves. It was no longer they who lived, but Christ Jesus who lived in them. They no longer wanted to be in first place. They wanted to take the lowest place but, instead, were given the highest place, in and with Jesus—*a sign of contradiction*.

What does all this have to do with *The Two Shall Become One?* The marriage between one man and one woman prefigures the marriage between Jesus, the Bridegroom, and the Church, his bride. Before Jesus returned to the Father, he prayed for his disciples and his Church:

> I do not pray for these only, but also for those who believe in me through their word, that they may all be one; even as you, Father, are in me, and I am in you, that they also may be in us, so that the world may believe that you have sent me. The glory which you have given me I have given to them, that they may be one even as we are one, I in them and you in me, that they may become perfectly one, so that the world may know that you have sent me and have loved them even as you have loved me. Father, I desire that they also, whom you have given me, may be with me where I am, to behold my glory which you have given me in your love for me before the foundation of the world. O righteous Father, the world has not known you, but I have known you; and these know that you have sent me. I made known to them your name, and I will make it known, that the love with which you have loved me may be in them, and I in them. (ICSB Jn 17:20–26)

This unity that Jesus keeps stressing throughout the Gospels, takes us back to Genesis: *Therefore a man leaves his father and mother and clings to his wife, and they become one flesh*. From the beginning, God's plan was that we might all be one, as a bride and groom become one. This is the marriage between Jesus, the Bridegroom, and his bride, the Church. Jesus said to his disciples: "If anyone comes to me and does not hate his own father and mother and wife and children and brothers and sisters, yes, and even his own life, he cannot be my disciple" (Lk 14:26). This sounds extreme. But, just as a man and woman must love each other above everyone else, and become one flesh, Jesus is asking his disciples to leave everything, all natural loves, and follow him to be joined to the bride, his Church; to become one with her. The relationship between the disciples and the Church, and the marriage between one man and one woman, prefigures the marriage between the "Lamb and his bride" when Jesus returns.

Before Jesus returns again, his bride, the Church, will be prepared for the marriage feast through tribulation in the world. When he returns, the marriage feast will begin. Then, all will rejoice.

> "Let us rejoice and exult and give him the glory, for the marriage of the Lamb has come, and his Bride has made herself ready; it was granted her to be clothed with fine linen, bright and pure" –for the fine linen is the righteous deeds of the saints. (ICSB Rev 19:7—8)

27

Into the Future

*W*hen I was young, growing up in America, we were supposedly a Christian nation. There was no noticeable separation between Church and state. Church and state were on the same page, in most things that affected our life-style. Christians and non-Christians shared the same values, ethics, morality, and laws. There was no visible difference between Christians and atheists. There was no visible difference between those of the *world* and those of the *kingdom of God*, on earth; at least, not that I was aware of. Christianity was not a *sign of contradiction* or counter-cultural.

We all wanted the same things in life: prosperity, money, success, possessions, fame, power, prestige, physical beauty, strength, knowledge, education, good health, entertainment, lavish vacations, travel, professional status, security, comfort, and pleasure. We all wanted *The American Dream*. We wanted to be winners, to be first, and to be the best. Everyone climbed onto the ladder of success. We wanted everything the world had to offer. These were all the things that would guarantee our happiness.

We believed that as long as we were *good* people, obeyed the laws, went to Church, and were charitable, we deserved to have the best of everything. Of course, everyone had skeletons in their closet and *dirty linen* that we were not about to let the neighbors see. Everyone had suffering and losses to cope with. Most people, however, were in denial and able to put on a good face for the world to see. We all knew something was missing in our lives, so we tried to fill that vacancy with more and more riches of the world. We looked for anything to numb the pain, and to hide our fears; like romantic relationships, parties, alcohol, drugs, gambling, sex, and porn; any distraction that we could find. We were looking for love, but in all the wrong places. We did not know how to recognize it or where to find it.

What a different picture this is from the Gospel that Jesus preached. He taught: "For what does it profit a man if he gains the whole world and loses or forfeits himself?" (ICSB Lk 9:25). We do not realize what priceless gifts our life and our soul are.

> There is great gain in godliness with contentment; for we brought nothing into the world, and we cannot take anything out of the world; but if we have food and clothing, with these we shall be content. But those who desire to be rich fall into temptation, into a snare, into many senseless and hurtful desires that plunge men into ruin and destruction. (ICSB 1 Tm 6:6—9)

> Do not love the world or the things in the world. If anyone loves the world, love for the Father is not

in him. For all that is in the world, the lust of the flesh and the lust of the eyes and the pride of life, is not of the Father but is of the world. And the world passes away, and the lust of it; but he who does the will of God abides forever. (ICSB 1 Jn 2:15—17)

Do not lay up for yourselves treasures on earth, where moth and rust consume and where thieves break in and steal, but lay up for yourselves treasures in heaven, where neither moth nor rust consumes and where thieves do not break in and steal. For where your treasure is, there will your heart be also. (ICSB Mt 6:19—21)

Blessed are you poor, for yours is the kingdom of God. Blessed are you that hunger now, for you shall be satisfied. Blessed are you that weep now, for you shall laugh. Blessed are you when men hate you, and when they exclude you and revile you, and cast out your name as evil, on account of the Son of man! Rejoice in that day, and leap for joy, for behold, your reward is great in heaven; for so their fathers did to the prophets. (ICSB Lk 6:20—23)

The poor were free to hear the *Good News*. They were free to recognize the *pearl of great price* (Mt13:46). There was no place in the *world* for them, and so they welcomed the kingdom of God and the hope that was held out to them. Jesus taught them that the suffering they have now is nothing compared to the glory that awaits them; that life is eternal and does not end in the grave. He told them that he would prove it by rising from the dead in his body and ascending into heaven. He taught them how much the Father loves them and that they were "blessed" by God.

Jesus taught the difference between the *world* and the *kingdom of God*. The *world* believes that *freedom from want* comes by obtaining everything we want. Jesus taught that the more we have, the more we want. He taught that *freedom from want* comes to those who are not dependent or controlled by their wants: those who let go of their wants; those who will what God wills; those who want goodness, harmony (order), beauty (light), and truth. Progress and prosperity are good things when they are for the common good; when they lead to deliverance, healing, wholeness, peace, joy, beauty, truth, harmony, love, and life. When they do not, they lead to the opposite of life; to death.

Progress is a good thing for everyone but the values of the world lead to sin: pride, anger, hatred, jealousy, greed, envy, lust, gluttony, and sloth. These sins of the heart lead to amorality and immorality: divorce, adultery, slavery, and tyranny; loss of identity, idolatry, wars, divisions, factions, violence, abuse, destruction and death. When we lose our moral compass, darkness covers the world and the only light is the light shed by the body of Christ in the world; those who choose Jesus.

From the beginning, sin separated the world from the kingdom of God. Jesus came to establish the kingdom of God upon the earth so that he might save the whole world. Those who are in Christ (believers) are in the world, but not of it. We live in two opposing worlds: the kingdom of God and the kingdom of the world. Christians are called to be a light for the world (Mt 5:14).

We are under a different law than the world, "the Law of the Spirit." (Rom 8:1—2)

Jesus offered a choice to all the people of the earth. They could choose to follow in his footsteps or choose to remain *of the world*, and suffer the consequences and fate of those who remain *of the world*. (1 Jn.5:19)

> Again, the devil took him to a very high mountain, and showed him all the kingdoms of the world and the glory of them; and said to him, "All these I will give you, if you will fall down and worship me." Then Jesus said to him, "Begone, Satan! For it is written, 'You shall worship the Lord your God and him only shall you serve.'" (ICSB Mt 4:8—10)

Christians believe in the kingdom of God that Jesus was sent to establish upon the earth. This kingdom is radically different from the existing kingdom of the *world*. These two kingdoms represent two different mind-sets. The kingdom of the *world* does not acknowledge God, or that he is the Creator, but believes that humanity is its own God, and no other God exists. These people decide for themselves what is good and what is evil. They make their own laws and are self-governing. They establish their own morality; their own values and ethics; their own goals and purposes; their own truth. Everything is relative and changing; there are no absolutes. They do not believe in life after death, or in a final judgment by God. They do not believe in heaven or hell or in angels or demons. They do not believe in sin or the need for forgiveness. They do not believe in miracles or in anything that is supernatural. For those with the mindset of the *world,* relativism seems to suggest a compassionate, inclusive, peaceful, non-judgmental, and unifying way of life. They do not recognize the deception. They do not realize that relativism makes people robots, programed by the existing culture. They have no free will or free choice. They have no resistance except against anything that opposes the existing program.

The fruit of these two mind-sets do not become visible until the *harvest*. When the mind-set of the *world* is on the verge of destroying the world, the truth and reason behind these two mind-sets become apparent. One brings life and the other brings death. The fruit of relativism and individualism begin to show their true colors, and makes Christianity their *scapegoat.*

Many Christians in the world, today, are double-minded. They go back and forth in their thinking and beliefs, or they reject some parts of the Gospel and try to combine the mind-set of the *world* with that of the kingdom of God. However, this is not what is meant by being *in the world, but not of it.* Christians are called to *put on the mind of Christ*; to live in the world as citizens of the *kingdom of God*, "so that we may no longer be children, tossed back and forth and carried about with every wind of doctrine, by the cunning of men, by their craftiness in deceitful wiles." (ICSB Eph 4:14)

The marriage between a man and a woman prefigures the marriage between Christ and his Church. The marriage between man and woman is temporal, only meant for life in this world, for the sake of intimacy and procreation; so that man would not be alone. In heaven, there is no distinction between man and woman, and no marriages or procreation; however, there is relationship among persons that is pure and holy, and there is love. In heaven, we will be like the angels: "For in the resurrection they neither marry nor are given in marriage, but are like angels in heaven" (ICSB Mt 22:30).

Humanity, and all creation, is continually changing and evolving. However, due to the disorder caused by sin, creation *missed the mark* from her original design. Creation has to be re-created, or transformed back to her original design; while at the same time, continue the process of change and evolution. It has always been God's plan to unite God and humanity, and to make them one. This is why he sent his only Son to be incarnated as a human being, so that humans could share in his divinity as he shares in our humanity. It has always been God's plan to unite heaven and earth by transforming the earth and making them one; and so we pray, "Thy kingdom come. Thy will be done on earth as it is in heaven." (ICSB Mt 6:10)

The disorder caused by sin affects our intellect (reason and understanding), our will (knowledge and choices); our memory, imagination, and emotions; and our desires and appetites (senses). They are at variance with our original design, and cause disorder and disharmony. The chemical and biological evolutionary changes taking place in the human person makes it even more difficult to resist disorder. There are no perfect men or women, males or females; everyone is flawed. Everyone, except Jesus and Mary, has been contaminated by sin. We have to continue to strive to resist the disorder within us by following God's revelation in spite of our evolutionary changes; so that we can live in the will of God.

We know what these disorders are, because God revealed a moral law to us for how we are to live in this world through our biological bodies. When we act contrary to this moral law, it brings fear, shame, guilt, and death. God also gives us the forgiveness of sin when we repent and get back up again. He gave us gifts, and the grace (power) to love others as God loves us, so that we can overcome our disordered inclinations; bring salvation to humanity; and prepare for a new life on earth and in heaven. We have to live this moral law in spite of evolutionary changes in our bodies, minds, and souls; or suffer the consequences.

Today, there is a dramatic increase in homosexuality and gender identity issues. This may be due to an increase of sin in the world or due to evolutionary changes in the make-up of humans; or both. Nevertheless, in this life—if this is our *cross* and we are Christians—we are called to live like angels; neither, male or female, and to obey the natural moral order for all humans. Therefore, we are called to shun sexual immorality, to remain celibate, and not enter into marriage. We are all called to be saints, to carry our cross and live for the kingdom of God. St. Paul reminds us:

> Do you not know that he who joins himself to a prostitute becomes one body with her? For as it is written, "The two shall become one." But he who is united to the Lord becomes one spirit with him. Shun immorality. Every other sin which a man commits is outside the body; but the immoral man sins against his own body. Do you not know that your body is a temple of the Holy Spirit within you, which you have from God? You are not your own; you were bought with a price. So glorify God in your body. (ICSB 1 Cor 6:16—20)

In the world, however, it seems that today there are many people who have more in common with animals, with the earth, rather than with their human nature or with angelic beings. They are controlled and driven by appetites and instincts, instead of their reason and will, and are incapable of unselfish love. Nevertheless, the whole human race was created for union with God, in his image and likeness. The Church has always taught that the moral directives from God are "absolutes" and do not change from person to person, age to age, or situation to situation as suggested by relativism. At the same time, this relativism is part of the world system. For those who are of the world, amorality is natural and moral. So, how are Christians supposed to judge those who are of the world? St. Paul tells us: "For what have I to do with judging outsiders? Is it not those inside the Church whom you are to judge? God judges those outside." (ICSB 1 Cor 5:12—13)

Christians cannot judge those who belong to the world, those who are non-Christians. They are under a different law. As Christians, we can only share our beliefs, values, ethics, and morals with non-believers, and invite them to come to Jesus. The choice is theirs to make. Why does this surprise us? It is normal for a world covered in darkness to be blind and lost. It is normal to see confusion and loss of identity; divorce, adultery, polygamy, same sex marriage, incest, violence, suicide, abortions, immorality, wars, division, and all manner of sin and evil, in a world that has no light. This is why Jesus came into the world. Humans have to choose; they are either with Jesus or against him; they are either part of the light or part of the darkness.

When darkness covers the earth, it affects every institution and form of government, including the institutions of the Church and of marriage. Christianity becomes a *sign of contradiction*, and initiates *the rise and fall of many* in the world (Lk 2:33). Christians become the enemy of the world. They suffer the same fate that Jesus suffered; the same persecution and condemnation. The good news is that they will also share in his resurrection. Darkness has covered the world of today, and even seeped into the Church. The world is as it was when Jesus came two thousand years ago. Have we had enough of the darkness? Are we ready to come back into the light? Are we ready to make the future a bright new world? Will Jesus find any faith upon the earth when he returns? (Lk 18:8)

As we step into the future, what will we see? If we are reading the *signs of the times*, we can go back two thousand years ago and listen to the words of Jesus in Matthew Chapters 24 and 25, and see how the signs of the times were fulfilled. Then, we will know what we can expect in our day. It is written, "I will strike the shepherd, and the sheep of the flock will be scattered" (ICSB Mt 26:31). When Jesus was arrested, the disciples scattered. When he was crucified, they all went into hiding. Jesus came to them after he had risen, and revealed himself to them. He sent the Holy Spirit down upon them. They were transformed. Thousands of people converted. The apostles were sent out to evangelize the world. Many Christians were martyred, including the apostles. The temple was desecrated and destroyed. There was great tribulation throughout the world, for believers and non-believers. The Roman Empire fell. But, the kingdom of God continued to grow, up to the present time, producing many wonderful fruits of the Spirit.

What are some of the signs of the times today? I think that most people would agree that there is a de-Christianization taking place in America and throughout the world. Atheism is on the rise. There is a resurgence of paganism and old heresies of the past. There is great corruption and division, not only in secular government, but also in the hierarchy of the Church. Apostasy is rapidly increasing in all the churches and world religions. Judeo-Christian morality has been replaced with relativism. People call good, evil, and evil good. For many people, their own understanding and experience has become their god. Marriage and family life is breaking down and being replaced by the State. Life has become a curse for many people, and they turn to abortion, suicide, euthanasia, drugs and alcohol to escape from life. Nature is rebelling against humans, with an increase in natural disasters: floods, tornados, hurricanes, earthquakes, droughts, and famine. Wars are increasing and nuclear war is on our doorsteps. Lawlessness seems to reign everywhere. Christians throughout the world are being persecuted and martyred. The stage is being set for the Anti-Christ, the *man of lawlessness,* to take the throne of the world. It almost seems like the world is on the brink of total destruction and the end of the world is near.

In our time, will the Church begin to flourish again or will Jesus return to judge the nations? We will have to wait and see! Whether we are alive when these things happen, or not, I believe that the Lord wants us to be prepared and awake. We should not be afraid, however. God is in control, and Jesus has already won the victory. Our God is a God of love and mercy for all. All the popes of the last century, and many prophets, have been praying for and prophesying a *new Pentecost* upon the earth, a *new Evangelization.* Many of the Early Church Fathers, many popes and prophets, and even Fatima have prophesied an *era of peace* before the Second Coming, preceded by a universal cosmic sign that will produce an *illumination of consciousness;* an era when the Church will reign triumphant after being purified; a time when all Christians will be reunited as one Church; a time when the will of God will be done on earth as in heaven. May we all pray for this! In conclusion, let me repeat a segment of a previous prophecy (Chapter 12):

> Listen, my people, I have not come to condemn you. I have come to prepare you. I want you to be ready for what is to come. In the past you have celebrated the Lenten season by choosing you own deserts, your own sacrifices and fasts. But, a Lenten season is coming upon the world of which no man has any control. I am leading you into a desert that you did not choose. I am preparing you for a time of glory, for victory. Trust me! Follow me! If you love me and love one another, the desert cannot hurt you. You will be victorious and through you I will save the world. I have warned you that days of darkness are coming upon the world, days of trial and tribulation. A great light will soon go out in Rome. When that happens, greater darkness will come upon the earth. Do not rely on any of the supports you have had in the past. I am going to strip you of everything you depend on now so that you will depend only on me. For my power is strongest in weakness. I will pour out all the gifts of my Spirit and when you are completely empty you will be able to fully yield to my Spirit and my power will be manifest in you and through you. Be prepared to lose everything for my sake and you will gain everything. You will have to suffer for a little while but your sorrow will be turned into joy. Nature will cry out in birth pangs and there

will be famines and floods and earthquakes. But, I will renew the face of the earth. Trust in me. Many people will be given over to evil, rejecting God and hating all that is good and holy. You will be hated and persecuted, and some will even be martyrs for my name. I have told you all this so that your faith will not be shaken. Band yourselves together in me, for I will triumph and my glory will be seen upon the earth. A new day is coming and when that day comes your joy will be great. In that day you will have everything. But, you must let me prepare you.

A word about prophecy: When God gives a prophecy of the future to his Church, it is not to make us fearful, but to give us hope; to warn us, prepare us, and call us to repentance and change. God does not tell us the day or the hour because he always leaves the door open for our response; *a day can be a thousand years*. Instead, God tells us to *read the signs of the times*. If we were reading the signs of the times we would be forewarned, and hopefully, take the right action.

A new day is coming! A glorious day is coming! The kingdom of God will reign upon the earth. The will of the Father will be made one with the will of humans—the will of the Father will be done on earth, as it is in heaven. All humans will worship God in Spirit and Truth. The Church—the bride of Christ—will be made spotless and beautiful. But, first, the Church has to follow in the footsteps of Jesus. She must be washed in the blood of Christ. She must enter into the passion and death of Jesus in order to be resurrected with him. The *man of lawlessness* must be destroyed. Then, Jesus will draw all people unto himself.

REFERENCES

Catechism of the Catholic Church, Second Edition, United States Catholic Conference, Inc.Washington DC 1997

The Holy Bible, Revised Standard Version Catholic Edition, Thomas Nelson Publishers for Ignatius Press, San Francisco 1966

The Ignatius Catholic Study Bible: The New Testament, Revised Standard Version, Second Catholic Edition, Ignatius Press, San Francisco 2010

The Jerusalem Bible, Doubleday & Company, Inc. Garden City, NY 1966

The New American Bible, Oxford University Press, Inc. New York 2004

The New American Bible, Catholic Publishers, Inc. New Jersey 1971

The New International Bible, Zondervan Publishing House, Grand Rapids, MI 1984

De Sales, St. Francis. *Introduction to the Devout Life*, Translated by Michael Day, Cong. OratThis Golden Library Edition, Burns & Oates, London 1962. 165—166

Francis, Pope. *Amoris Laetitia: On Love in the Family*, Apostolic Exhortation, Our SundayVisitor Publishing, Huntington, IN 2016

Francis, Pope. *The Joy of the Gospel: Evangelii Gaudium,* Apostolic Exhortation, United StatesConference of Catholic Bishops, Washington DC 2013

Iannuzzi, Joseph. *The Splendor of Creation,* Missionaries of The Holy Trinity, Inc. Distributed by: St. Andrew's Productions, McKees Rocks, PA 2004

Martin, Ralph. *Catharine of Sienna: Growing in Love,* Six CD Series, Saint JosephCommunications 2003

Martin, Ralph. *The Urgency of the New Evangelization: Answering the Call,* Our Sunday Visitor, Inc., Huntington, IN 2013

Paul VI, Pope. *Address of Pope Paul VI to Women,* Closing of the Second Vatican Ecumenical Council, Liberia Editrice Vaticana 1965

Pio, Padre. *Biography of Pio of Pietrelcina: Padre Pio, the Man,* L'Osservatore Romano 1999

Sheen, Bishop Fulton J. *Three to Get Married,* Scepter Publishers, New York 1951

Beckman, Kathleen. *Foundation of Prayer for Priests,* 2013 www.kathleenbeckman.com/about-us/ www.foundationforpriests.org

Benkovic, Johnnette. *Women of Grace,* Clearwater, FL 1988, www.womenofgrace.com/en-us/about/default.aspx

Mallett, Mark. *NOW WORD: Reflections on Our Times,* 2003–2018 www.markmallett.com/blog

Ross, Donna. *Magnificat, A Ministry to Catholic Women,* New Orleans, LA 1981 www.magnificat-ministry.net

ABOUT THE AUTHOR

*L*enora Grimaud is a woman of many lives. She was married to a Military Officer and Deacon in the Catholic Church for twenty-four years; raising a son and three daughters. When her marriage came to an end, she became a Nun for ten years. After being refused for *final vows*, she returned home and presently, lives as a single lay woman in *private vows*. Lenora has been very active in the Catholic Church since 1968, serving in the United States and Europe. She has served in many different ministries: the leadership of the Military Council of Catholic Women in the United States and Europe; Diocesan Director of Divorced and Separated; Right of Christian Initiation for Adults (RCIA), Coordinator; Magnificat Ministry to Catholic Women; Women of Grace; and the Charismatic Renewal. She is also a certified Spiritual Director. Her gifts have involved her in giving retreats, bible studies, women's study groups, public speaking, writing, and spiritual direction. She was also a blog editor for parishworld.net for several years, and has posted many of her articles on-line. After many years of self-study and experience, Lenora received her BA in Religious Studies and Psychology when she was sixty-two. Presently, she is a grandmother of twelve and is expecting her tenth great-grandchild.

CPSIA information can be obtained
at www.ICGtesting.com
Printed in the USA
FSHW02n1223060618
49028FS